The Cost Disease

The Cost Disease

Why Computers Get Cheaper
and Health Care Doesn't

William J. Baumol

with contributions by
David de Ferranti
Monte Malach
Ariel Pablos-Méndez
Hilary Tabish
Lilian Gomory Wu

Yale UNIVERSITY PRESS
New Haven & London

Published with assistance from the foundation established in memory of
Philip Hamilton McMillan of the Class of 1894, Yale College.

Permission to reprint is hereby gratefully acknowledged for previously
published extracts of this text. Figures 4.3 and 4.4 appeared in BAUMOL/
BLINDER, *Economics*, 12e, © 2011 South-Western, a part of Cengage
Learning, Inc., reproduced by permission, www.cengage.com/permissions.

Yale University Press books may be purchased in quantity for educational,
business, or promotional use. For information, please e-mail
sales.press@yale.edu (U.S. office) or sales@yaleup.co.uk (U.K. office).

Set in 10.5/14.5 Janson type by Westchester Book Services.
Printed in the United States of America.

ISBN: 978-0-300-17928-6 (cloth)

Library of Congress Control Number: 2012938269

A catalogue record for this book is available from the British Library.

This paper meets the requirements of ANSI/NISO Z39.48–1992
(Permanence of Paper).

10 9 8 7 6 5 4 3 2

In memory of Pat Moynihan, who took the cost disease analysis and ran with it.

Contents

Acknowledgments   xi
Introduction   xvii

PART I   *The Survivable Cost Disease*

ONE
Why Health-Care Costs Keep Rising   3

TWO
What Causes the Cost Disease, and Will It Persist?   16

THREE
The Future Has Arrived   33

FOUR
Yes, We Can Afford It   43

Contents

FIVE

Dark Sides of the Disease: Terrorism and
Environmental Destruction   69

SIX

Common Misunderstandings of the Cost Disease:
Cost versus Quality and Financial versus "Physical"
Output Measures   77

SEVEN

The Cost Disease and Global Health   94

PART 2   *Technical Aspects of the Cost Disease*

EIGHT

Hybrid Industries and the Cost Disease   111

NINE

Productivity Growth, Employment Allocation, and the Special
Case of Business Services   116

PART 3   *Opportunities for Cutting Health-Care Costs*

TEN

Business Services in Health Care   141

ELEVEN

Yes, We Can Cut Health-Care Costs Even If We Cannot
Reduce Their Growth Rate   154

Contents

TWELVE
Conclusions: Where Are We Headed and What
Should We Do? 180

Notes 183
References 207
About the Authors 237
Index 239

Acknowledgments

This book is based on work first done in the early 1960s by my longtime friend Bill Bowen, then a young assistant professor at Princeton University, and myself. Most of the credit goes to Bill, who organized our thinking on the subject and laid the plans for our research enterprise. Our analysis of rising costs originally focused on the live performing arts—theater, music, and dance—under a project generously funded by the Twentieth Century Fund and the Rockefeller Brothers Fund. In carrying out this research, we were struck most intensely by one observation: the universal, virtually uninterrupted upward movement of theater production costs and ticket prices. The search for an explanation of this striking trajectory soon led us to the idea of the "cost disease," which we then applied to other activities with a large handicraft component, notably health care and education. Thus, the cost disease literature was launched.

That first research project was a vast endeavor that entailed data collection from well over one hundred audiences and theater groups throughout the United States and England, a task that was carried out masterfully by our wives, Mary Ellen Bowen and Hilda Baumol. It is not possible to list the names of all of those who provided us with encouragement, insights, and information almost half a century ago. However, I must acknowledge the support and helpful guidance we received from August Heckscher and John Booth of the Twentieth Century Fund, as well as from Nancy Hanks and John D. Rockefeller II of the Rockefeller Brothers Fund.

I will mention only in passing the upsurge of interest in the cost disease analysis during the Clinton administration's effort to secure passage of legislation that would institute a governmental health-care program. On this, I worked closely with the late Senator Daniel Patrick Moynihan, my wonderful friend, an intellectual giant, and an unusually effective politician who was the first elected official to understand the cost disease analysis and put it to use in promotion of the general welfare. We had a number of exchanges with Hilary Clinton and her staff, seeking to avoid excessive promises regarding the cost slowdown that they hoped to achieve. Such promises, we feared, would endanger the entire proposal.

I also owe a great debt to Professor Alice Vandermeulen, who coined the term "Baumol's cost disease." A major contribution was provided by Sue Anne Batey Blackman and Professor Edward Wolff, my coauthors in *Productivity and American Leadership* (1989), which expanded the factual evidence and deepened the cost disease analysis.

Next, and perhaps most urgent, is a report on the roles of my collaborators in the current volume. I am deeply indebted to the Rockefeller Foundation for its generous support of this book. To my coauthors, too, my debt is enormous. Here, I address their contributions in the order in which their chapters appear in his book. The first of these comes from three capable analysts associated with the Rockefeller Foundation, Ariel Pablos-Méndez, Hilary Tabish, and David de Ferranti. In Chapter 7, they expand the cost disease analysis to include low- and middle-income countries. The data they provide show an upward path with surprisingly small deviations—rare in economic relationships—between rising per capita incomes in selected countries and per person expenditures on health care. Their chapter also reminds us that the cost disease is surely not the only cause of this relationship: improved health care enhances longevity, which in turn increases costs.

In Chapters 9 and 10, Lilian Gomory Wu provides empirical substance for Nicholas Oulton's analysis of the cost disease in relation to business services. She shows that the role of the disease in the cost of services can be very different when these services are final products (for example, a doctor's observation of a patient), compared with its role when services are used as *inputs* to another final product, as in the case of software that guides the progress of an assembly line. Lillian's role at IBM afforded her ample access to examples of business services in action.

Chapter 11 and portions of Chapter 6 are provided by Monte Malach, a noted cardiologist and retired faculty member at New York University Medical Center and the State University of New York Downstate Medical Center. Chapter 11 builds on the observation that while no one seems to have found a way to curb the disturbingly fast rate of increase in health-care costs, there are many ways to cut the *current magnitude* of those costs. An earlier version of this chapter appeared as the lead article in the *Journal of Community Health* (see Malach and Baumol 2009, 2010). The revised version published here provides pragmatic recommendations for reducing health-care spending through modification of current medical practices.

I owe additional thanks to Professor Edward Wolff of New York University for his guidance in calculating health-care spending projections for the book; to Aurite Werman, who gave up a summer to research data that were more current and illuminating; and to Rebecca Sela, formerly a doctoral student in statistics at New York University's Stern School of Business, who double-checked our calculations.

I also must acknowledge my debt to those at Yale University Press whose skill and dedication is responsible for the emergence of this well turned-out volume. In particular, our editor, William Frucht, made invaluable suggestions related to presentation and emphasis. Even on the one occasion when we differed substantially (albeit on a trivial matter), our exchanges proceeded in a productive and civilized manner. Thanks also are due to Jaya Chatterjee, Mary Pasti, Michael Haggett (of Westchester Book Services), and their many colleagues who contributed to this book—with whom it was always a pleasure to work.

Finally, I come to my greatest obligation, to my two indispensible colleagues, Anne Noyes Saini and Janeece Roderick Lewis. It must be conceded that Janeece had little direct role in the book itself. But her competent and reliable control of all other activities in my office, while Anne and I worked on the book, was surely indispensible to the publication process. Of course, Anne's role was much more than editing—full justice would require that she be listed as principal coauthor. She coordinated the work of all the participants in the preparation of the book, ensured the mutual consistency of the different chapters, put our editor's valuable suggestions into practice, translated the medical terminology of Dr. Malach's chapter into terms comprehensible to general readers, and much more. Acknowledgment of my gratitude to (and affection for) Anne and Janeece is surely the appropriate way to end this inadequate listing of the many debts I owe those who have contributed so much to this book.

Acknowledgments

Ariel Pablos-Méndez, Hilary Tabish, and David de Ferranti would like to thank William Baumol, Anne Mills, Timothy Evans, Jacques van der Gaag, and Marie Beylin for their input and critical review of earlier versions of Chapter 7, as well as Dianne Langham-Butts, Marian Jamieson, and Tom Helmick for assistance in finalizing their chapter. The views expressed in Chapter 7 are solely those of the authors and not of their institutions.

Lilian Gomory Wu would like to thank the following people for their contributions to Chapters 9 and 10: Susan Andrews, Daniel Z. Aronzon, M.D., Paul Baffes, Edward Bevan, Marcia Chapman, Liam Cleaver, Lynette Coleman, Brian Goodman, Therese Hudson-Jinks, Larry Kasanoff, Stephen A. Katz, M.D., Kristine Lawas, David Newbold, and Margaret Vosburgh.

Monte Malach would like to thank William Baumol for a rapid education in the economics of the "cost disease" with regard to the cost of medical care and Anne Noyes Saini for extensive editing help with Chapter 11.

Introduction

Many years ago, I received a handwritten note from the extraordinarily creative economist Joan Robinson, commenting on the "cost disease" that is at the center of this book. The cost disease asserts that the costs of health care, education, the live performing arts, and a number of other economic activities known as the "personal services" are condemned to rise at a rate significantly greater than the economy's rate of inflation, as indeed they have throughout the period for which data are available.[1] This is so because the quantity of labor required to produce these services is difficult to reduce.

Since the Industrial Revolution, labor-saving productivity improvements have been occurring at an unprecedented pace in most manufacturing activities, reducing the cost of making these products even as workers' wages have risen. In the personal services industries, meanwhile, automation is not always possible, and labor-saving productivity improvements occur at a rate well below average for the economy. As a result, costs in the personal services industries move ever upward at a much faster rate than the rate of inflation.

In her note, Professor Robinson did not disagree with this assertion but drew attention to an even more important point. With productivity rising almost everywhere in the economy of the twentieth and twenty-first centuries—in some industries more slowly, in others more rapidly—she pointed out that *all* industries must be growing less costly in the amount of human labor they require. This labor, she noted, is surely the real cost humanity incurs in producing a commodity. I sent her a note expressing my agreement, but at the time I did not understand the full implications of her comment. They are indeed profound. The updated analysis of the cost disease presented in this book focuses on the key conclusion that follows from this: no matter how painful rising medical and educational bills may be, *society can afford them*, and there is no need to deny them to ourselves or to the less affluent members of our society, or indeed to the world. Overall incomes and purchasing power must rise quickly enough to keep these services affordable, despite their persistently rising costs.

This conclusion—that our descendants will likely be able to afford more health care and education as well as more of all the other goods and services they consume—may seem strikingly implausible in light of the data and analysis presented in this book. We all know that health-care and educational costs are rising at a disturbingly fast rate. But how will these increases affect us? The answer is suggested by a straightforward calculation, which shows that if health-care costs continue to increase by the rate they have averaged in the recent past, they will rise from 15 percent of the average person's total income in 2005 to 62 percent by 2105. This is surely mind-boggling. It means that our great-grandchildren in the year 2105 will have only a little less than forty cents out of every dollar they earn or otherwise receive to spend on everything *besides* health care—food, clothing, vacations, entertainment, and even education! Yet as this book will show, this prospect is not nearly as bad as it sounds.

But is this really plausible? Of course events may change the current trends in productivity and economic growth—wars, earthquakes, and myriad other things that cannot be foreseen by anyone, most notably by the economists. (As the saying goes, economists are qualified to predict anything but the future.) But it should be noted that the bulk of the cost disease analysis presented here was first offered almost exactly half a century ago by me and a colleague, William Bowen.[2] The predictions we made in that original work for the future costs of health-care and other labor-intensive services were fully borne out. Recently, an independent study of a complete set of industry accounts data for 1948 through 2001 by the eminent economist William Nordhaus concluded that "Baumol's hypothesis of a cost-price disease due to slow productivity growth is definitely confirmed by the data."[3] An even more recent study of the economic challenges facing symphony orchestras in the United States, by Robert Flanagan (2012), confirms that relentlessly rising costs and slow productivity growth still plague the performing arts. In the half-century since our analysis first emerged, our predictions have achieved what is surely a special status: they may well be the longest valid forecast ever to emerge from economic analysis.

It must be confessed that when our analysis was first offered, Bowen and I were too cowardly to venture such bold claims. Instead, we referred to the theory's future implications as "extrapolations" rather than predictions. But now, almost fifty years later, the authors of the current book are tempted to make bolder claims.

Overview of the Book

Briefly, the book's central arguments are these:

1. Rapid productivity growth in the modern economy has led to cost trends that divide its output into two sectors, which I call "the stagnant sector" and "the progressive sector." In this book, productivity growth is defined as a labor-saving change in a production process so that the output supplied by an hour of labor increases, presumably significantly (Chapter 2).

2. Over time, the goods and services supplied by the stagnant sector will grow increasingly unaffordable relative to those supplied by the progressive sector. The rapidly increasing cost of a hospital stay and rising college tuition fees are prime examples of persistently rising costs in two key stagnant-sector services, health care and education (Chapters 2 and 3).

3. Despite their ever increasing costs, stagnant-sector services will never become unaffordable to society. This is because the economy's constantly growing productivity simultaneously increases the community's overall purchasing power and makes for ever improving overall living standards (Chapter 4).

4. The other side of the coin is the increasing affordability and the declining relative costs of the products of the progressive sector, including some products we may wish were less affordable and therefore less prevalent, such as weapons of all kinds, automobiles, and other mass-manufactured products that contribute to environmental pollution (Chapter 5).

5. The declining affordability of stagnant-sector products makes them politically contentious and a source of disquiet

for average citizens. But paradoxically, it is the developments in the progressive sector that pose the greater threat to the general welfare by stimulating such threatening problems as terrorism and climate change. This book will argue that some of the gravest threats to humanity's future stem from the *falling* costs of these products, rather than from the rising costs of services like health care and education (Chapter 5).

The central purpose of this book is to explain why the costs of some labor-intensive services—notably health care and education—increase at persistently above-average rates. As long as productivity continues to increase, these cost increases will persist. But even more important, as the economist Joan Robinson rightly pointed out so many years ago, as productivity grows, so too will our ability to pay for all of these ever more expensive services.

Unfortunately, none of these ideas seem to have found their way into current political discussions.[4] If governments cannot be led to understand the ideas presented here, then their citizens may be denied vital health, education, and other benefits because they *appear* to be unaffordable, when in fact they are not.

PART I

The Survivable Cost Disease

ONE

Why Health-Care Costs Keep Rising

This strange disease of modern life.
—MATTHEW ARNOLD

In 1980, it cost $3,500 per year, on average, to attend a four-year undergraduate school in the United States (including room and board). By 2008, that figure was ancient history: a single year of undergraduate study cost nearly $20,500.[1] That's an average annual increase of more than 6 percent—well above the rate of inflation. If this trend continues, by 2035 annual tuition at a top-tier private school could cost nearly $200,000.[2]

College tuition is not an isolated case. Medical care and live theatrical performance are also victims of a widespread pattern of increasing costs that has come to be called "the cost disease," "Baumol's disease," or in educational circles, "Bowen's curse." The data are striking in both their magnitude and their persistence.

The Cost Crisis

The exploding cost of health care is the focus of widespread concern. There is rarely an election in an industrialized country in which every candidate is not expected to proclaim a commitment to containing these costs. In the United States, contenders in the 2008 presidential election repeatedly stressed this issue as one of the most critical facing society. Participants in these debates often point out that people in other nations pay far less for health care than Americans do, yet they live longer and enjoy better health.[3] But as we will see, even though their total costs are lower, those nations also are beset by strikingly rapid and persistent increases in the cost of their health-care programs. The cost disease is universal.

Those of us with children or grandchildren in college are only too painfully aware that education suffers similar problems, which also elicit growing political attention. The National Center for Public Policy and Higher Education reports that nearly two-thirds of Americans "believe that college prices are rising faster than the cost of other items."[4] Data from the Bureau of Labor Statistics confirm the accuracy of these perceptions.[5] Since the early 1980s, the price of college tuition in the United States has increased by a much greater percentage (up 440 percent) than the average rate of inflation (110 percent), median family income (150 percent), and even medical care (250 percent).

My purpose in this book is to show not only that health care, education, and a number of other service fields share the problem of growing costs but that these increases have a common source. Until that source is recognized, programs to deal with the issues are likely to prove ineffective or worse—but once the problem is understood, promising courses of action become visible. The beginnings of this discussion will appear suitably grim, but the rising-cost portion of the story will have a rather happier ending—though that ending still depends on the rationality and insight of policy makers.

My argument, in brief, is that the cost disease is largely a product of the unprecedented and spectacular productivity growth that the world's industrialized nations have achieved since the Industrial Revolution, commonly said to have begun in the eighteenth century, which has contributed so much to standards of living and reduction of poverty. This unprecedented productivity growth— carried out primarily by the partnership of inventors and entrepreneurs and expanded to a large scale by companies, governments, and nonprofits—has all but eliminated famine in wealthy countries, created technology unimaginable in earlier eras, given us ever rising standards of living, and greatly reduced poverty in both extent and severity. But it has also brought the rising costs of health care, education, and other important services. The argument here is that the productivity growth that gives rise to the cost disease also gives society the means to deal with it.

Rising Health-Care and Education Costs in the United States

It is often noted that Americans pay considerably more for health care than citizens in most other industrialized countries. Judging by the statistical evidence, we can be fairly certain that this is true, despite the well-known pitfalls besetting cost comparisons among different countries with different currencies. The main shortcoming of this conclusion is not that it is factually incorrect but that it focuses on the wrong issue. The pain society experiences from the costs of health care and education does not derive primarily from their *levels* at some particular date, but rather from their *growth rates*. As expensive as health care and education may have been yesterday, they are considerably more so today, and will be costlier still tomorrow.

Here it is important to note that I refer not to price inflation but to what economists call "real price increases"—that is, price increases above the rate of general inflation in the economy. (For noneconomist readers, an explanation of "real" versus "nominal" prices appears in the appendix at the end of this chapter.) The magnitude and persistence of these real prices' growth rates are sufficiently striking as to leave little doubt that even if they are not the only difficulty, they are surely a major component of the problem.

Consider that between 1948 and 2008 the consumer price index (CPI), which measures overall price rises in the U.S. economy, increased by nearly 4 percent per year. In comparison, the cost of physician services rose by about 5 percent annually during that period (Figure 1.1). This difference may seem trivial, but it signi-

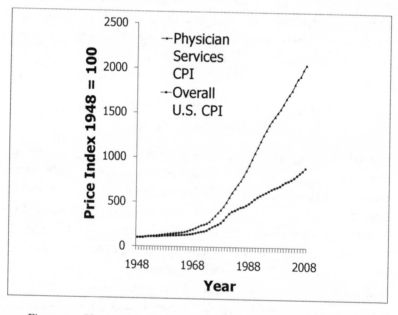

Figure 1.1. Physician services consumer price index (CPI) versus overall CPI in the United States, 1948–2008. (Based on data from the U.S. Bureau of Labor Statistics.)

fies an increase in the price of a visit to the doctor of approximately 230 percent (adjusted to eliminate increases due to inflation) over that sixty-year period.[6]

In the last thirty years, the cost of hospital services, as reported by the U.S. Bureau of Labor Statistics, rose even more sharply— nearly 8 percent a year between 1978 and 2008. In comparison, as shown in Figure 1.2, the costs of physician services and overall CPI grew by rates of just over 5 percent and just under 4 percent, respectively, during that thirty-year period. Corrected for inflation, this represents an increase of nearly 300 percent. In comparison, during that thirty-year time period, the real cost of physician services grew by almost 150 percent. Increases of this magnitude clearly constitute a serious threat to the quality and quantity of

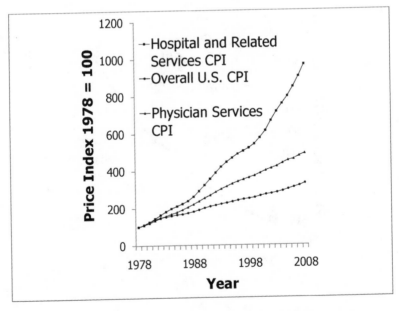

Figure 1.2. Hospital services consumer price index (CPI) versus physician services CPI versus overall CPI in the United States, 1978–2008. (Based on data from the U.S. Bureau of Labor Statistics.)

medical care that middle- and lower-income Americans can afford. In an affluent society that is dedicated to promoting the general welfare—including a minimum standard of acceptable medical care—the rising cost of health care clearly represents a pressing problem. (Later, however, we will see that this problem may be less serious than it seems.)

When we look at similar data for educational costs, we find very similar patterns. As Figure 1.3 shows, the average consumer's expenditures on college tuition and fees, for instance, have risen steadily at rates markedly outstripping inflation. According to the Bureau of Labor Statistics, college tuition and fees increased by just over 7 percent per year during the last thirty years. Measured in dollars of constant purchasing power, tuition increased by more

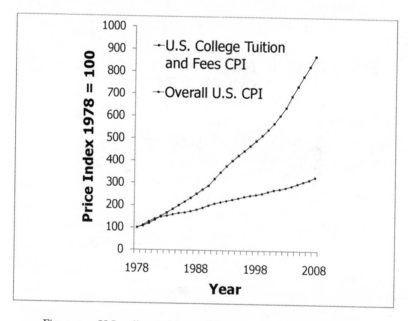

Figure 1.3. U.S. college tuition and fees consumer price index (CPI) versus overall CPI in the United States, 1978–2008. (Based on data from the U.S. Bureau of Labor Statistics.)

than 250 percent during this period—a growth rate that lags behind the increase in hospital services costs but easily surpasses that of physician services.

Global Comparison: Rising Health and Education Costs

Are these steadily growing real costs peculiar to the United States? Several commentators have suggested that other countries exercise firmer control over their health-care costs and thus continue to offer better and more affordable public services. There is undoubtedly much truth to this contention, which reflects, among other influences, differences in public policies. Chief among these are other nations' greater commitment to social services, financed by tax rates that are far higher than those in the United States, and stricter controls on physicians' fees. Even so, the *rates* of cost increases in health care and education affect other industrialized countries as well as the United States (for data on health-care costs in low- and middle-income countries, see Chapter 7).

When we compare U.S. health-care and education costs with those elsewhere,[7] we see that between 1995 and 2004 educational expenditures per student increased significantly in every one of the seven industrialized countries for which we have data. American expenditures on education were consistently higher than those in the other six countries, but three others—the United Kingdom, the Netherlands, and Denmark—were not far behind. As shown in Figure 1.4, the *rate* at which U.S. expenditures grew was also the highest—at nearly 5 percent each year. The United Kingdom, Denmark, and the Netherlands again followed closely behind. As for health care, virtually every major industrial nation has tried to prevent these costs from rising faster than its rate of inflation—and all have failed. Between 1960 and 2008, as shown in Figure 1.5, the

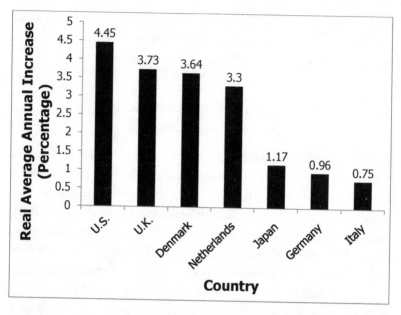

Figure 1.4. Real average annual growth rates in expenditure on educational institutions in all levels of education in the United States, the United Kingdom, Denmark, the Netherlands, Japan, Germany, and Italy, 1995–2004. Data for 1995, 2000, 2001, 2002, 2003, 2004, and 1996–1999 were not available. (Based on data from *OECD Education at a Glance 2007*, Table B2.3: Change in Expenditure on Educational Institutions, Paris: OECD.)

United States spent more on health care per capita than Canada, Germany, Japan, the United Kingdom, and the Netherlands. But as Figure 1.6 shows, the United States did not have the highest *rate of increase* in real health-care spending per person during that period. Japan's growth rate, for instance, easily exceeds that of the United States. Although health-care spending in the United States is comparatively high, its rate of increase resembles that of other affluent industrialized countries.

Finally, although real health expenditures have increased faster than inflation in the United States, the wages of employees in health-

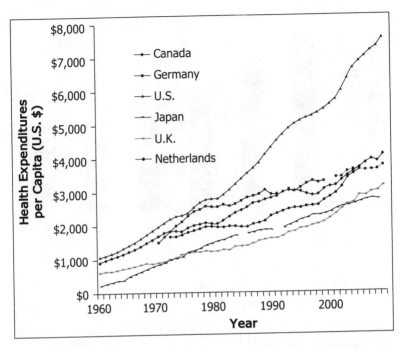

Figure 1.5. Real annual health expenditure per capita in Canada, Germany, the United States, Japan, the United Kingdom, and the Netherlands, 1960–2008. Gaps in the trend lines correspond to missing data. (Based on data from the OECD, Health Data 2010: Total Expenditure on Health, Per Capita U.S. $ PPP, http://stats.oecd.org.)

care professions have not. Over the last fifty years, according to data from the U.S. Bureau of Labor Statistics, health-care workers' salaries have barely kept up with inflation. The wages of employees at American colleges and universities, meanwhile, actually failed to keep pace with inflation, starting in the mid-1970s (Figure 1.7). The rapid rise in health-care and education costs cannot be blamed on the people working in these sectors.

The first lesson to draw from this is that other countries' systems suggest no quick fix for the problem of rising health-care costs in

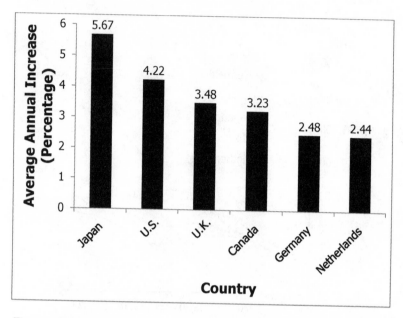

Figure 1.6. Average annual growth rates in real health expenditure per capita in Japan, the United States, the United Kingdom, Canada, Germany, and the Netherlands, 1960–2006. (Based on data from the OECD, Health Data 2008: Total Expenditure on Health, Per Capita U.S. $ PPP, http://stats.oecd.org.)

the United States. The universality and persistence of the problem— the fact that it has endured for more than four decades and affects countries throughout Europe, North America, and Asia—indicate that its roots go far deeper than America's particular administrative or institutional arrangements. There are many reasons for increased spending on health care, including an aging population, technological change, perverse incentives, supply-induced demand, and fear of malpractice litigation. The broader point is that the basic underlying problem does not entail misbehavior or incompetence but rather stems from the nature of the provision of labor-intensive services.

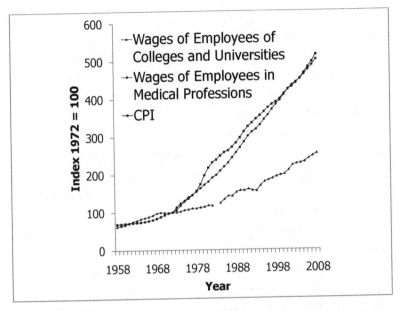

Figure 1.7. Wages of employees of colleges and universities versus wages of medical workers versus overall consumer price index in the United States, 1958–2008. Gaps in the trend lines correspond to missing data. "Medical workers" include all those employed in physicians' offices. (Based on data from the U.S. Bureau of Labor Statistics.)

Appendix: "Real" versus "Nominal" Costs

Economists have adopted two ways of looking at changes in cost. One is called *nominal* change, and the other is called *real* change. The nominal change in cost is the cost modification that meets the eye directly. If the price of a newspaper goes from $1 to $2, we say that the nominal cost to the consumer rose by $1—a 100 percent increase. But if *all costs and wages in the entire economy* (that is, inflation) also happened to rise 80 percent during that same year, we must take this into account. Though we are paying more dollars for our newspaper, each of those dollars is worth less than before.

These two changes partially offset one another. To evaluate how much the newspaper's real cost has risen, we subtract the increase attributable to inflation (80 percent) from the nominal increase (100 percent), which gives us the real increase in cost. In this example, the real cost increase is 20 percent (100 percent − 80 percent = 20 percent).

It is important for many purposes to be able to separate out these two influences on costs. Failure to distinguish between them can lead to poor policies that, rather than ameliorating a problem, actually make it worse. For example, suppose the cost of automobiles rises by 15 percent in one year, but in that same year wages double for all workers. Workers everywhere will be able to afford to buy a new car more easily than they could the year before, even though the nominal cost of buying a car increased. If we were to punish the automobile manufacturers for their greed in raising prices, it might force them to build inferior cars or even drive them out of business—their workers' salaries, remember, have increased along with all others. Real cost is an economic concept created to avoid such misunderstanding.

How to Calculate Changes in Real Cost

The method economists use to calculate changes in real cost is straightforward and not deeply interesting in itself, but it is worth explaining here to make it easier for noneconomist readers to follow the analysis in this book. The real cost of any commodity is calculated simply by taking its nominal cost and dividing that by a measure of the *average change in cost* for all of an economy's products (or a representative sample of its products, such as the consumer price index, or CPI). Thus, to calculate the real cost in 2010 of product X, simply use this equation:

$$\text{Real Cost of Product X in 2010} = \frac{\text{Nominal Cost of Product X in 2010}}{\text{Index of Costs for the Whole Economy in 2010}}$$

Note that if the percentage increase in the cost of product X is less than the percentage increase in the index of costs for the whole economy, the real cost of product X will fall, even though its nominal cost has risen. From this, we deduce an observation that is quite obvious, though generally overlooked: in any economy in which the costs of the various goods rise at different rates, the costs of some goods must rise more rapidly than average, while the costs of others must rise more slowly than average. This must be so because, by the definition of an average, some cost increases must be higher than average, while others must be below average.

Inevitably, then, there always will be some commodities whose real costs are rising and others whose real costs are falling. Commodities whose nominal costs are increasing at rates that are *less* than the average of all costs in the economy, for instance, will see their real costs *decrease*. There should be nothing surprising, therefore, in the fact that some goods and services, such as health care and education, are characterized by rising real costs, while others, such as computers and telecommunications, have falling real costs.

What should be more surprising—but not much more, as we will see—is that the goods and services whose real costs fall in any given year generally tend to have falling real costs year after year. Items whose real costs rise follow a rising pattern year after year. As we will see, this persistence is what gives rise to the cost disease.

TWO

What Causes the Cost Disease, and Will It Persist?

Since rates of labor-saving productivity growth are uneven, the growth in some activities *must* be below average.
—WILLIAM BAUMOL

Why are the costs of health care, education, and other services rising so persistently at rates faster than the economy's rate of inflation? This chapter seeks to explain what drives that phenomenon.

Obviously, such an explanation is of considerable interest in itself, but there are many other reasons why it merits our attention. First, the explanation enables us to infer whether rising costs are likely to be transitory or can be expected to persist. I will argue that, while there are no guarantees, assuming no catastrophic developments undermine our economic system, these rising costs can be expected to endure for the foreseeable future. Second, the explanation will enable us to evaluate the damage it threatens to inflict on the general welfare. Does it foretell a future of poverty, with steady deterioration in the standard of living? We will see that nothing of the sort is at stake and that, curiously, these rising costs are an inevitable part of economic progress.

These steadily rising costs can damage the public interest, I will argue, only if the nature of the phenomenon is misunderstood, and policy makers are led to reactions that appear rational but in fact are the opposite. Still, we are not quite home free. As we will see, the other side of that is the cost disease, represented by those products (computers are a good example) whose costs are falling in real terms, may constitute a more serious threat to the general welfare.[1]

Causes of Health-Care Cost Increases: Three Common Misconceptions

What accounts for the ever increasing costs of labor-intensive services? Can the increases be attributed to inefficiencies in government management or to political corruption? The issue is surely complex, and no single hypothesis can pretend to account for a set of problems whose roots are undoubtedly sociological and psychological as well as economic. Many conditions, actual or alleged, may help to explain the high levels and rapid increase of those costs. In the case of health care, for instance, among the most commonly cited are aging of the population, pricing by pharmaceutical and medical technology manufacturers, lawsuits against doctors and others involved in health care, a lack of competitiveness in the medical profession, and physicians' high earnings.[2]

All of these do have some influence, and no doubt there are other factors as well. But none of them appears to constitute a major source of the continuing and rapid rise in health-care costs. For instance, the number of medical malpractice payments declined steadily after 2002.[3] Granted, average malpractice payments and median jury awards for medical malpractice suits both increased steadily (adjusted for inflation) during roughly the same period.[4] But the incidence and size of malpractice awards would have to be increasing much faster than they are in order for persistently rising medical costs to be attributable to malpractice litigation.

Similarly, if a lack of competitiveness in the medical profession was the cause of growing health-care costs, the degree of competitiveness would have to have been declining over many years. The evidence does not support this. In the last decade and a half, the number of physicians per capita in the United States actually increased slightly—from 2.1 physicians per 1,000 people in 1993 to 2.4 per 1,000 in 2007—which certainly does not suggest that competition among doctors has declined.[5] During the same period, the number of matriculants in American medical schools also increased slightly.[6] Competition in the medical field apparently has not decreased, so we would expect that wages in the health-care industry would not have risen much faster than the rate of inflation (confirmed by the data in Figure 1.7) and therefore could not have contributed significantly to rising health-care costs.

Finally, if doctors' incomes were a valid explanation for rising costs, these would have risen over time, despite inflation. Again, the facts show otherwise. In the early 1970s, medical workers' earnings were increasing faster than inflation, but by 1980, as shown in Figure 1.7, these increases were easily outstripped by the rate of inflation.[7] Despite impressive increases in the number of dollars they earn, medical workers' purchasing power actually has declined since 1980. Thus, the problem cannot be attributed to physicians' greed, unscrupulous overcharging, or other forms of villainy. Although the ethics of doctors are probably no better than those of professors or other professionals, attributing the bulk of the cost increases to doctors' unchecked avarice is surely misguided.

How the Cost Disease Works: A Basic Explanation

The cost disease can best be explained using an analogy: in 1946, a British newspaper headline shocked readers by reporting that "Nearly Half of U.K. Student Grades Are Below Average." The cost disease functions the same way. To see this, we must remember that any index of the overall price level is just an average of the prices in the economy. These prices, in turn, reflect the costs of producing goods and services. The rate of inflation, then, is an *average* of the rates of growth of many different prices. It follows immediately and unequivocally that *if the prices of all commodities are not rising at the same pace, then some must be increasing at a rate above average.* That is, their inflation-adjusted—or real—prices must be rising. The real prices of other commodities, meanwhile, *must* be falling. Health care is one of the commodities whose costs are rising at a rate above average, for reasons we will see. This means that, by definition, health-care costs *must* be rising faster than the economy's overall (average) rate of inflation.

Beyond that rudimentary analysis, true by definition, the only additional element of the cost disease is the observation that the list of those items whose real costs are rising remains roughly constant, decade after decade, while the same appears to be true of those items whose real costs are falling. That is, the cost of health care is rising faster than the average rate of inflation today, and we can be reasonably confident that it will continue to do so tomorrow as well as the day after. The opposite is true of computers, whose cost will continue to fall behind the economy's average inflation. The reason is not difficult to identify. The items in the rising-cost group generally have a *handicraft* element—that is, a human element not readily replaceable by machines—in their production process, which makes it difficult to reduce their labor content. Items whose prices are falling are predominantly manufactured via much more easily automated processes. Their steadily falling real costs simply reflect their declining labor content.

This idea, then, is fundamentally simple. The growth rate of costs in some industries must be below the average, while others must be above it. The former group is composed substantially of industries in which the production process offers few opportunities for labor-saving changes, while the latter, the industries with the relatively falling costs, are those that offer abundant opportunities for labor-saving changes.

A More Extensive Explanation

The clue to a fuller explanation lies in the nature of the products whose real costs are driven upward. The cost disease stems from the nature of what I will refer to as "the personal services," which usually require direct, face-to-face interaction between those who provide the service and those who consume it. Doctors, teachers, and librarians all have jobs that require in-person contact.

Other parts of the economy—car manufacturing, for instance— require no direct personal contact between the consumer and the producer. The buyer of an automobile usually has no idea who worked on its assembly and does not care how much labor time went into its production. Moreover, suppose a new production process is introduced that allows an automotive plant to increase its annual production by, say, 25 percent without increasing its workforce. If the size of the labor force is left unchanged but wages are increased by 25 percent, the rise in output will exactly offset the cost of the higher wages. The workers are just as productive as before, if we measure productivity by the labor cost per car, even though they're spending less time on each car. But a reduction in the amount of time put into a personal service is likely to make the service worse. In other words, an increase in labor productivity in health care or education—that is, a rise in the number of patients or students treated or educated in a given amount of time—is difficult to attain without an accompanying decline in quality.

As a result, it has proved far easier for technological change to save labor in manufacturing than in providing many of the economy's services. In the period after World War II, for instance, productivity in the U.S. nonfarm business sector grew by roughly 2 percent on average each year.[8] Meanwhile, labor productivity in elementary and secondary education, for example, actually *declined*, with the average number of pupils per teacher in public schools falling from about 25 in 1960–1961 to about 15 in 2006–2007.[9]

When growing productivity raises wages throughout the economy, it should be clear how differing productivity growth rates lead to rising real costs in some industries and relatively declining real costs in others. Take, for example, manufacturing—if wages in this sector rise by 2 percent, the cost of manufactured products need not rise because increased output per worker offsets the higher wages. In contrast, the nature of many personal services makes it very difficult to introduce labor-saving devices. A 2 percent wage increase for teachers or police officers is not offset by higher productivity and therefore must lead to equivalent increases in municipal budgets. A 2 percent wage increase for hairdressers must lead beauty salons to raise their prices.

In the long run, wages for all workers throughout a country's economy tend to go up and down together. Otherwise, an activity whose wage rate falls seriously behind will tend to lose its labor force. Auto workers and police officers will see their wages rise at roughly the same rate in the long run, but if productivity on the assembly line advances while productivity in the patrol car does not, then the cost of police protection will increase—relative to manufacturing. Over several decades, the two sectors' differing cost growth rates add up, making personal services enormously more expensive than manufactured goods.

Sustained Patterns

Historical evidence confirms the resulting remarkable persistence of this pattern of differences in productivity growth. Economic sectors usually do not fluctuate haphazardly between periods of relatively slow and relatively rapid advance in productivity. Rather, the industries in which productivity was expanding slowly a century ago are by and large still the laggards today. The endurance of productivity stagnancy in these industries has imposed upon the services they provide a distinctive cost history that is the fundamental symptom of the cost disease: cumulative and persistent cost increases that significantly exceed the larger economy's rate of inflation.

In addition to health care and education, these industries include legal services, welfare programs for the poor, the postal service, police protection, sanitation, repair services, the performing arts, restaurant services, and many others. Their common element is the handicraft—or in-person—attribute of their supply processes. None of these has yet been fully automated and thus liberated from this requirement of substantial personal attention by their producers. Although most of these sectors have seen some rise in productivity over time (that is, their labor productivity growth rates have not always been zero), it has increased far more slowly than productivity has risen in the larger economy. Innovations have not been very effective in bringing labor savings to these industries. For this reason, I call these the *stagnant services*.

There are at least two reasons why productivity growth has eluded the stagnant services. First, some are inherently resistant to standardization. Thousands of identical automobiles, for instance, can be manufactured on an assembly line, with much of the work done by industrial robots—but the repair of a car hauled to a garage after an accident cannot be automated. After all, before one can try to cure a patient or repair a broken piece of machinery, one must determine exactly what is wrong and tailor the treatment to the individual case. A second reason why it has been difficult to reduce the labor content of these services is that quality is—or at least is believed to be—inescapably correlated with the amount of labor expended on their production. That is, it is difficult to reduce the time needed to perform certain tasks without also reducing the quality of their product. If we try to speed up the work of surgeons, teachers, or musicians, we are likely to get shoddy heart surgery, poorly trained students, or a very strange musical performance.

But there is also self-deception by the providers of those services and the customers who obtain them. At least some medical activities can be carried out better by computers than by doctors. For instance, a set of symptoms may be compatible with a dozen different illnesses—three of which may be rare and apt to be overlooked by physicians—but computers do not forget. Moreover, a filmed lecture by an extraordinarily talented teacher may provide better instruction than the same material presented live by a mediocre local professor. And recorded music is sometimes even preferable to live performance.[10]

This is not to deny that the personal attention of a doctor or a live instructor has important benefits. Live contact permits questions to be asked and answered by doctors and teachers, which is surely important and beneficial. Still, professors and medical doctors often have an inflated view of the benefits of their personal attendance in the lecture hall and the operating room. These attitudes are widely shared by medical patients, students, and others who benefit from such person-to-person interactions. This creates yet another obstacle to labor-saving modifications in stagnant-sector activities, even as labor-saving efforts are constantly under way throughout the progressive sector. Psychological resistance to labor-saving change in the personal services increases the lag in productivity growth that characterizes these services.

The divide between these stagnant and other services is evident when one examines job losses and gains during the current recession. Between December 2007 and June 2009, for example, the motor vehicles and parts sector lost 35 percent of its jobs—the largest loss of any U.S. employment sector.[11] The twenty sectors with the largest declines in employment also included textile mills (24 percent job loss), construction (17 percent), and manufacturing (14 percent). Ever increasing efficiency in these nonstagnant sectors—a key component of the cost disease—has allowed them to keep up with demand despite laying off workers.[12] In contrast, the stagnant sectors actually gained jobs during that period.[13] Because these sectors are far less amenable to labor-saving changes, they cannot continue to provide their services with fewer workers.

Not All Services Are Stagnant

Many of the published comments on the cost disease imply that the cost disease affects *all* services. This is not so. Many services have benefited from rapid productivity growth and therefore are not part of the stagnant sector. Telecommunications, for instance, though clearly a service, is undoubtedly in the progressive sector. Productivity growth in this industry has been not merely substantial but at the forefront of the economy. The advent of the Internet, mobile telephones, and a host of other advances make it clear that the telecommunications industry's superior productivity growth is not likely to slow any time soon. Moreover, among progressive sector services—especially those connected with computers, this industry's impressive productivity growth is hardly alone.

The Fate of the Stagnant Sectors

We have divided the economy into two sectors—the progressive sector, in which productivity is rising, and the stagnant sector, in which productivity is constant or growing very slowly. Let us simplify this with a thought experiment. Suppose the first sector produces only automobiles, while the second only performs Mozart quartets. Let us assume that in automobile production, where technological improvements can increase efficiency, output per work hour is rising at an annual rate of 4 percent, while the productivity of quartet players remains unchanged year after year. Now imagine that the auto workers recognize their own productivity growth and persuade management to agree to a matching rise in wages. The effect on the automobile industry is easy to trace. Each year, the average worker's wage goes up by 4 percent; meanwhile, average output increases by exactly the same percentage. Each effect on cost is thus exactly offset by the other, and labor cost per unit (that is, the ratio of total labor cost to total output) remains unchanged. This process can continue indefinitely, with auto workers earning more each year, but with increased efficiency preventing an increase in the cost of production per automobile, thereby allowing both automobile prices and manufacturers' profits to remain constant.

But what of the other industry in our little economy? How is quartet performance faring in this society of growing abundance? Suppose that the quartet players somehow succeed in getting their wages raised by 4 percent each year so that their standard of living maintains its position relative to the auto workers. How does this situation affect the costs of quartet performance? For a while, perhaps, the musicians could also increase their performances by 4 percent a year, but because they cannot keep doing this forever, let us assume that the number of performances is fixed. If each string player provides just as many performances as in the previous year but his wage is 4 percent higher, the cost per performance must rise by 4 percent. There is nothing to prevent this cost from rising indefinitely. So long as the musicians are successful in resisting erosion of their incomes relative to those of the auto workers, the cost per performance must continue to increase along with the performers' incomes. Thus, the performing arts will be beset with perpetually rising costs.

Note that ordinary price inflation plays no role in this analysis.[14] So long as the wages of musicians in this two-sector economy continue to increase, the cost of a live performance will rise cumulatively and persistently relative to the cost of an automobile, whether or not the general price level in the economy is changing. The extent of the increase in the relative cost of the performance will depend directly on the relative rate of productivity growth in the respective industries. Moreover, though it is always tempting to seek some villain to explain such cumulative cost increases, there is no guilty party here. Neither wasteful expenditure nor greed need play any role. Instead, the irreducible time and labor required for a live musical performance, which resists productivity improvements, accounts for the compounding rise in the cost of attending a Mozart quartet.[15]

This analysis can be applied to many personal services. For instance, the output per hour of police patrol time, postal delivery time, or street cleaning time has been enhanced—in terms of territory covered—by the use of motor vehicles. But this increase in productivity has been modest and certainly has not been continuous and cumulative. Moreover, in the case of police work, the productivity of criminal activity also has been enhanced (in terms of the labor time needed to achieve the criminal's goal) by the use of motor vehicles—thus offsetting some of the police officers' productivity gains. Among other personal service industries, productivity has risen by a minuscule amount at most. Automotive insurance appears to be an example because the purchaser of an insurance policy is simply acquiring a bundle of several stagnant services—health care, automobile repair, legal services, and so on.

A final class of stagnant services is particularly significant. Government welfare and related programs, which do not benefit from any significant source of productivity growth, are essentially handicraft activities whose technology remains fundamentally unchanged. This has substantial consequences for taxation and fiscal policy, among other important matters.

Rising productivity clearly makes a nation wealthier and helps to contain poverty, but it also underlies the cost disease and the rising real costs of the affected services. A disturbing moral of the story is that the products most vulnerable to the cost disease include some of the most vital attributes of civilized communities: health care, education, the arts, police protection, and street cleaning, among others. All of these services suffer from cost increases that are both rapid and persistent. They threaten the strained budgets of families, municipalities, and central governments throughout the industrialized world and, as we will see in Chapter 7, those in developing countries as well. As financial stringency inevitably becomes more pressing, spending on these services is apt to be cut back or, at best, increased by amounts that are barely sufficient to stay abreast of overall inflation. As a result, the supply of these services may fall in both quantity and quality. This is not the only source of increasing public squalor, but it surely is apt to make a significant contribution.

In other words, it is inherent in the economic growth process that the economic activities for which labor-saving innovation is difficult to come by are often the very activities that are generally considered most critical for society's welfare. They are condemned to a pattern of spiraling increases in their real costs that appears to put them beyond the reach of both the individual and the state. Thus, rising productivity and the attendant cost disease threaten to create both private affluence and public squalor. We will see, however, that despite these unavoidable increases in real costs, such outcomes are not inescapable. The very nature of the cost disease ensures that we can cover these cost increases, though if government intervention is lacking, this remains an urgent problem for the impoverished members of society. But that paradoxical assertion is a different part of the story.

Further Evidence from the Stagnant Sectors

If the lagging productivity explanation is correct, the rising real costs that are the symptom of the cost disease should be present in a wide range of personal services industries. Funeral services, for instance, have more than doubled in cost since 1987, suggesting the presence of the cost disease.[16] Between 1987 and 2008, a period when overall inflation grew at roughly 3 percent each year, the cost of funeral services increased by nearly 5 percent each year.[17] Similarly, the Bureau of Labor Statistics' price index for legal services suggests that between 1986 and 2008 lawyers' fees outpaced inflation by about 1.5 percent each year (Figure 2.1).[18] It is easy to extend the list of personal service industries in which labor productivity has grown at much slower rates than it has in the manufacturing sector. Productivity in the funeral homes and services sector, for instance, grew by just over 1 percent a year between 1986 and 2008.[19] In the same period, productivity in the overall manufacturing sector grew by an average of just over 3 percent per year.[20] Such lagging productivity is precisely what the cost disease analysis would lead us to expect from these industries.

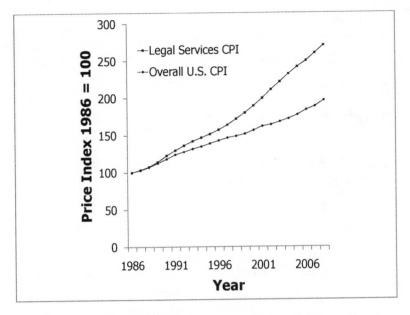

Figure 2.1. Legal services consumer price index (CPI) versus overall CPI in the United States, 1986–2008. (Based on data from the U.S. Bureau of Labor Statistics.)

Productivity Growth, Innovation, and Entrepreneurship

Figure 2.2 shows estimates of GDP per inhabitant of China, Italy, and the United Kingdom since 1500.[21] Notice that for the sixteenth, seventeenth, and eighteenth centuries, the graph is almost horizontal, meaning that productivity growth was almost zero. Despite the significant accomplishments of the Italian Renaissance in the fourteenth and fifteenth centuries, the difference between the Italian and English curves during this period is hardly discernible. Not until the onset of the Industrial Revolution in the first part of the

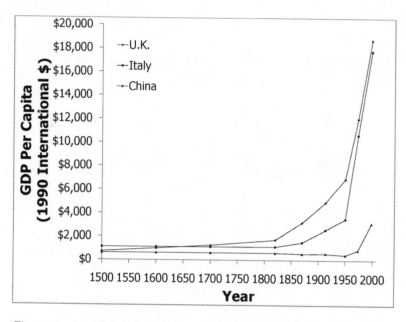

Figure 2.2. Gross domestic product per capita, 1500–2006: China, Italy, and the United Kingdom. (Based on data from Angus Maddison, *The World Economy: A Millennial Perspective*, Paris: OECD, 2001, p. 264.)

nineteenth century does growth in England begin to increase significantly. In Italy, this starting point occurs perhaps half a century later, and in China it begins even later—in the late twentieth century.

What happened to bring on this truly revolutionary era and its unprecedented explosion of productivity growth? The sharply varying opinions of economic historians confirm that there cannot be a single answer. Clearly, however, one key contribution was the outburst of breakthrough inventions such as the steam engine, railroads, and electricity, as well as institutional innovations such as contract law, the patent system, and the rule of law. These changes materially enhanced the incentives for innovative entrepreneurs, who ensure that inventions are put to effective use. Moreover, as the great economist Joseph Schumpeter has emphasized, competition among business firms evolved such that the principal weapon used to combat rivals became innovation—new products and new processes. In such an environment, no firm dares to fall behind in the innovation race, in which the penalty for the laggards is often death of the company.

Several conclusions follow from this. First, because there was little productivity growth before the Industrial Revolution in the economy as a whole, and probably not much in any particular industry, no industries leaped quickly ahead or fell far behind. Instead, few industries, if any, seemed to have achieved much more than zero average productivity growth. As a result, there probably was little growth in the disparity among these industries' relative costs, and no products were beset by any substantial cost disease.

The absence of institutions that rewarded inventors and innovative entrepreneurs surely helps to explain the lack of growth from 1500 to 1800, and the same is likely true for the bulk of history before that. But what about the future—the remainder of the twenty-first century and beyond? Here, caution on our part is surely called for because, as we know, economists are able to predict anything except the future. Still, more than a half-century of data are a strong indication that the cost disease is not a transitory phenomenon. The arms race among business firms, especially in the high-tech sectors of the economy, suggests that management will not lag in innovation and that labor-saving processes will continually appear in those industries where they are relatively easy to implement. So we can expect the cost disease to be with us for the foreseeable future. This is one disease for which we have no cure.

The long-term historical view makes it clear that the existence of a sector of the economy with persistently rising real costs is indissolubly married to the existence of a substantial sector with a very different performance pattern—one in which real costs are forever falling because market forces push productivity to grow at an above-average rate. You cannot have one sector without the other. This may seem to impart at least a partially happy ending to the cost disease story, but unfortunately it is not quite as felicitous a prospect as it seems. Over the next three chapters, we will see that, paradoxically, the rising costs of the economy's stagnant sector are not nearly as serious a threat as they appear to be, while the falling costs of the progressive sector are not a pure blessing.

THREE

The Future Has Arrived

Longevity has its place.
—Martin Luther King Jr.

The rising real (inflation-adjusted) costs that constitute the cost disease are both persistent and dramatic, but they cannot force us to give up our customary patterns of consumption. Instead, the flip side of the cost disease—the near universality of rising productivity in the economy as a whole—means that we *can* afford health care, education, and other personal services despite their disturbingly persistent rates of cost increase. Indeed, we can even afford steady expansion in the amounts of these services we consume.

This does not mean, however, that society is unaffected by the cost disease. Over the years, general standards of living have increased, and our material possessions have multiplied. But our communities have experienced a decline in the quality of many public and private services, arguably because of these services' rising costs and the resulting cuts in employment needed to reduce budgetary pressure. As workers' wages have risen—not only in the United States but throughout the world—streets and subways have grown dirtier, and bus, train, and postal services have been cut back.[1] Suburban Londoners in the mid-1800s, for instance, received twelve mail deliveries each weekday and even one on Sundays. Today the Royal Mail, with its single daily delivery and other declines in service quality, no longer inspires our admiration.

Similarly, the quality of private services has been cut back. In the past, speaking with a human being at the bank, the doctor's office, or the utility company did not involve answering a series of automated questions with button-push responses. We seem headed toward a future in which personal services demand greater expenditures of both money and time and constitute a rising share of the budgets of individuals and governments.[2]

The Triumph of Do-It-Yourself

Entrepreneurs, who introduce products that stimulate consumer demand and keep pace with competition, seek ways of keeping costs down. This is particularly urgent for products or services that are subject to the cost disease. One widespread approach toward that goal is obvious: one can make some modification to a product, which reduces the amount of labor required to supply it and thus avoid the corresponding wage outlay. The simplest way to do this is to shift some of that labor from the supplier to the consumer. This gambit, in essence, is the logic of the "do-it-yourself" feature of so many products and services that are sold today. In effect, the entrepreneur demands that the technicians who update the products modify their design so that part of the labor entailed in making them functional is simplified to the point that it can be carried out by the consumer.

In the developed world, for instance, most of us do our own cleaning and other household tasks, now that maids and butlers have all but disappeared.[3] These professions were largely gone by the time I obtained my first teaching position some six decades ago, but my older colleagues at the time had previously employed maids, even when they were only assistant professors. Today, even people who still employ such help get by with far less of it than earlier generations. Once, when a former professor of mine and his wife were staying at my home, they received a lunch invitation from another former student, one of the world's wealthiest men. The chauffeured car was sent to pick them up, but when they returned after lunch, the host had to drive them himself because, he explained, it was the driver's afternoon off.

Many other personal services are now relegated to the do-it-yourself realm. Until the 1960s or so, milkmen would deliver dairy products from house to house. Before World War II there was also an iceman who made the same rounds, as refrigerators were a rarity. And when illness struck, the physician would arrive carrying his little black bag. At that time, office visits were a rarity, employed only for routine examinations. Today, milk and ice are purchased from grocery stores and stored in refrigerators, and house calls by doctors have disappeared—sick patients normally travel to their doctors or emergency rooms to receive treatment.

But for academics perhaps the biggest change is the disappearance of secretaries. Early in my career, I would write articles by hand and give them to a secretary, who would type multiple copies with carbon paper. No matter how smart the secretary—or how superb her typing skills—it often took three weeks to decipher a professor's handwriting and to type out and correct the obscure hieroglyphics. By the 1980s, when I was appointed to head a committee that allocated research grants to colleagues, we found that most of the grant applicants had requested around $10,000 to fund secretarial and research help. It occurred to us that there was an alternative: We offered each applicant the choice between the requested assistants and a new computer. Every applicant chose the computer, saving us some $7,000 per grant.

Perhaps the most striking change, however, is the advent of the disassembled product, available for purchase in a large carton stamped with the terrifying message "easy to assemble." Most of us dread the assembly process that such products entail. We know that one or more days that could have been better spent likely will be eaten up, as we run into various dead ends—broken, ill fitting, or lost parts—and must suffer the humiliation of turning to our children or grandchildren for help.

The "Throw-Away" Society

People often complain that American citizens lack social conscience and that one extreme manifestation of this is the "throw-away" society, in which we simply dispose of valuable products that are essentially still functional but have run into some problem—a malfunctioning part or an exhausted battery. Not only is this a waste of the product itself, but it also exacerbates the community's waste disposal problem, which in turn contributes to pollution.

This conception of disposable products, however, is largely a misunderstanding. Take, for instance, my father's gold-filled pocket watch, a Waltham dated 1915, which I still own. It is a beautiful mechanism, but to keep it running accurately my father had it cleaned once a year at a cost of $10. Anyone who has ever disassembled such a watch, cleaned the parts, and reassembled it (as I have done, sometimes even successfully) knows that it entails several hours of skilled labor. Today such a thorough cleaning job, with complete manual disassembly, costs a few hundred dollars. A few watch enthusiasts still get this done, but my current wristwatch cost less than $7 and has kept amazingly accurate time for more than three years. When the battery inevitably expires, it will simply be logical to replace this watch with a new one.

Things were not always this way. Until the end of the eighteenth century, when paper was very expensive and the rubber eraser had not yet been invented, people wrote notes on fan-shaped booklets made of ivory that could be erased with a wet rag and reused. Jefferson used one, and Franklin was both a seller and a user of such ivory booklets.[4] Meanwhile, the fortunate few who could afford paper for writing customarily erased their notes by rubbing them with fresh bread and reused the paper. In the sixteenth century, experiments with "erasable paper" abounded. One such "table book" asserted on its title page that what the user had written upon it "you may erase with a wet finger. And when you have worn out [the erasable surface], so that you cannot write on it any more, you can get it repaired by Jan Severszoon, parchment maker, for a little money, and you can write on it as if it was new. . . ."[5]

The point is that maintenance and repair of products inherently resist automation. A mechanical watch can suffer many different forms of damage. Just as the doctor must examine each sick patient individually to determine just what the problem is, the person who repairs an antique watch or fountain pen must personally disassemble the item and inspect it. For a modern, mass-produced item, it is typically far too expensive to arrange for the handicraft task entailed in its repair. Simply throwing it away and buying a mass-produced replacement is often a far less expensive alternative.

Similarly, the cost disease analysis would lead us to expect that the cost of automobiles made on the assembly-line would increase far more slowly than the handicraft work of automobile repair, which often requires item-by-item inspection and special treatment. Of course, matters do not always conform with theory.[6] Earlier data did appear to confirm this prediction, but it must be admitted that that has not been true of the more recent data.

Automobile insurance, however, does seem to display the predicted pattern. Figure 3.1 shows thirty years of data on the cost of automobile repairs and automobile insurance compared with the Consumer Price Index. It is clear that the cost of automobile insurance has risen significantly faster than the economy's overall rate of inflation even though the cost of automobile repairs has not. This is because insurance entails not only the cost of automobile repair—which cannot be fully automated and thus remains a labor-intensive task—but also the medical costs of accident victims, who also require bodily "repairs" that are hardly standardized and homogeneous.

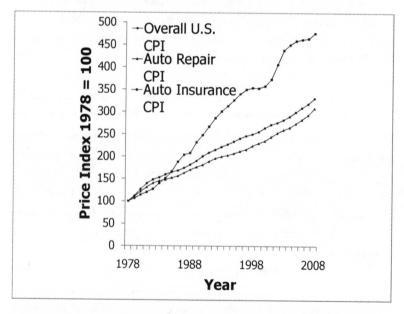

Figure 3.1. Automobile maintenance and repair consumer price index (CPI) versus automobile insurance CPI versus overall CPI in the United States, 1978–2008. (Based on data from the U.S. Bureau of Labor Statistics.)

The Automation Revolution and the
Do-It-Yourself Incentive

The rise in the cost of personal services has served as an incentive for labor-saving innovations—many of which help to transform labor-intensive paid tasks into do-it-yourself activities, often leaving all but the very wealthy with little choice in the matter. The marvelous machinery now found in every middle-class kitchen—the dishwasher, the in-sink garbage disposal, the automatic toaster, and much more—helps facilitate the replacement of hired cooks. Outside the home, one can find many other illustrations. The automatic teller machine, for example, is designed to have users do for themselves what was once done by a bank teller. The insult in the arrangement is the occasional charge for ATM use, by which bank depositors are expected to pay for the privilege of doing their own work in depositing or withdrawing cash.

Another obvious but more complicated example is the disappearance of elevator operators. Interestingly, this disappearance is not yet complete: it remains as an example of what Veblen called "conspicuous waste"[7]—that is, spending carried out simply to show the world that the person making the outlay can afford the useless expenditure. Very elegant hotels that want to advertise their luxury retain uniformed elevator operators wearing handsome gloves to push the buttons.

Production of newspapers also has been modified in ways that serve to combat the cost disease. Typesetting is no longer done by hand, or even with a Linotype machine. Today, page layout software programs and laser printers make typesetting and correction far less labor-intensive. Still, reporting and writing the news resist automation, and their cost has continued to increase, as is evident in the price of the *New York Times*, which has exploded (in money terms) from about two cents in the 1920s to (at this writing) $2 on weekdays and $5 on Sundays. Surprisingly, however, this price increase translates into an average annual increase below that of inflation.

Automation is spreading even into realms that sound like science fiction. Health care provides many startling examples. A notable one, described at the American Philosophical Society's 2003 meeting, involves robotics and X-ray technology.[8] The patient undergoes an advanced form of radiology that is far more sophisticated than a computed tomography scan. The output, which resembles a credit card, contains a set of photographs of the patient's innards, layer by layer—from the skin to the skeleton. Then, if the patient needs surgery, this can be carried out by a robot, preprogrammed by computer for the task and guided by the set of photos on the "credit card." Several dry-run presurgeries can be done to ensure that the robot has it right; a surgeon is in attendance during the operation but only assists if there is an emergency. This process has already been carried out on live patients—at least one of whom was far from the location of the supervising human surgeon. Here, the primary purpose, clearly, was not saving human labor but giving medical care to a patient in a remote location. This example suggests the imaginative forms that the pursuit of labor-saving goals may take.

Productivity Growth and Survival of the Stagnant Services

The glimpse of the future described here shows that the cost disease is changing how personal services are provided, even though the supply of some of these services, such as health care and education, has not been reduced. Do-it-yourself procedures and disposable products are only two examples of this new reality.

One of the issues raised by the cost disease, however, is whether we will begin to see reduced demand and supply of certain items and services. As we have already seen, productivity growth ensures that both wages and per capita income will continue to increase, making most products and services cheaper relative to consumers' buying power.[9] This means that we can afford not merely the current quantities of these items and services but also ever greater

Table 3.1. Automobile Maintenance and Repair Consumer Price Index (CPI) versus Automobile Insurance CPI versus Overall CPI in the United States, 1978 to 2008.

Country	1980 (years)	2000 (years)	Increase (%)
Italy	74	80	8.1
Germany	72.9	78.2	7.3
Japan	76.1	81.2	6.7
France	74.3	79.2	6.6
United Kingdom	73.2	77.9	6.4
Canada	75.3	79.3	5.3
United States	73.7	76.8	4.2

Source: Based on data from the U.S. Bureau of Labor Statistics.

Table 3.2. Percentage of 18- to 21-Year-Olds Enrolled in Postsecondary Education in Belgium, France, Germany, the Netherlands, the United Kingdom, and the United States, 1985 versus 2005.

Country	1985 (%)	2005 (%)	Increase (%)
Netherlands	14	29	107
France	19	36	89
United Kingdom	15	28	87
Belgium	25	43	72
Germany	9	13	44
United States	37	45	22

Source: Based on data from the National Center for Education Statistics, *Digest of Education Statistics: 2008 Tables and Figures*, Table 401: Percentage of Population Enrolled in Secondary and Postsecondary Education, by Age Group and Country, http://nces.ed.gov. Data for Germany for 1985 are for the former West Germany.

quantities and ever rising quality in the future, despite their rising costs. Thus, there is no need to contemplate reductions in the provision of health care, education, or the performing arts. Here, too, the future is already with us.

This is evident in Tables 3.1 and 3.2, which show that despite steadily rising health-care and education costs,[10] health-care quality and access have improved steadily and substantially in much of the world in recent decades, while secondary and postsecondary education has become more common.

Although the cost disease has constricted some personal services, such as household servant labor and secretarial assistance, this constriction need not apply to health care and education, where demand not only persists in the face of cost increases but even expands when rising productivity enhances consumers' purchasing power.[11] Despite the appearance of dramatic cost increases and ensuing reductions in quantity and quality induced by ill-considered reactions to those increases, the future promises more and better health care, education, and police protection—to name just three of the most critical stagnant-sector services. In short, society can afford to expand its consumption of these services, despite their rising costs. That, then, is not the real and ultimately unavoidable danger associated with the cost disease.

FOUR

Yes, We Can Afford It

If the amount that can be produced by an hour of labor increases for almost every commodity and decreases for none, then more of *everything* can be provided for the public to consume.
—WILLIAM BAUMOL

We saw in Chapter 3 that the cost disease has brought profound changes in the way we live. If it continues to influence the workings of the economy, the consequences may be even more far-reaching. With continued growth in general productivity, the typical household may enjoy an abundance of goods, but if governmental responses are poorly considered, citizens also may suffer from great deterioration in public services such as garbage removal. The services of doctors, teachers, and police officers may become more automated and impersonal, and the arts and crafts may be increasingly supplied only by amateurs—the cost of professional work in these fields may be too high. In these circumstances, people may begin to question whether the explosion of the supply of material goods has really improved their quality of life.

Yet the cost disease does not make this future inevitable. To see why, one must understand that the source of the problem, paradoxically, is the growth of our economy's labor productivity—or rather the unevenness of that growth. Trash removal costs go up not because garbage collectors become less efficient but because less labor is needed to manufacture a single computer, for instance, and wages in that industry (and others, as well) continue to climb. Although the sanitation worker's productivity is barely increasing, her wages must go up in order to keep her at her garbage removal job—otherwise, she might be tempted to join the computer assembly line. Productivity growth in some sectors of the economy—and the wage increases that accompany it—thus raises the cost of garbage removal and other personal services.

Despite this trend, increasing productivity does *not* make an economy unable to afford what it could afford in the past. Productivity growth makes a society wealthier, not poorer, and able to afford more of all things—televisions, electric toothbrushes, and cell phones, as well as medical care, education, and other services.[1] This outcome is particularly likely, given the impressive speed at which overall productivity is increasing, relative to the costs of personal services.

But productivity growth alone does not solve all of our economic problems. Workers with no great skills cannot expect wage increases commensurate with overall productivity growth or the rising costs of health care and education; neither can the unemployed. The state must help equalize matters by providing such services to those who otherwise could not afford them.[2] The tax increases required to fund the provision of such services by the government, however, come with political and economic consequences.

Unprecedented Productivity Increases: Past, Present, and Future

The statement that the global economy's productivity is growing is misleading—not because it is wrong, but because it fails to make clear the economy's fantastic growth, which is so remarkable and unprecedented that it strains our comprehension. Figure 4.1, already familiar from Chapter 2, showed the record of productivity growth, measured as gross domestic product (GDP) per capita between A.D. 1500 and 2000 for China, Italy, and the United Kingdom. I omitted the United States for the obvious reason that its records do not go back to 1500, and I included Italy because its prosperity

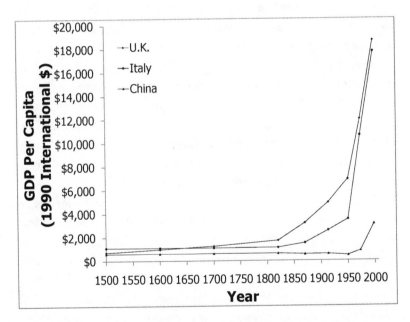

Figure 4.1. Gross domestic product per capita, 1500–2006: China, Italy, and the United Kingdom. (Based on data from Angus Maddison, *The World Economy: A Millennial Perspective*, Paris: OECD, 2001, p. 264.)

during the Renaissance constitutes a suggestive comparison. China is included because its data show the twentieth-century sequel—unparalleled anywhere apart from England's nineteenth-century Industrial Revolution—to its sixteen centuries of invention that were accompanied by relatively modest overall growth.

According to the best available estimates, between the fall of the Roman Empire in A.D. 476 and the American Revolution thirteen centuries later, the worldwide average growth in output per worker was not materially different from zero. It probably declined until about the tenth century and then began to crawl upward at a barely discernible pace. Although Figure 4.1 does not include data from before 1500, it does depict the crucial era when the Renaissance, already well established in Italy, got under way in England under Henry VIII. Between 1500 and the middle of the eighteenth century, per capita GDP in the three countries was virtually flat—a striking record of snail's-pace progress. We see also how very slightly the economic welfare of the Italians exceeded that of the English in that era, despite Italy's achievements in banking, cloth manufacturing, merchandising, and other fields. But from then on, it is clear that the rate of improvement grows ever faster, until the curves jut sharply upward, and China pulls ahead of both England and Italy in the second half of the twentieth century, as Figure 4.2 shows.

What is striking here is China's poor economic performance before the late twentieth century, at which point it began its dramatic productivity growth.[3] This recent explosion in output contrasts dramatically with China's earlier centuries of astonishing invention, which failed to produce anything like the past three centuries' growth in the West. One can argue that despite medieval China's profusion of inventors, entrepreneurs sought roles in the bureaucracy rather than in industry. In recent decades, entrepreneurship in China has instead directed itself to the business sector, while invention has fallen well short of its incredible earlier performance.

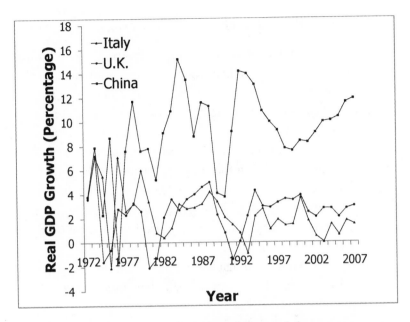

Figure 4.2. Annual real gross domestic product growth from 1972 to 2007: China, Italy, and the United Kingdom. (Based on data from *OECD Factbook 2009*, Economic, Environmental and Social Statistics, Paris: OECD.)

As for twentieth-century America, the most conservative estimates indicate that the average American's purchasing power in 2010 is about seven times as great as her ancestor's a century earlier. This means that an average American family living around 1900 could afford only *one-seventh* the food, clothing, housing, and other amenities that the average family today enjoys.[4] This change, too, is incredible in light of the world's previous economic performance. Its magnitude can perhaps be best understood by imagining how your family's life would change if it lost more than $6 out of every $7 it now earns, spends, and saves.

But What Happened to Costs?

We can look at this enormous economic progress from another angle: by examining how much work time it takes to acquire the income needed to buy the things we purchase. This arguably constitutes the best measure of their true cost to us. According to a 1997 report by the Federal Reserve Bank of Dallas, in 1919 the average worker labored thirteen minutes to earn enough to buy a pound of bread compared with just four minutes in 1997.[5] The work time required to buy one dozen eggs in 1919—eighty minutes—had fallen to just five minutes by 1997.[6] Figure 4.3 shows how the work time required to buy a variety of snack foods also has declined over the past century.

Food is not the only item that has become much less costly by this measure. In 1910, 345 hours of work time bought a kitchen range,

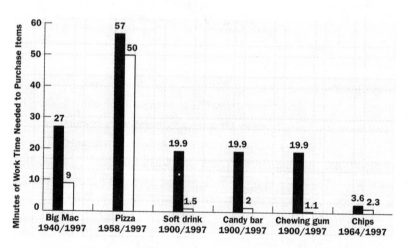

Figure 4.3. Declining real labor price of junk foods in the twentieth century. (From Baumol/Blinder. *Economics*, 12E. © 2011 South-Western, a part of Cengage Learning, Inc. Reproduced by permission. www.cengage.com/permissions.)

and 553 hours bought a clothes washer. By 1997, those numbers had dropped to 22 and 26 hours, respectively.[7] Purchasing a 1908 Ford Model T automobile required 4,696 hours of labor versus 1,365 hours for a 1997 Ford Taurus.[8] Figure 4.4 shows the dramatic reduction in the labor time, over a shorter time period, required to buy various electronic devices.

The most sensational decrease of all has been in the cost of computers. Computer capability is standardized in terms of the number of MIPS (millions of instructions per second) a computer can handle. In 1997, one MIPS of computer capacity cost about twenty-seven minutes of labor at the average wage. In 1984, it cost fifty-two *hours* of labor; in 1970, the cost was 1.24 *lifetimes* of labor; and in 1944, the cost was a barely believable 733,000 lifetimes of labor.[9] The data cited here are more than a decade old, and I have not been able to find any studies of the subject that are more recent. Still, there is

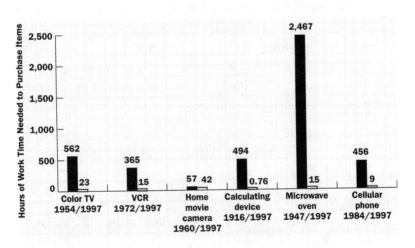

Figure 4.4. Declining real labor price of electronic products in the twentieth century. (From Baumol/Blinder. Economics, 12E. © 2011 South-Western, a part of Cengage Learning, Inc. Reproduced by permission. www.cengage.com/permissions.)

every reason to believe that the price of computing power, by any measure, has continued to plummet. In 1997, you could buy a computer with the capacity to perform 33 million computations per second for $1,000. In 2006, $1,000 bought you a computer capable of 2 trillion computations per second—even though $1,000 in 2006 could only buy what about $800 in 1997 could have purchased.[10]

The rise in productivity that makes it possible to create commodities with less and less labor, thereby lowering what consumers pay, has occurred in almost every industry. Even services that seem most impervious to productivity growth have participated indirectly in this process. I frequently use the example of a Mozart string quartet written for a half-hour performance as an example of a service that resists reduction of its labor content. But even an activity like live musical performance has benefited from considerable savings in time expended. In 1790, when Mozart traveled from Vienna to give a performance in Frankfort am Main, the trip required six days of extreme discomfort. (At the time, however, that was considered swift—Mozart wrote that he was surprised at the speed of the journey.[11]) Today, the same trip takes only about six hours: 1.5 hours for the airplane flight and 4.5 hours for transit to and from the airport and other preliminaries. Surely this is a marked reduction in the time required for such a musical performance.

We *Can* Afford It All

With this explosion of purchasing power at our disposal, we can expect to afford even the sharply rising costs of services such as health care and education without cutbacks in quality or quantity.[12] The extrapolations in Figures 4.5, 4.6, and 4.7 show what will happen to our spending on health care and other products and services if current productivity growth continues.[13] In that future world, we

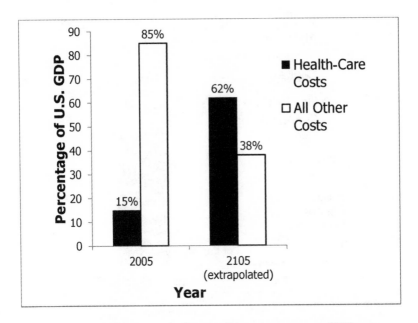

Figure 4.5. Health-care and other spending as a percentage of U.S. gross
domestic product: 2005 and extrapolated 2105. (Based on data from *OECD in
Figures 2007*, Health Spending and Resources, Paris: OECD, pp. 8–9.)

can have much more of *all* of these goods. By 2105, the amounts we
can consume will have gone up about 700 percent, leaving us far
better off.

The only thing that will change, in terms of the cost to us, is
how we will have to divide our money among these items. Because
manufactures and agricultural products are growing steadily
cheaper in real dollars while health care and education are growing
more expensive, we will have to increase the share of money we
devote to the latter services. The proportions will change drasti-
cally. In Figure 4.5, which projects relative spending on goods and
services from 2005 to 2105, I have kept the height of the bars (total

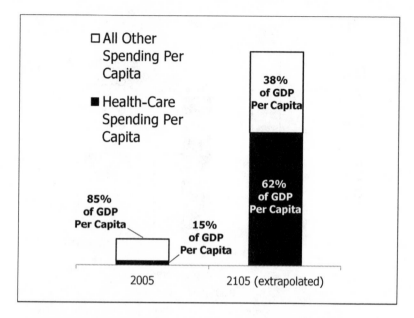

Figure 4.6. Percentages of U.S. gross domestic product per capita devoted to health care and all other purchases: 2005 and extrapolated 2105. (Based on data from *OECD in Figures 2007*, Health Spending and Resources, Paris: OECD, pp. 8–9; and from Angus Maddison, *The World Economy: Historical Statistics*, Table 8c: World Per Capita GDP, 20 Countries and Regional Averages, 1–2001 A.D., Paris: OECD, 2003, p. 262.)

spending) the same for ease of comparison. But the *share* of the spending devoted to health care will have exploded from about 15 percent of GDP in 2005 to roughly 60 percent in 2105.[14]

Yet because output is growing so fast, the *total* amount of purchasing power left over for other products and services will increase dramatically. Figure 4.6 shows the eightfold increase in total output per person by 2105 if overall economic productivity grows as it did during the twentieth century.

Health-care spending also will increase enormously in the next century, as Figure 4.7 shows. But despite this great increase,

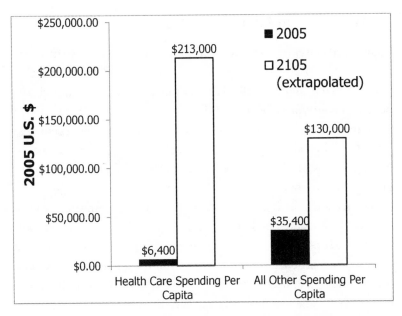

Figure 4.7. Change in U.S. gross domestic product per capita devoted to health care and to all other purchases, from 2005 to extrapolated 2105. (Based on data from *OECD in Figures 2007*, Health Spending and Resources, Paris: OECD, pp. 8–9; and from Angus Maddison, *The World Economy: Historical Statistics*, Table 8c: World Per Capita GDP, 20 Countries and Regional Averages, 1–2001 A.D., Paris: OECD, 2003, p. 262.)

the amount left over for all other purchases also will grow greatly— by more than three-and-a-half times—thanks to the eightfold rise in total income in the United States. We will be so much richer overall that, despite dramatically increasing health-care costs, we will be able to afford much more of everything. The cost disease, which was a cause for great gloom in Chapter 1, turns out to affect only the way in which we divide up the money we spend. It does not force us to decrease how much we buy. Thus, with no increase in the work we expend, our standard of living will have improved dramatically.

Why We Can Afford It All: No Historical Accident

I have used statistics to argue that, in the present state of the economy, the rising cost of services such as health care and education will not make them unaffordable to most consumers, though the poor will continue to be denied their benefits without some form of assistance. But is this affordability a mere accident of recent history? Could productivity and costs at some period in the future—perhaps very soon—behave very differently and force consumers to give up these beneficial services? The answer is no.

The reason is straightforward. In the world's community of consumers, if someone spends a dollar, someone else must earn that dollar. Thus, if people in that community choose to purchase all the commodities produced in all sectors, even if they must beg or borrow to obtain the necessary funds, then the members of that community as a whole automatically will earn the amount that is required to make those purchases. (Of course, the poor, unfortunately, are likely to get a much lesser share of the economy's output, but the shortfall in their purchasing power *must* be offset by the overabundant earnings of the wealthy.)

Although this may seem like the illusion of a professional magician, it is simply an inescapable feature of the sales process, and it remains true no matter how quickly (or slowly) the cost of any product rises. Thus, the statistical evidence provided in this chapter cannot be attributed to some set of freak circumstances. The rising costs of stagnant-sector products will never leave consumers, as a group, unable to afford to buy them.

The implication is clear. We can surely afford it—cars and computers as well as health care and education. The quantity and quality of the cost disease-affected services we obtain in the future will depend on how we order our priorities. If we value them sufficiently, we can have more and better services—at some sacrifice in the rate at which our consumption of manufactures grows. Society *does* have a choice, but if we fail to take steps to exercise this, our economy could continue to drift toward a world in which material goods are abundant, but many things we consider primary requisites for a high quality of life are too scarce, particularly for the poor.

Will Productivity Continue to Accelerate?

There is more to this story than mere accounting. The more relevant issue is whether productivity in the industrialized and rapidly developing countries of the world will continue to increase as it has in recent centuries. The evolution of free markets has created an environment that drives private firms constantly to invest funds and energy in the innovations that spur productivity growth. Elsewhere I have called this arrangement "the free-market innovation machine."[15] Key to this story are the giant oligopoly firms that have accounted for about 70 percent of the vast private spending on research and development (R&D) in the United States since the nineteenth century. The R&D activities of oligopoly firms in the high-tech industries can be described as an "arms race."[16] In keeping with the theories of that noted economist Joseph Schumpeter, who contributed much work on the topic of innovative entrepreneurship, these firms now regard pricing and advertising as secondary weapons in their competitive battles.[17] The primary weapon has become the new or improved products that these firms race to introduce before their rivals can bring more attractive alternatives to market. No firm dares to fall behind in the race to create new and better products because protracted failure to do so can be fatal. Just as the Red Queen's subjects in Lewis Carroll's *Through the Looking Glass* had to run as fast as they could in order to stay in the same place,[18] so too must each firm constantly come up with new products in order to preserve its position in the market. This "Red Queen game" is a key attribute of advanced economies that helps to account for their continuing outpouring of innovations. Corporate survival is a far more powerful incentive than monetary reward, which allows successful firms to rest on their laurels and withdraw from further innovative activity. Thus, an innovation arms race permits no rest.

The Red Queen game is automatically introduced by oligopolistic competition—that is, competition among a small number of large firms that dominate many industries—and is part of the normal workings of the market. Large, competitive high-tech firms cannot avoid—indeed, cannot survive without—constant and substantial reinvestment in R&D, whether conducted in-house or outsourced. The Red Queen game ensures that these high-tech firms are forced to keep investing in the innovation that drives productivity growth. Thus, there seems to be little reason to worry that productivity growth will slow down in the near future. Because greater productivity obviously means more abundance and more purchasing power, the Red Queen game provides another reason for our optimistic expectation that consumers in industrialized countries will continue to be able to afford ample products and services, even with rapidly rising costs.

The Other Source of Growth

Giant firms that invest heavily in R&D do not carry the burden of improving productivity all by themselves.[19] Much of the innovative activity of the economy comes from another group, the individual inventors and entrepreneurs who have created many of the breakthrough inventions of recent centuries.[20] Indeed, much of the large-firm R&D activity described in the previous section has been devoted to improvement of the breakthroughs contributed by these independent inventors and entrepreneurs, who often sell or lease their creations to larger enterprises.

This raises yet another important question: can we be optimistic about the continuing supply of inventors and entrepreneurs? Some earlier societies created an abundance of invention. The ancient Romans, for instance, probably invented the water mill that was the main source of inanimate power before the age of steam. In the first century A.D., they also invented a working steam engine. During the Middle Ages, the Chinese not only invented gunpowder and the compass, which are commonly attributed to them, but also paper, printing, the spinning wheel, playing cards, elaborate clocks, and much more. Yet these inventions were rarely put to widespread productive use, arguably because the Roman and Chinese entrepreneurs who would have brought the inventions to market were engaged in other tasks. In ancient Rome, those with entrepreneurial ambitions focused instead on supporting and carrying out military activity, while in medieval China, enterprising individuals seem to have focused their energies mainly on passing the imperial examinations and obtaining governmental or judicial positions that allowed them to accumulate wealth through bribery.

There is, then, ample reason to conclude that entrepreneurship plays a crucial role in innovation. Consequently, it is also important to examine what determines the long-run supply of *productive* entrepreneurial activity, as opposed to entrepreneurship that is unproductive or even destructive as in ancient Rome and medieval China. After all, private mercenary armies and drug cartels need entrepreneurs to get them started, and their activities can surely be rewarding, though they are more likely to damage the economy's output than to enhance it.

In the economics literature, it is often asserted that an abundant supply of entrepreneurs stimulates growth, while shrinkage in the cadre of entrepreneurs is a significant impediment to growth. But the appearance and disappearance of entrepreneurs is left as a mystery, perhaps related to cultural developments and vaguely described changes in other psychological and sociological influences. But the historical evidence suggests a less magical explanation.[21] Entrepreneurs do not suddenly appear from nowhere or vanish just as mysteriously. Rather, potential entrepreneurs—talented and ambitious people looking to establish a business enterprise that promises profits, whether legitimate or illegitimate—are always with us, but as the structure of the rewards offered in the economy changes, they switch their activities, gravitating toward arenas where the payoff prospects are most attractive. In doing so, they may move between activities that are generally recognized as entrepreneurial *and productive* and those that require considerable enterprising talent but may not involve production of goods and services—or may even *impede* production. Just as technological change led workers and engineers to reallocate themselves from canal building to railroad construction and then to still more modern enterprises, entrepreneurs have reallocated themselves in accordance with changes in the payoffs for different occupations. As they do so, the set of *productive* entrepreneurs appears to expand or contract.[22]

Thus, innovative entrepreneurship is a resource that can be reallocated between productive and unproductive activities, influenced by the institutional incentives that determine the relative payoffs of the two types of activities. In free-market economies, these incentives include rules that protect private property from expropriation, rules for the enforcement of contracts, a system of patents, and rules of bankruptcy protection that encourage risk taking. With these institutions in place, independent inventors and innovative entrepreneurs can expect earnings and prestige if they are successful. It follows that we may be optimistic about a continued supply of independent inventors and productive entrepreneurs.

A Sanguine Conclusion with Caveats

If we can expect productive innovation to continue, the most pressing problem created by the cost disease is the rise in relative costs of personal services and the resulting illusion that these services are no longer affordable. In reality, we will enjoy more from both the progressive and stagnant sectors, even though the products of the latter sector will grow relatively more expensive over time. But even this desirable outcome brings complications and perils.

Caveat 1: The Cost Disease Disproportionately Affects the Poor

Even if the average American can afford to purchase ever increasing quantities of those goods and services whose real costs are raised by the cost disease, there remain many inhabitants of the United States, and still more elsewhere in the world, whose incomes are far below the average. Here, too, the constantly rising productivity that underlies the cost disease should enable society to mitigate poverty to a substantial degree by providing larger quantities of all goods and services. But will this occur? In the United States, progress has been far from universal. As shown in Figure 4.8, for instance, as of 2007 a dramatically significant number of Americans are uninsured and thus are apt to have difficulty paying for health care. Obviously this problem is far worse during periods of recession, when many more people than usual are without jobs and thus without health insurance. It has been reported that "at least half of all bankruptcies by American families in 2005 were eventuated by medical events and catastrophic health expenditures."[23] As we will see in Chapter 7, enormous medical bills also place a disproportionate burden on the poorer citizens of low- and middle-income countries. Despite measures such as Medicaid and scholarship grants, the rising cost of health care and education serves as an effective access

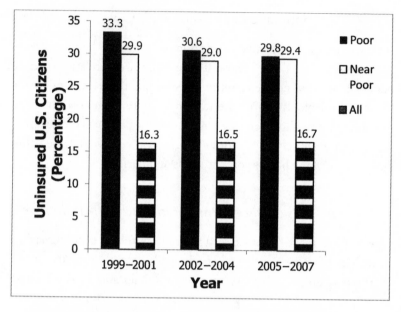

Figure 4.8. Percentages of uninsured U.S. citizens under age 65, 1999–2007: total population, near-poor population, and poor population.
(Based on data from the Centers for Disease Control and Prevention, *Health Insurance and Access* [interactive report], No Health Insurance under Age 65: U.S., 1999–2007 [table], 2007.)

barrier to poor and even middle-class Americans who seek these services.

Caveat 2: Ill-Advised Government Intervention Can Transform the Cost Disease into a More Serious Problem

It is wrong to interpret the cost disease as a failure of the market's pricing behavior, which, as standard economic analysis tells us, ensures that supplies approximate the amounts of each commodity that consumers demand. In this instance, the market *does* give the appropriate cost signals, reporting correctly that the amount of labor required to supply the affected services is declining at a rate far below the average, and perhaps may not be declining at all. As a result, the costs of these services rise persistently in comparison with those of manufactured products, which induces consumers to switch their purchases to those commodities that are easier and less costly to produce. Stagnant services, like the runner who never stops but runs far more slowly than the others, will never win the productivity race. Still, as we have seen in this chapter, rising purchasing power promises to keep even the rising-cost services affordable to the public as a whole. But the public and the government may misunderstand this. After all, the numbers are startling. If current trends continue for the next century, outlays on health care and education alone will far exceed half of the nation's GDP. This gives the appearance of a problem crying out for a dramatic solution.

Such frightening projections, along with their budgetary manifestations, may lead governments to make decisions that do not promote the public interest. For example, because health-care costs are increasing faster than the rate of inflation, if we want to maintain standards of care in public hospitals it is obviously not enough to keep health-care budgets growing at the economy's prevailing inflation rate. Those budgets must grow *faster*, or there must either be an increase in private financing of those services or a decline in quality. Suppose the current inflation rate is 4 percent, but hospital costs are rising at 6 percent a year. A political body that increases its hospitals' budgets by 5 percent per year will feel that something is wrong—even though the budgets steadily outpace the inflation rate, standards of quality at the hospitals are constantly slipping. If legislators do not realize that the cost disease is causing this problem, they will look for other explanations, such as corrupt or inefficient hospital administrators. The result can be a set of wasteful rules that inappropriately hamper hospitals' and doctors' freedom of action or tighten hospital budgets below the levels that would be determined by market forces.

Legislators often propose *cost controls* for sectors of the economy affected by the cost disease—for instance, medical services and insurance services. But cost controls often create problems that are more serious than the disease itself. As we saw in Chapter 1, many economies that have tried the cost-control approach to health-care services—Canada, the United Kingdom, Germany, and others— have had no more success than the United States in controlling cost increases.

We can see manifestations of the problems resulting from cost controls in countries where the systems of medical care and the measures to restrain its costs are touted as models. Surgery that is not an emergency may be subject to long delays or sometimes prohibited altogether. Some Canadians reportedly cross the border to the United States to avoid delays in medical treatments in their own country.[24] In the United Kingdom, as of 2003, at least 10 percent of all people had purchased costly private medical insurance in order to bypass the long wait lists that prevail under the health-care system operated by their government.[25]

The critical point here is that because politicians do not understand the mechanism and nature of the cost disease, and because they face political pressures from a similarly uninformed electorate, they do not realize that *we can indeed afford these services* without forcing society to undergo unnecessary cuts, restrictions, and other forms of deprivation.

Similarly, the public may perceive that it cannot afford the continually increasing cost of health care. People may be unwilling to revise household budgets to cover rising health-care costs, even as rising per capita incomes make this financially feasible. One cannot argue with such preferences; people are entitled to spend their earnings as they choose. But if retrenchment in the quality or quantity of health care stems from misunderstanding of what the public can really afford, then surely it is important to try to educate the public about this misapprehension. This brings us to our next caveat.

Caveat 3: Educating the Public Will Not Be Easy

Not the least of the problems we face is the difficult task of helping the public recognize the difference between the reality and the illusion of the cost disease. For instance, it surely will be difficult to convince intelligent nonspecialists that although costs of personal services appear to be out of control, they are actually falling in terms of the labor-time required to earn enough to pay for them. Such assertions can sound to the uninitiated like a statistical sleight of hand or theoretical gibberish. This is all the more true if the quality of the product simultaneously increases—for instance, by providing better health and enhanced life spans through more effective medical services. That evidently means that we are getting more—possibly *far* more—for the money spent on this service.

The task of explaining this to the public should not be beyond the abilities of skilled journalists and others who specialize in effective communication. This is an indispensable task—for without it, governments' efforts to reorient their budgets to respond effectively to the cost disease will fail politically in any democratic society.[26]

Caveat 4: The Public Sector Share of GDP Will Increase Dramatically

The extrapolations presented in this chapter suggest that if health care, education, and other services with similar cost characteristics are supplied largely by government, then by 2105 well over 60 percent of the U.S. GDP may flow through the public sector, thereby insulating it from control by the market.[27] The experiences of planned economies indicate that this is not a promising arrangement. Taking so much of the economy out of the control of private enterprise will substantially impede efficiency and handicap economic growth.[28]

Our municipal governments also face a particularly difficult task in raising the revenues necessary to prevent municipal services from collapsing even more completely than they already have. A large portion of a city government's budget consists of health care, education, police protection, libraries, and other services subject to cost disease-induced cost increases. Expenditures on these services will have to rise enormously over the next century if the quantity and quality of these services are not to fall behind the outputs of agriculture and manufacturing. Even if the difficult political task of acquiring such increases in government revenues is accomplished, that such an enormous increase in the share of GDP will have to flow through government, rather than private channels, is hardly an attractive prospect.

Caveat 5: Privatization Is Susceptible to Ill-Advised Cost Controls

Projects that call for the huge expansion of the public sector are often met with calls for greater reliance on privatization. But privatization is no cure for the cost disease. There are good grounds for public opposition to complete privatization of the public school system, police protection, and national defense. The threat to liberty posed by reliance on private armies, for instance, has been demonstrated by many historical examples.

Moreover, any private industry beset by the cost disease will surely be suspected of greed and malfeasance. Calls for cost controls in such privatized industries will be politically irresistible. But if rising costs are caused by unavoidably slow productivity growth in personal and handicraft services, cost controls can only lead to deterioration in the quality of those services or, worse, to their partial or total disappearance.

It is important to emphasize once again that, in addition to health care and education, the cost disease affects many other services that are vital for a good quality of life, such as the live performing arts, libraries, police protection, restaurants (from which the most labor-intensive dishes have all but disappeared), and welfare support for the poor. If we do not address these cost increases with carefully considered adaptations, our society increasingly will be characterized, in the words of John Kenneth Galbraith, by "private affluence and public squalor."

Caveat 6: The Rising-Cost Story Is Basically Reassuring, Unless . . .

Despite these reservations, the picture of the future that emerges is mostly reassuring. Universally and persistently rising productivity promises a life of abundance and prosperity that we cannot imagine. If we stop and think of the variety of gadgets that are commonplace in every middle-class home—and how inconceivable they were to our ancestors three or four generations back—we will have a vague inkling of what the future promises. As I noted earlier, if productivity over the next century grows at an average annual rate of just over 2 percent, the purchasing power in the hands of an average American will rise eightfold. One way to understand what this means is to imagine yourself eight times richer than you are now—except that you would also have an array of new ways to spend this wealth that are as inconceivable to us as an iPhone was to Calvin Coolidge.

One would think that with such abundance we could deal effectively with problems like world poverty, but this is by no means guaranteed. In particular, this ignores the terrifying noneconomic threats that hang over us—most prominently climate change and weapons of mass destruction, as well as less lethal forms of mismanagement, from misbehavior of private business to misguided governmental intervention. We will see later in this book that all of these problems are apt to be exacerbated by the cost disease.

Some Final Reservations

Before I turn to the really threatening consequences of the cost disease, I must bring out a more immediate reservation about the optimistic story presented in this chapter. I have argued that continued universal productivity increases will enable society to afford the increasing costs of personal services—such as health care, education, police protection, and live theatrical, musical, and dance performance—whose relative costs are driven up by the irreducible labor content of these activities, making it difficult to introduce productivity-enhancing changes.

The disturbing increases in the relative costs of these services are not likely to end soon. Whatever remedial cost-cutting steps may be attempted, their effect will be negligible and disappointing. This is surely confirmed by the many policies adopted throughout the prosperous countries of the world to reduce health-care expenditures. Moreover, as we will see in Chapter 7, rising health-care costs are now increasingly afflicting fast-developing middle-income countries as well. Some countries have imposed ceilings on doctors' earnings; others have restricted the treatments available to patients. Yet these countries almost always have failed to prevent health-care costs from rising faster than the rate of inflation.

The reason for this general failure lies in the nature of health care and other personal services. Such industries simply do not lend themselves to automation or similar labor-saving strategies. Whatever the virtues of various efforts to curtail health-care costs—such as the landmark health-care legislation adopted in early 2010 in the United States, which is intended to extend insurance protection to millions who are now uninsured—any hope that these measures will bring the rising costs to an end will lead to disappointment.

Still, the costs of health care and other personal services will remain within our reach. The innovation that drives our economy is likely to continue, and productivity in the economy as a whole will continue to rise, giving us the means for everyone to afford to pay for health care, education, and other vital services. These words, written during a severe recession, are apt to strike some readers as naïve. Yet, in the long run, the forces of competition will relentlessly drive innovation forward. We can expect productivity to continue to grow at rates unequaled in earlier history.[29]

The role personal services play in the future depends on how we order our priorities. If we value services sufficiently, we can have more and better services at surprisingly small (if any) sacrifice in what we spend on manufactured goods. Whether this is a good choice is not for economists to say. We, as a society, must decide. If we fail to do so, we may find ourselves in a world where material goods are abundant but the services that sustain our high quality of life continue to deteriorate.

Contrary to appearances, we can afford more ample health care, more abundant education, more adequate support of the indigent, and a growing abundance of private comforts and luxuries. That we cannot afford all of these is an illusion—one that must be dispelled if we are to deal effectively with the fiscal problem that triggers the cost increases, which, in turn, leads to the service cuts that ultimately cause growing public squalor. This conclusion may sound simplistic, but if future productivity bears any resemblance to that of past decades, which brought the United States and the rest of the industrial world better health care and more education despite rising costs, we must recognize that the increasing costs of services, coupled with rising productivity, are clearly less fear-worthy than they appear to be. As one *Washington Post* editorial aptly noted, "People sometimes say that the country has no money to deal with the growing tragedy of the inner cities. That's incorrect. The country has a lot of money. It's only a question of how we choose to spend it."[30] Thus, the late Senator Daniel Patrick Moynihan was precisely right when he characterized these prospects not as a deplorable outlook but rather as constituting a fundamentally *optimistic* forecast.[31]

FIVE

Dark Sides of the Disease
Terrorism and Environmental Destruction

The AK-47 assault rifle is "the world's most prolific and effective combat weapon, a device so cheap and simple that it can be bought in many countries for less than the cost of a live chicken."
—LARRY KAHANER

While I have argued that the rising-cost side of the cost disease is not as worrisome as it may appear, I have also hinted repeatedly that other consequences of the disease are more threatening. These dangers stem, paradoxically, from some of the products whose costs are driven *downward* by the cost disease. In this chapter I will focus on two prime examples of this: military armaments and threats to the environment.

Cheaper Is Not Always Better

Warfare is surely the activity that punishes the second-best combatant the most. Driven by this threat, nations spend generously on preparation for self-defense or aggression, including an unending search for more powerful weapons. This unrelenting drive to stay ahead has two critical consequences. First, humanity now has it in its power to commit suicide via nuclear holocaust. Second, new developments in military technology have produced an outpouring of powerful and often bargain-priced weapons.[1] These new tools of warfare are predominantly manufactured goods, which, like other manufactures, invite labor-saving innovation in their production. As productivity increases, the real cost of manufacturing these weapons decreases, and the price of many of them—for instance, an AK-47 rifle—falls.[2] Continual reduction in the cost of weapons, energetically pursued by entrepreneurs, places these products in the progressive sector of the cost disease scenario, where their falling costs bring consequences that are often far from beneficial to humanity.

We should not underestimate the threat posed by these military commodities—the tools of warfare, terrorism, and genocide—whose abundance results from the fact that the relative cost of many weapons is being driven downward by the cost disease. Compared with the threat of ongoing violence and political instability, which surely is exacerbated by the *falling* cost of weapons, the financial consequences of the *increasing* costs of health care and education seem far less frightening.

Terrorists and guerillas have shown how effectively these products can be put to use, proving in the process how powerful such basic weaponry can be in stymieing even the most determined counter efforts of major powers equipped with extensive manpower, organized forces, and sophisticated new devices. For perhaps the first time in history, vastly superior wealth has ceased to be a guarantor of military success, as it was, for instance, when Ulysses S. Grant's much larger Union Army destroyed the apparently far more brilliant Confederate General Robert E. Lee's forces in the American Civil War.

The facilitation of terrorist activities brought by cheaper weapons is clearly a major threat to the general welfare. In Iraq and Afghanistan, the media have told us of the continuing misery of life beset by terrorist bombings and other acts of violence. The casualties inflicted upon soldiers and innocent civilians in these countries are horrifying enough. Meanwhile, sensational terrorist attacks throughout the world continue to make headlines.

A similarly frightening potential for the destruction of life underlies Iran's and North Korea's nuclear ambitions, as well as the troubled relations between those nuclear-armed neighbors India and Pakistan, whose ongoing conflict could escalate at any time.[3] The growing ease and declining real costs of producing weapons more powerful than any available before have helped to create these threats.

The Environmental Impact of Continual Productivity Growth

Beyond terrorism and potential nuclear war, environmental damage looms as a second man-made threat to our welfare—and even to our collective survival. I claim no expertise on the conflicting claims that characterize the debate on this subject, but many knowledgeable observers have identified humanity's damage to the environment as a source of peril. This damage is perhaps exemplified by climate change, which carries many possible consequences such as drought, widespread famine, floods, ensuing displacement and disease, and other horrors that have not yet elicited a serious response from those who design policy.[4] For example, little attention has been paid to the prospect of rising sea levels, which threatens to create millions of refugees and cause great geopolitical instability.

This, too, is a phenomenon in which the cost disease plays a disquieting role. For example, the falling-cost sector ensures that the real cost of manufacturing automobiles continues to fall. As a result, cars no longer crowd *only* the roads in the United States and western Europe; traffic jams pervade the far more populous cities of China and India, where bicycles increasingly are replaced by the cars and motorcycles that are now within reach of many consumers who previously could not afford them. With the growing abundance of fossil-fuel-devouring vehicles have come increased levels of carbon dioxide and other greenhouse gases. By making manufactures cheaper and more accessible, the cost disease threatens to pollute our world.

But this story does not apply only to the recent proliferation of automobiles. Coal-fired electric power plants, emissions from airplanes, and even apartment building furnaces also are said to be among the causes of climate change. Paper manufacturing and the production of electronic goods have polluted our waterways, killing fish or making them dangerous to eat. Various forms of machinery have resulted in noise pollution that has been suspected as a cause of birth defects and hearing impairment. The list goes on and on. As rising productivity has made products cheaper to produce—and to purchase—their output has exploded. Thus, the cost-lowering side of the cost disease is a primary stimulant to the consumption of many of the manufactured products that are most damaging to the environment.

One of the means that has been suggested for amelioration of environmental destruction is an effort to shift the output of the world economy away from manufacturing and toward the services sector.[5] The proposed incentives would reorient taxation, reducing the amounts levied on services industries and raising those on manufacturing industries. Services—products that are not physical items that literally can be touched—use raw materials and power sources to a much smaller degree than manufactured products. Greater consumption of services and lower consumption of manufactures may reduce both emissions into the atmosphere and the need to dispose of waste products, while slowing the depletion of resources. This, in turn, should materially decrease the pace of environmental damage and the accompanying threat to the general welfare.

But the incentives generated by the cost disease conflict directly with the logic of such an effort. They take us in precisely the wrong direction. As we know, the disease makes many services more expensive while reducing the relative price of manufactures—a pattern that inevitably drives consumer spending away from the services and toward less costly manufactured products.[6] Surely such an incentive structure can only be deemed perverse.

Of course, considered dispassionately, the falling cost of manufactures also offers great benefits. These include poverty reduction, growth in general prosperity, and the wide availability of better living standards than our ancestors could have ever imagined. But as the economists' cliché goes, there is no free lunch. These benefits are offset by the destruction of earth's natural beauty and widespread health effects from environmental toxins. These potential outcomes, rather than government budget deficits, are the real disservice we may be providing to our grandchildren.

Constraining the Cost Disease

I close this chapter by reemphasizing the observation that while rising prices for services are understandably disquieting, they are paradoxically the *less threatening* side of the cost disease. The consequences of the rising-cost side of the disease are less serious than they appear to be, but the other side of this story—the steadily declining prices of progressive-sector manufactures—is a key source of some of the most urgent perils facing humanity. We can afford to pay more for the services we need—chiefly health care and education—and probably will always be able to do so. What we may not be able to afford are the consequences of falling costs: environmental destruction and continual warfare.

This is not the place for a detailed exploration of how we may counter the threats that stem from rising costs in the stagnant sector of the economy and falling costs in the progressive sector, but it seems appropriate to provide a few observations. First, we may hope that rising costs can be mitigated by the market's (or the government's) encouragement of cost saving and productivity-enhancing innovation and entrepreneurship in stagnant-sector industries. Although there are limits to what can be expected, such efforts surely should not be neglected. Taking health care as a prime example, Chapters 10 and 11 will describe some very promising opportunities for reduction of the costs incurred in this field. Chapters 9 and 10 also address the use of business services, with their twofold productivity growth, to offset the cost disease.

Although the falling-cost side of the disease may be more threatening, effective countermeasures for the problems exacerbated by the disease—environmental destruction and continual warfare—are arguably within reach. Particularly noteworthy is the substantial literature devoted to environmental policy and to other damaging consequences of economic growth. Many scholars have suggested promising approaches to containment of these perils.

The policy approaches generally favored by economists who deal with such issues focus on the restructuring of taxation: reducing taxes or granting subsidies on beneficial products whose availability is threatened by increasing costs, and imposing higher taxes on less beneficial items such as those manufactures whose increased productivity and falling real prices facilitate their dissemination *and* are the source of the major environmental threats.[7] Economists agree that taxes substantially affect incentives. They also are aware of the widespread impression that these incentive effects are always damaging to the general welfare. But they point out that, on the contrary, many taxes provide inducements that favor the community's interests. If, for example, we tax labor at a lower rate than gasoline, we will encourage employment by making it cheaper for firms to hire new workers and will reduce the emission of pollutants from automobiles by making it more expensive to drive. This need not entail any increase in the total tax burden. It merely shifts existing taxes so that activities that benefit the community are rewarded while those that threaten the general welfare are penalized.

Some such taxation strategies are already in place. Taxes on alcohol and tobacco and "cap and trade" pollution-reduction programs, an increasingly employed substitute for emissions taxes, are key examples. But in the future, as many leading economists have argued, we may have to think more radically and consider revising the entire tax system along these lines. Taxes that bring beneficial incentives—those that discourage us from activities that threaten society's well-being—would replace taxes whose incentive effects are damaging to the general welfare, such as those that place a heavy burden on new and small business firms and thereby discourage both employment and economic growth. Economists have long favored this general approach, and it is high time that legislators reexamine the entire tax structure from this point of view.[8]

The bottom line is that the cost disease is indeed a *disease*. Contrary to appearances, its disquieting consequences threaten not just our pocketbooks but also our way of living. Indeed, the cost disease conceivably may even help us along the path toward self-destruction. We are not powerless to deal with its most damaging prospects, but as even Adam Smith warned, we cannot afford to sit back and rely on the invisible hand of the market to provide *all* the necessary remedies.

SIX

Common Misunderstandings of the Cost Disease

Cost versus Quality and Financial versus "Physical" Output Measures

From 1970 to 2004, the percentage of Americans aged 45 and older who died in hospital following a heart attack declined by more than 50 percent.
—National Heart, Lung, and Blood Institute

In the last decade, the average real cost per hospital stay in the United States increased by roughly one-third—from $6,410 in 1997 to $8,690 in 2007.
—Healthcare Cost and Utilization Project

The explosive growth of college tuition and the rising cost of hospital services—two very visible symptoms of the cost disease—have generated many fallacies and misunderstandings. Some have blamed rising costs on greedy college presidents, doctors, and hospital administrators, who are suspected of paying themselves more generously. True, there may be some hospital administrators and college presidents who have grown profligate or self-serving, but it is hardly plausible that all or even most of them are changing in this manner. This alone could hardly make overall costs *rise* at the pace we observe. It is simply not plausible to pin the responsibility for rising costs on such behavior.[1]

To this confusion, let us add two other misunderstandings about the cost disease, generated by economists themselves. The first concerns the manufacturing sector's share of gross domestic product (GDP), which has declined steadily and significantly in the past three decades. This decline is a measurement phenomenon resulting from the *fall in the prices* of manufactures that, as noted in Chapter 5, is the other side of the cost disease. The *actual quantity* of manufacturing output has not declined; rather, its real prices have fallen because of rapid productivity growth. After all, the output of a commodity whose price has fallen by 25 percent may not have declined at all, even though its market value has decreased. It is reasonable to conclude that the manufacturing sector's share of the total "physical" output of any given industrialized country has not changed very much.

The second misunderstanding arises from a debate regarding which measures of productivity growth provide the most appropriate data for analyzing the sectors of the economy affected by the cost disease. There are two types of productivity measures that are apt to be cited in these discussions: quality-adjusted figures and quality-*un*adjusted figures. The issue is whether the analysis of productivity growth should take into account improvements in the quality of a product, such as cardiac care, or should consider only the inputs required to create it, such as the time spent by the doctors, nurses, and other health-care workers in dealing with a patient's problem.

Financial versus "Physical" Measurement of Manufacturing Output

We really do not know how to measure total national output because this inescapably entails adding apples and oranges. Suppose, for example, that during a ten-year period the production of computers rises by x percent, production of autos increases by y percent, and the output of cellular telephones declines by z percent. How can we determine the change in the output of the three items in total? In other words, how many cell phones add up to one car? And what would any such number mean?

The standard approach to answering that question is to convert the production numbers to dollars and add up the total spending on computers, cars, and cellular telephones. But that does not give us the answer we seek. Because the cost disease has lowered the real prices of all three items, a net monetary measurement is likely to tell us that the items' total output has declined—even though we know that this is not true. If the prices of all three items fell by exactly one-half during the decade we wish to study, and the annual numbers of autos and cell phones produced in that time doubled, then the money value of their output would stay the same, leading to the illusion that production of these items had not changed. Meanwhile, if the number of computers produced did not rise, then the calculated revenue from their sale would fall by about 50 percent, leading to the impression that production of computers had fallen by half. Even if the outputs of each of the three products had risen by 30 percent but the price of each had fallen by one-half, the money-value calculation would tell us that production of all three items had fallen, even though it rose substantially.

The data confirm that the money value of manufactures, taken as a share of GDP, has been falling steadily as ever increasing efficiency and productivity have lowered production costs.[2] But the actual physical output of manufactured goods has not fallen—or rather has not fallen as much as the declining money value of manufactures would lead us to expect.

The Cost Disease and the Allocation of Labor

Although it is not necessarily true, let us assume for simplicity that the share of the economy's total output that comes from the progressive sector, as measured in physical units rather than money, does not change. Because the economy has only two sectors, progressive and stagnant, whose production together accounts for all of its output, it follows that the stagnant sector also must maintain a constant share of the total.[3]

This has significant implications for the distribution of an economy's labor force. By definition, labor productivity grows significantly faster in the progressive sector than in the stagnant sector, so to keep a constant proportion between the two sectors' output, more and more labor has to move from the progressive sector into the stagnant sector. For example, suppose that at the beginning of the last century, the two sectors each produced 100 units of output and employed 10 million workers. Next, suppose that productivity quadruples in the progressive sector but increases by only 4/3 in the stagnant sector. A 50 percent shift of labor from the progressive to the stagnant sector will result in a precise doubling of both outputs. If the progressive sector had no reduction in its workforce, its production would quadruple. But cutting its workforce in half and quadrupling its productivity will yield 200 units of output. In the stagnant sector, the 50 percent larger labor force would increase the sector's output to 150 units so that a 4/3 rise in productivity also will result in 200 units of output: $150(4/3) = 200$. The point is that the sector with slower productivity growth requires a growing labor force to maintain its share of overall output. The sector with rapid productivity growth requires a shrinking labor force to reach the same result.

Even if the stagnant and progressive sectors do not maintain constant output ratios, this tendency exists, and it helps explain the declining share of employment in the manufacturing industries of most developed economies. Rising productivity means that fewer workers are needed to produce a given amount. Thus, in the United States, Germany, and the United Kingdom, these industries provide a declining share of each nation's jobs. This also explains my assertion that the loss of manufacturing jobs in the United States cannot be attributed primarily to the capture of those industries by rival economies such as China and Japan. In these countries, manufacturing productivity also is growing rapidly, meaning that it requires fewer workers to meet the world demand for its manufactured products. Of course, in some countries, notably China, there has been an offsetting increase in volume of output—the country added some 21 million new manufacturing jobs between 2002 and 2008.

But what about the stagnant services purchased directly by consumers? Here again, the problem is easier to understand if we continue to use the simplifying assumption—realistic or not—that the two sectors' shares of the economy's total output do not change over time. As we have seen, this means that more and more of the economy's labor force must migrate from the progressive to the stagnant sector. Moreover, if their share of the total physical output stays unchanged, their share of the money value of the economy's total product also must fall because the real prices of the progressive sector's outputs are fated to decline steadily. The money value of the stagnant sector outputs must therefore rise. In sum, we have the situation shown in Table 6.1.

Table 6.1. Share of Economy's Total Output: Progressive Sector versus Stagnant Sector.

Method of Measurement	Progressive Sector Share	Stagnant Sector Share
Physical quantity	Unchanging	Unchanging
Share of labor force	Falling	Rising
Share of money value	Falling	Rising

It should be clear that *if we measure the economy's total output in terms of money value*, with the fast-growing progressive sector's output seeming to shrink because of its constantly declining costs and prices, then the average growth rate we calculate for the overall economy will be more and more influenced by the growth rate of the stagnant sector. Thus, average growth will seem to decline more or less steadily. But if we measure output in physical terms—as the number of units of product—there is no reason for the growth rate of the economy to level off as a consequence of the cost disease, as productivity will continue to increase in virtually all industries.

Thus, although there is no one uniquely legitimate method of measuring economic growth, one could argue in favor of the physical output measure. The argument is simply that if we want to consider a product in terms of its benefits to society, neither money value nor the amount of labor employed in its production gives us the correct measure. If, for example, a way is found to cut the labor content of an automobile by 30 percent, a two-car family will be none the worse off—indeed, they may be better off when replacement time arrives. Even though their two cars now cost less than before and the cars' production requires less labor, the usefulness of the product has not declined one iota. Two cars remain two cars regardless of their drop in price or labor content. Moreover, their contribution to living standards, the ultimate measure of labor productivity growth, is likely to rise as the number of people who can afford cars increases.

Quality-Adjusted versus Quality-Unadjusted Productivity Measures

The innovations brought to market by entrepreneurs generally have at least one of two purposes: *quality improvement*, whose goal is to attract more customers by offering them a better product, and *cost saving*, typically achieved through a reduction in the labor time required to produce the commodity. There are two corresponding productivity-growth concepts, which we can call *quality-improving productivity growth* and *cost-saving productivity growth*. Both are vital for the general welfare, but in this book, with its focus on the cost issue, the latter concept is the more relevant.

In practice, however, most measurements of productivity seek to deal with both kinds of improvement. If an economist wants to determine what is happening to the productivity of labor in the manufacture of some product, she takes the quantity of the output produced during some period and divides it by the number of hours of labor that were devoted to the task, thus getting the number of units of the product created per hour of labor. This figure is called *quality-unadjusted productivity*. If there has been some change in the quality of the product, she adjusts this output quantity, increasing it by an amount that indicates how much more the improved product is worth relative to its more primitive predecessor.[4] Let us call this figure *quality-adjusted productivity*.

Each of these productivity concepts has its appropriate domain of usefulness, but each can be misleading if it is used where the other is called for. This distinction may seem like a mere methodological quibble, but it is critically relevant to understanding the cost disease. If we want to test for the presence or absence of the disease, quality-*unadjusted* figures are most pertinent because we are merely asking how much money consumers must pay for a product, not how desirable that product is. The use of adjusted figures has misled some analysts to conclude that the cost disease is no longer with us. What these analysts have observed is enhancement of *benefits* that the consumer receives from a product or service, but no accompanying decrease in its *monetary cost.*

Much of the literature on productivity refers to the need to take full account of progress in improving the quality of products. Workers' output is surely increased, goes the argument, if the products they turn out have greater capacity, last longer than they used to, or do a better job for the consumer. If a measure of productivity growth fails to take these quality improvements into account, the resulting numbers are spurious and misleading.

This argument is quite valid: productivity statistics that do not take quality developments into account can be seriously misleading *if used inappropriately.*[5] But if employed with care and for appropriate purposes, quality-unadjusted figures also can provide insight of their own. For analyzing the rising costs that constitute the cost disease— which, as its name implies, is a problem of cost, not product quality, quality-*unadjusted* productivity figures are most relevant. After all, the cost disease analysis deals with the rising costs of some services and does not concern itself with evolution of the benefits that those services provide.

Cost versus Benefit: That Is the Question

To see what is really at issue in this apparently esoteric discussion, we must keep in mind that we are examining the mechanism that determines what outputs *cost* to produce and consequently what consumers must pay to purchase them. We are discussing how much a product *costs* the consumer, not its *benefits*—that is, how good the product is for the money that consumers spend. These are very different things.

A few examples will bring out the significance of this difference and show why, for cost disease analyses, measures of the cost to consumers are more important than measures of the quality of the product or service. Consider an innovation in cardiac surgery that doubles the patient's cost but trebles his subsequent life expectancy compared with the procedures that were available earlier. Surely one can conclude that the patient is getting his money's worth despite having to pay more for the new method.

But what if the same patient has barely enough income to pay for the older, less expensive procedure? Might the result be a reduction in basic medical care for such impoverished patients? Or suppose the hospital would like to avoid passing on the cost increase to impecunious patients. What if the hospital is on the verge of bankruptcy? In these instances is not the cost increase imposed by the new procedure a legitimate concern in itself, even if the outcomes of the procedure are worth every penny? (For more on this, see the discussion of the costs and benefits of some specific medical innovations later in this chapter.)

The same is true of education. There is considerable evidence that, for some subjects such as writing and mathematics, smaller class size improves student performance. But a school that cuts class sizes in half by doubling its teaching staff courts financial trouble. In a publicly financed school system, a municipality that is hard-pressed financially simply cannot afford to make such a change, despite its future benefits.

The point is that in evaluating cost increases there are two critical issues: first, and perhaps ultimately most important, does the higher cost, if affordable, offer a net benefit? Second, if this change in cost is instituted, will it lead to financial disaster and perhaps undermine an organization's other activities?

Selecting the Correct Productivity Measure

The misunderstanding of the cost disease among some economists arises from the widespread idealization of quality-adjusted productivity as the only useful measure of productivity growth. Many analysts believe that a measure that does not take quality improvement into account is a distortion. Indeed it is, if the figures are used to evaluate (1) the amount of benefit the consuming public derives from some amount of labor or (2) the magnitude and rate of improvement of standards of living. But quality-unadjusted figures are *not* misleading if they are used to measure the cost consequences of productivity improvements for those who pay the bill.

Use of the wrong productivity measure has led to the contention that there are significant sectors of the economy in which the cost disease has disappeared, even though prices in these sectors continue to rise faster than inflation. This argument maintains that what looks like lagging productivity growth is in fact something else: spectacular and continual increases in product quality often prevent the implementation of labor-saving measures. This can impede quality-unadjusted productivity growth in these industries, leading some researchers to conclude that "true productivity" (that is, quality-adjusted productivity) is not lagging at all.

In an article published in 2003, for instance, Jack Triplett and Barry Bosworth point out that quality-adjusted productivity in the field of health care has been rising at an impressive rate. This, they correctly assert, is good news because it indicates that those who use the health-care system are getting more for their money. Although that may be true, it will hardly placate hospital directors, who often do not know where they will find the money to cover their hospitals' rising expenses.

Other studies of the subject, notably a 2008 paper by William Nordhaus and a 2012 book by Robert Flanagan that test the disease against relevant data, have avoided the problem described in this chapter, and their results appear to confirm fully the price and cost developments predicted by the cost disease analysis nearly half a century ago. This does not mean that research that focuses on product quality is pointless and wrong, merely that it deals with a different issue.

Some Quality Advances in Health Care

The health-care sector has achieved outstanding improvements in the quality of its services via a seemingly endless stream of miraculous innovations. As a result, the average human life span has increased dramatically, and new and sometimes astonishing ways have been found to limit the ravages of many illnesses and to make life easier for those who require medical attention. In this sense, there can be no doubt that quality-*adjusted* productivity in health care has increased dramatically.[6]

But when examined in terms of labor saving and cost reduction, the sources of improvements in quality-*unadjusted* productivity, the record of these health-care innovations is decidedly mixed—or worse. As noted in Chapter 1, the prices American consumers pay for health care have increased significantly in recent decades. These steadily growing costs cannot be wholly unaffected by the huge costs associated with inventing, continuously improving, and teaching doctors how to make effective use of the virtually magical innovations that have revolutionized the health-care field.

In order to see this more clearly, let us look at several health-care innovations whose quality and cost implications vary substantially.

These examples bring out the difference between the two valid productivity concepts discussed in this chapter: quality-*adjusted* and quality-*unadjusted* productivity growth.

Case Study 1: Robotic Surgery

The use of robots to perform surgery, under the visual control of a surgeon who may or may not be thousands of miles away from the patient, was introduced to brain surgery in 1985. By the late 1980s, robots were in use in prostate and hip replacement surgery, and since then the list of surgical procedures that can be performed using robots has expanded even further.[7]

Robotic surgery offers several appealing advantages for patients. Perhaps most miraculously, the procedure can be carried out remotely, allowing patients in isolated locations access to expert surgeons in distant cities. The operations, guided by surgeons who use patients' computed tomography (CT) scans to direct the robot's work, also make smaller and more accurate incisions and usually require shorter postoperative hospital stays, which result in reduced postoperative hospital costs.[8]

But robotic surgery itself is far more costly than conventional surgery. According to one study, it costs $1,500 more, on average, than standard surgical procedures.[9] For some procedures, the increase is much larger—a robotic coronary artery bypass, for instance, may cost $5,000 more than the same procedure with the surgeon in the operating room.[10]

These high costs can be attributed to several factors. In 2008, one machine used in robotic surgery, the da Vinci™ Robotic System, cost $1.3 million.[11] In addition to this high purchase price, the unit also comes with annual maintenance costs and requires special training for surgeons, nurses, and technicians to use it. Moreover, physicians and nurses must still be on hand during robotic surgery in case medical complications arise in the operating room. In addition to the expensive equipment, these highly trained stand-by personnel add much to the expense of robotic surgery. No doubt, with the passage of time, these costs will be reduced, but we can be confident that expensive, future inventions will offset these gains.

Case Study 2: Kidney Dialysis

With increased longevity of the general population, more patients are being diagnosed with chronic kidney disease. Kidney dialysis replaces kidney function in clearing the blood of wastes, and the large number of kidney dialysis centers throughout the United States makes it easier for these patients to get medical care for this condition.

In the past, kidney failure was treated exclusively with peritoneal dialysis, which involves pumping fluids containing sodium, chloride, lactate or bicarbonate, and a high percentage of glucose into a patient's abdomen. The fluid is pumped in via a catheter that has been surgically inserted into the abdomen, with one end protruding through the skin of the belly; the catheter remains in place for the duration of the dialysis treatments. In each round of dialysis, the fluid stays in the patient's abdomen for several hours, and the concentrated chemicals in the fluid pull waste out of the blood through the abdominal arteries. When the fluid is removed, it brings with it these extracted waste materials, thereby cleansing the blood of these wastes that the patient's failing kidneys are unable to remove. This process must be repeated three to four times a day.

The chief advantage of peritoneal dialysis is that it has remained relatively inexpensive. It does not require doctors with highly specialized training and expertise, and it involves relatively simple and affordable equipment. But patients receiving this type of dialysis are at high risk for infection because it is very difficult to keep the area around the catheter completely sterile. Some peritoneal dialysis patients have also suffered serious complications when their catheters accidentally punctured their intestines.

In the early 1960s, a new method called hemodialysis was introduced. This process removes a patient's blood via an arterial shunt inserted in the arm, filters it through a semipermeable membrane contained within an external machine, and then returns the cleansed blood to the patient's circulation. Hemodialysis offers obvious advantages for patients. It cleans the blood much more efficiently and effectively than peritoneal dialysis, and patients receiving this treatment have much longer lifetimes and a far lower incidence of related infections, making them eligible for kidney transplantation. Hemodialysis also allows a better quality of life for patients: they receive one round of dialysis just three times a week—rather than several times each day—and can continue to live otherwise normal lives.

But hemodialysis requires expensive equipment. Even if the equipment itself is declining in price, the procedure demands highly trained doctors, nurses, and technicians to monitor patients continuously during each four- to six-hour session and thereby costs far more than the older peritoneal method. In recent years, the cost of hemodialysis in the United States has grown by more than 60 percent—from just over $50,000 per Medicare patient in 1995, according to one study, to roughly $82,000 in 2009.[12] In the next decade, as survival rates improve, the cost of dialysis for all patients with end-stage renal disease in the United States is expected to grow by an estimated $14 billion.[13]

For patients with kidney failure, hemodialysis is clearly preferable to older methods of dialysis—it provides better clearance of body wastes with fewer complications. But the costs associated with this more sophisticated technique will continue their inexorable increase.

Benefits but No Savings

Because in an earlier era robotic surgery and hemodialysis were unavailable, we can draw two pertinent conclusions from this discussion. First, these new techniques require the labor time of more and better-trained medical professionals—above what was required for more primitive treatments in earlier decades. Second, the new treatments clearly bring additional costs. These may include the expense of maintaining the machines used in the procedures, replacing them when manufacturers bring out new and improved versions, the salaries of additional technicians to run and maintain the equipment, and the cost of training medical professionals to use the new technology. Moreover, there are costs incurred in the research and development of new technology, which are passed on to hospitals that purchase the equipment. In most cases, these procedures are clearly beneficial, but given the substantial costs of these medical innovations it should be clear that while they provide *quality*-adjusted productivity gains, they do not represent labor-saving or cost-saving enhancements of productivity.

Many medical innovations promise seemingly miraculous results for patients, and some even deliver. There is no reason to think that these breakthroughs will stop coming. What must not be forgotten are the huge costs associated with these new techniques and the machines many of them require. This is true of almost all the great medical innovations. The complexities entailed in their creation and use ensure that health-care costs will continue their steady rise.

My purpose is not to argue with those who focus on product quality or financial measures of manufacturing output but rather to dispel the confusion that surrounds these two measurement concepts. Quality-unadjusted productivity figures and "physical" measures of output play a fundamental role in analyses of the cost disease; quality-adjusted productivity data and financial output measures do not, despite their importance for the general welfare. Quality-adjusted productivity is a measure of how much benefit consumers are getting from their purchase of a product. Quality-*unadjusted* data tell us how much money must be raised to purchase the product. Similarly, financial measures of manufacturing output indicate the money value (that is, price) of manufactured goods. In contrast, physical measures give us the quantity of these goods produced. These are different issues, though all four are vitally important.

The cost disease analysis does not conflict with the observation that product improvement often ensures that consumers get more for their money—nor is the disease merely the result of dollar cost decreases in manufacturing. Monetary costs in manufacturing clearly are declining, no matter what output measure we use. And the rising costs of services are often associated with marked improvement in their quality. In health care especially, the public appears to have an insatiable appetite for such improvements, yet that same public simultaneously seems to have serious doubts about paying the requisite costs.

Finally, it is important to emphasize that nothing I have said in this book suggests that cost savings in health care are impossible. On the contrary, as we show in Chapter 11, there exist substantial opportunities for cost reduction in health care without damage to either the quality or the quantity of care. We must remember, however, that the cost disease tells us that even if society takes advantage of all these opportunities, we still can expect a relentless rise in monetary costs. Our leaders will have to explain to taxpayers that the cost increases are not caused by criminal neglect, incompetence, or greed, but rather that they are an unavoidable consequence of the essentially irreducible quantity of labor entailed in the provision of health care. If this is not made clear, the public are likely to demand cost reductions regardless of the consequences, and the unavoidable result will be the cutting of corners with accompanying declines in quality. All this will occur even though we can afford to pay the rising costs required to preserve and even continue to improve the quality of our health care.

In seeking ways to address the cost disease, we must not ignore the quality of the affected services or the fact that costs in the progressive sector are indeed falling. But quality improvements and differing manufacturing output measures are not the issue here. The point is to understand the persistently rising costs of personal services and to recognize the virtual certainty that, despite appearances, we will be able to afford them.

SEVEN

The Cost Disease and Global Health

Ariel Pablos-Méndez, Hilary Tabish, and David de Ferranti

> We see in all other pleasures there is satiety, and after they be used, their verdure departeth. . . . But of knowledge there is no satiety.
>
> —Francis Bacon

The rapidly rising cost of health care in the United States is hardly atypical. The cost disease is universal, so it applies to health care throughout the world. Although some economists and policy makers recognize the fundamental role that economic forces play in health-related cost increases, the worldwide rising trend in health spending is too often attributed to the aging of populations and the high cost of novel technologies.

In discussing the cost disease to this point, we have largely relied on evidence drawn from the world's wealthier economies. In this chapter, we turn to the rest of the world, focusing on a related phenomenon: the strong relationship between gross domestic product (GDP) per capita and total health spending per capita. This simple and powerful relationship holds important implications for foreign aid and health systems planning—especially now, when unprecedented economic growth in developing countries makes it likely that their health spending will increase substantially. The cost disease is one of the important drivers of this process.

The First Law of Health Economics

Many health-care advocates, assuming that one can identify an optimal level of health spending that will ensure a healthy population, judge this spending to be too high in rich countries and too low in poor ones. They may then prescribe policies to "correct" the perceived excesses (such as cost controls) or deficiencies (such as foreign aid). Yet statistical analysis consistently shows that each country's spending on health is highly dependent on its GDP per capita, regardless of its other characteristics or how its health spending is allocated.

This finding is not new. It was demonstrated in developed countries more than thirty years ago[1] and in a group of less developed nations in the 1990s.[2] Recent statistical analyses indicate a stable relationship between GDP per capita and health spending per capita across the entire spectrum of the World Health Organization's 178 member countries.[3] Figure 7.1 shows how remarkably strong the correlation is: the dots representing income and health spending form a pattern amazingly close to a perfectly straight and uniformly rising line. Expenditure on health per inhabitant rises at a predictable and steady rate whenever a country's GDP per capita grows. There are, however, two significant exceptions to this pattern. First, there are countries like Angola, Oman, Bhutan, United Arab Emirates, Congo, Qatar, Singapore, and Kuwait that spend

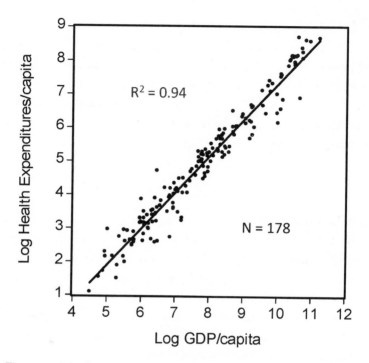

Figure 7.1. The first law of health economics: a strong relationship between total health spending per capita and gross domestic product per capita across 178 countries. (Reproduced with permission from Jacques van der Gaag and Vid Štimac (2008a), Towards a New Paradigm for Health Sector Development, Amsterdam Institute for International Development, www.rockefellerfoundation.org/uploads/files/9b109f8d-0509–49fc-9d0c -baa7ac0f9f84–3-van-der.pdf.)

little on health relative to their income levels. Second, there are countries that spend a lot on health relative to their GDP per capita, such as the United States, Kiribati, Malawi, and Timor-Leste. Both of these categories merit further study. Despite these exceptions, the relationship appears to be robust enough to justify broader consideration by policy makers.

The robustness of the evidence over long periods of time—the near universality of this pattern, found consistently in multiple studies—led Jacques van der Gaag and Vid Štimac to label it "the first law of health economics."[4] Yet despite the strength of the evidence, donors and policy makers have tended to ignore this relationship.[5] After all, they argue, there are so many causal variables, and it is within their jobs to adjust levels of spending in their respective sectors.

Further preliminary analysis shows that health spending per capita does not depend significantly on the breakdown between public and private spending on health in a given country or on the level of international development assistance or debt relief a country receives.[6] Government commitment to improve the population's health may increase public budgets for health, or other competing interests may limit such spending. Yet total health spending per capita—the sum of public, private, and external funds—does not appear to deviate significantly over several years from that predicted by a country's GDP. Private spending,[7] which accounts for 50 to 80 percent of total health expenditures in low- and middle-income countries (mostly in the form of regressive out-of-pocket payments, in which the poor pay a larger proportion of their incomes than the rich), shrinks or expands in reaction to the amount of public spending, adjusting itself to fund the health services demanded by the population.[8]

This relationship does not seem to be affected by the level of official development assistance.[9] In fact, a recent analysis shows that development assistance for health serves mainly to depress domestic government health spending.[10] Every dollar of development assistance for health brought a *reduction* in domestic public health spending of $0.43 to $1.14.[11] If this evidence is confirmed in future studies, donors and governments may decide to redirect their efforts in ways that enhance their impact. These findings also suggest that crude attempts at budget reductions or price controls in health spending are unlikely to be effective, equitable, or efficient.[12] Private spending will simply make up the difference in ways that benefit fewer people and impose a greater burden on those with lower incomes.

Economists continue to debate why this relationship holds and what it means for policy making.[13] What we know is that the relationship between total health spending per capita and GDP per capita does not vary much with economic and social profiles, governance structures, health systems, and financing mechanisms.

Drivers of the Rise in Health Spending

Total health spending per capita appears to be *income elastic*. In other words, if GDP per capita increases by 1 percent, total health spending per capita will increase by slightly more than 1 percent. As it grows richer, a country will spend a growing proportion of its GDP on health.[14] Exceptions notwithstanding, this finding has been obtained not only by analyses of cross-country data, such as that shown in Figure 7.1, but also by longitudinal studies of individual countries.[15]

Although we believe the first law of health economics should underpin health-financing policy, other factors also drive the rise in health spending.[16] As we noted, growing demand for health care by aging populations may explain *part* of the story,[17] and the relentless supply of expensive new medical technologies may contribute even more.[18] Other commentators blame greedy insurance companies, profligate governments, or unnecessary tests and treatments resulting from the practice of defensive medicine—though their significance is contested.[19] Still others point out that when patients and medical providers are distanced from the true cost of health care by third-party insurance, unnecessary services and unnecessarily high prices are more common.[20] However, none of these factors is as strong a predictor of health spending per capita as GDP per capita.

Then, of course, there is the fundamental role of the cost disease.[21] The standard cost disease idea rests on differential productivity levels in different sectors of the economy, but that is hardly the entire story.[22] Demand also plays a crucial role: there seems to be no satiety for health care, wellness, and certainty. Most of our needs and appetites—such as for food or clothing—are eventually satisfied by rising productivity and falling prices in the supply of goods. And most consumers give up personal services (for example, house maids) when they get too pricey. Yet as long as their incomes are growing from productivity gains elsewhere in the economy, people seem willing to pay the increasingly high prices for health services.[23] This demand is surely a significant source of upward pressure on the prices of health-care services. But at the same time, without social protection, the demand for medical services among the poor and lower middle classes must decline as prices increase.

The evidence of the cost disease gives us confidence that it plays a substantial role in the rising cost of health care,[24] which reached $2.5 trillion in the United States in 2009—just over 17 percent of the country's GDP—and could reach 60 percent of GDP by 2105.[25] (By comparison, the entire U.S. federal budget in 2007 accounted for approximately 20 percent of GDP.[26]) In response to those who say such enormous cost increases will never happen, we should recall that, to the skeptics of the last generation, our current levels of spending also seemed impossible.

The Economic Transition of Health

The first law of health economics is particularly significant because of the exceptional economic growth over the last fifty years, which has transformed the world. Economists expect this growth to continue in the next fifty years—even after discounting for periodic downturns, such as the exceptionally severe Great Recession of 2007–2009. Global GDP per capita growth rates began accelerating sharply around 1950 and had more than tripled by 2000.[27] Still higher growth rates appeared throughout most of the first decade of the twenty-first century,[28] and developing countries are expected to expand faster than developed countries for the next few decades.[29]

Given this strong economic growth and the high correlation between GDP and health spending per capita, most countries will likely see their health spending increase significantly in the decades ahead. The ramifications could be as significant as the last century's demographic[30] and epidemiologic transitions,[31] in which declining death and fertility rates changed the structure of the population, while the primary cause of death worldwide began to shift away from infectious to chronic diseases.[32] A huge expansion of health spending has occurred in developed countries during the last fifty years, and the developing world seems likely to follow suit.

The BRIC nations (Brazil, Russia, India, and China) and other emerging economies are already starting to see significant increases in health spending.[33] In China, for instance, total health spending (in nominal terms) grew fiftyfold from 1980 to 2005, and new estimates indicate that it could grow twenty times more by 2050.[34] If projections of double-digit GDP growth in the coming decades prove to be correct, domestic health spending in many African countries may naturally double or triple by 2020. These increases in health resources will create both challenges and opportunities for the financing and provision of health services. Health leaders in developing countries will be forced to shift their attention to managing growing domestic resources more effectively, improving performance, and providing a fair means of financing.

The less desirable outcome of this momentous transformation would be weak stewardship of the health system, dysfunctional service delivery, and inequitable health financing.[35] By itself, the increase in health resources does not guarantee that they will be used effectively or that they will result in greater health equity.[36] Given this, choices made in the near future may have huge impacts—positive or negative—for decades to come.

The implications of the economic transition of health will vary depending primarily on a country's baseline GDP, growth rate, political philosophy, and health system design. Societies in which economic development is accompanied by large income inequalities—where the few reap the rewards of growth, but all face the inflation of health-care costs—will have to establish a balance between solidarity and self-reliance, with vastly different outcomes for social well-being. In general, the specific implications will be different for poor, developing, and developed nations.

The Poorest Countries

In countries where GDP per capita is less than $1,000 (for example, Bangladesh, Ethiopia, Laos, and Rwanda), the transition will begin only when GDP growth accelerates—an event that, for the worst-off countries, may be decades away.[37] International assistance for health spending will remain important for these nations in order to help them to continue approaching the millennium development goal of reducing severe poverty by 2015.[38] As noted, foreign aid that simply buys health products and services in developing countries might crowd out local government health spending[39] and distort national priorities, but it also may redirect resources to the poorest communities and the right priorities. Global donors will have to redirect their support toward better, simpler, and more cost-effective health-care technologies, disease eradication, primary health care, and improving local capacity in both service provision and management. In such settings, financing "health for all" still remains a formidable challenge.[40]

Middle-Income Countries and Emerging Economies

Countries where GDP per capita is higher and growth is already robust—such as Mexico, Turkey, China, or South Africa—are likely to witness a transformation of their health sectors. Developing countries that historically have relied on governments and nongovernmental organizations to supply and finance their health services are likely to see a surge in private demand, provision, and spending on health. This increase in spending brings some perils. Initially, it may outpace public budgets and formal insurance schemes, causing an increase in out-of-pocket spending on health that is apt to be inefficient and regressive. Already, out-of-pocket spending in Africa and Asia (which, as noted, accounts for 50 to 80 percent of all health spending) is fast becoming a leading cause of impoverishment in these regions.[41] Current global estimates indicate that 150 million people each year incur catastrophic health expenditures, pushing 25 million families into poverty each year.[42]

For countries committed to improving health equity and financial protection, the transition to higher GDP and increased health spending may offer unprecedented opportunities to accomplish these goals. Although growth in health spending may be unstoppable, domestic health financing can certainly be reorganized away from out-of-pocket expenditures via public or private insurance. This, in turn, may lead many governments to explicitly pursue universal health coverage—prepaid risk-pooled financing that ensures everyone affordable access to appropriate health services.[43] Many developed countries accomplished this decades ago through social insurance, general tax revenues, or private insurance.[44] An increasing number of middle-income countries—for example, Colombia, Mexico, Thailand, and Ghana—are now following suit.[45] Such policies can help to improve health outcomes[46] and protect individuals and families from catastrophic health expenditures.[47] Although social preferences and efficiency will shape the particular arrangements in each country,[48] all of these changes will require new capacities and institutional arrangements that provide better oversight of national health systems.[49]

For example, Ghana, which at the start of the millennium had less than 5 percent of its population covered by any form of health insurance, launched its National Health Insurance Scheme, a network of community-based health insurance plans, in 2004.[50] By 2008, approximately 39 percent of Ghanaian women aged 15 to 49, and 29 percent of men in the same age group, were covered.

As of 2010, government figures indicate that more than 50 percent of the population has health insurance coverage. In addition, private expenditures, as a proportion of total health spending, declined from 59 percent in 2000 to 48 percent in 2007, while the proportion of Ghana's GDP consumed by health spending increased from 7.2 percent to 8.3 percent.[51] The National Health Insurance Scheme is funded primarily by Ghana's general tax revenues (2.5 percent of the national value added tax goes to fund the scheme), by payroll contributions from formal sector employers, and by direct premiums paid by members. The scheme offers a comprehensive benefits package that is said to cover 95 percent of all health problems reported in Ghanaian health facilities, with an emphasis on maternity care and child health. This was done without raising the country's national debt, which as a percentage of GDP declined during last decade thanks to debt relief provided by international donors.[52]

As GDP per capita and health spending rise in emerging econ-omies, political support for universal health coverage may increase worldwide.[53] In particular, if India[54] and China[55] succeed in provid-ing universal coverage to their citizens, the portion of the world population with health coverage could double from 40 to 80 percent by 2020. Currently there are 30 to 50 middle-income countries in the world where the transition to higher GDP and health spending will prompt calls for immediate health-sector reform. Forty-seven of these countries have experienced average GDP growth of more than 4 percent during the prior decade, as noted in Table 7.1.[56] In thirty-one of these, out-of-pocket spending accounts for more than one-third of all health expenditures, and twenty-nine of the thirty-one spend between 5 and 10 percent of GDP on health. These twenty-nine countries, we believe, can be expected to move more quickly to universal health coverage. In addition, eleven other coun-tries do not meet these conditions but are already moving toward the introduction of universal health coverage, with notable reduc-tions in out-of-pocket health spending achieved already. The inter-national community can facilitate this transition by financially supporting related research and learning, providing assistance to the institutions—often new government agencies—that implement and oversee reform efforts, and subsidizing health-insurance pre-miums for the world's poorest people in countries undergoing the early stages of reform.

High-Income Countries

Organisation for Economic Co-operation and Development (OECD) members and other high-income countries are much farther along in this health and economic transition. Most of these countries em-braced universal health coverage in the twentieth century, but their progress varies according to their differing cultural values and

Table 7.1. Countries Moving toward the Economic Transition of Health.

Selected World Health Organization Member States	Total Formal Coverage (%)[1]	Total Health Spending as a Percentage of GDP (2007)	Out-of-Pocket Spending as a Percentage of Total Health Spending	Average GDP Growth (2001–2010)[2]
Argentina	99.9	10	23.9	4.4
Armenia*	100.0	4.4	51.5	8.5
Bangladesh*	0.4	3.4	55.8	5.8
Belarus	100.0	6.5	17.3	7.4
Burkina Faso	0.2	6.1	39.4	5.4
Cape Verde	65.0	4.5	18.4	5.8
China*	23.9	4.3	53.9	10.5
Colombia*	31.3	6.1	6.4	4.0
Costa Rica*	100.0	8.1	19.2	4.3
Dominican Republic*	84.0	5.4	54.7	5.1
Ecuador*	73.0	5.8	48.3	4.3
Egypt	47.6	6.3	56.3	5.0
Gambia	99.9	5.5	29.3	4.3
Georgia*	55.0	8.2	72.1	6.2
Ghana*	18.7	8.3	50.0	5.4
Honduras*	65.2	6.2	45.5	4.1
India*	5.7	4.1	75.6	7.4
Indonesia*	54.6	2.2	32.9	5.2
Jordan*	80.0	8.9	44.4	6.2
Kazakhstan*	75.0	—	35.4	8.1
Lao People's Democratic Republic	16.1	4.0	74.1	7.1
Latvia*	87.0	6.2	35.8	4.0
Lebanon*	95.1	8.8	39.3	5.3
Mali	2.0	5.7	48.1	5.6
Mongolia	100.0	4.3	13.8	6.4
Morocco	41.2	5.0	48.7	5.0
Namibia	22.5	7.6	5.4	4.5
Niger	0.7	5.3	40.3	4.8

(continued)

Table 7.1. *(continued)*

Selected World Health Organization Member States	Total Formal Coverage (%)[1]	Total Health Spending as a Percentage of GDP (2007)	Out-of-Pocket Spending as a Percentage of Total Health Spending	Average GDP Growth (2001–2010)[2]
Oman	100.0	2.4	10.2	4.9
Panama	100.0	6.7	25.1	6.2
Peru*	71.0	4.3	33.2	5.7
Romania	100.0	4.7	24.7	4.12
Russian Federation	88.0	5.4	30.0	4.87
Rwanda*	36.6	10.3	22.7	7.61
Senegal	11.7	5.7	61.9	4.03
Serbia	96.2	9.9	25.1	4.19
Slovakia	96.2	7.7	23.0	4.93
Sri Lanka	0.1	4.2	43.6	5.1
Syrian Arab Republic	29.2	3.6	52.4	4.23
Thailand*	97.7	3.7	27.3	4.33
Tunisia*	99.0	6.0	46.0	4.54
Turkmenistan*	82.3	2.6	33.3	13.0
Uganda	0.1	6.3	37.9	7.44
Ukraine*	100.0	6.9	41.1	4.47
United Republic of Tanzania*	14.5	5.3	34.0	6.9
Viet Nam*	23.4	7.1	60.5	7.23
Yemen	6.3	3.9	51.0	4.3

Source: Based on data from the International Labor Organization (2008); the International Monetary Fund (2008); and the World Health Organization (2009).

Notes: Unless otherwise noted, data shown in Table 7.1 come from sources that are identified and discussed in this chapter. Asterisks denote countries that already are working toward universal health coverage, including some that are still struggling to control out-of-pocket expenditures. [1] "Total Formal Coverage" gives the percentage of people in each country who have access to health care, according to the International Labor Organization (2008). [2] Source: International Monetary Fund (2008).

historical circumstances.[57] Those that have not achieved universal coverage, like the United States, have seen their total health spending grow, despite vigorous cost-control measures such as managed care and hospital reimbursement schemes. Unfortunately for such countries, the barriers to universal coverage only increase as the cost disease advances and health spending increases. Paradoxically, it may be easier to implement reforms aimed at achieving universal coverage when a relatively poor country's total health spending accounts for just 5 percent of GDP. Once a country grows affluent and health spending consumes 15 percent or more of GDP, it is far more difficult to overcome political and fiscal hurdles.

The economic disparities between richer and poorer countries are likely to be exacerbated as countries go through this transition (albeit at different times and at different speeds). This will be manifested in growing tensions over brain drain (that is, the movement of trained medical personnel from the poorer societies to more affluent ones) and medical tourism—both of which lead to an increasingly integrated global health market. The growing importance of health in the economy is guaranteed to figure prominently in debates about national labor and fiscal policies, as well as in international trade and development.[58]

Developing countries are likely to repeat the experiences of already developed countries. As the overall burden of disease declines and more countries are able to afford ever higher levels of health spending, the burden of unfair and catastrophic health expenditures will increasingly fall on ordinary citizens—specifically, on the small subset of the population that falls seriously ill in any given year—unless these societies move toward universal health coverage. As health spending increases, the cost of health care generally will take a back seat to issues of inequality and the increasing difficulty of providing universal care.[59]

Decades ago, Brian Abel-Smith[60] emphasized the need for more awareness of the implications of health financing for global health. We believe those implications cannot be understood without the first law of health economics (that is, the close relationship between total health spending per capita and GDP per capita). The two factors together will make cost a more complex issue in countries that are accustomed to thinking of health care in isolation from productivity macroeconomics. As developing economies expand at an unprecedented rate, health reform debates around the world must shift away from simple attempts to increase aid or control costs and embrace new strategies that allocate health resources more efficiently and equitably.

PART 2

Technical Aspects of the Cost Disease

EIGHT

Hybrid Industries and the Cost Disease

Each plant has its parasite, and each created thing its lover and
poet.
—RALPH WALDO EMERSON

The cost disease affects research and development (R&D) much as
it does education, medicine, the performing arts, and other techno-
logically stagnant personal services. Even though researchers employ computers and other equipment whose real costs tend to decline
markedly and therefore decidedly belong to the progressive sector,
the disease nevertheless can lead to a persistent rise in the real cost of
research. Like other services whose productivity is not easily increased, the portion of research that consists of sheer thinking does
not benefit from the labor-saving offset to rising wages that characterizes economic sectors whose productivity is constantly increasing.

Many industries rely heavily on a variety of inputs with different
technical attributes, some coming from the progressive sector and

others from the stagnant sector. Products that use inputs from both sectors in more or less unchangeable proportions tend to follow the cost behavior of the stagnant inputs, with the progressive inputs steadily losing their influence upon the overall cost of the final product over time.[1] This is neither coincidence nor accident but is inherent in the structure of the cost disease. Of course, it must be recognized that the patterns of cost behavior will vary from case to case, at least to some degree. However, the basic story described here surely is widely applicable.

The Asymptotically Stagnant Sector

Some years after Bill Bowen and I first introduced the cost disease model, it was extended to include a hybrid sector, called the *asymptotically stagnant* sector.[2] Products of this sort use some inputs from the progressive sector of the economy and some from the stagnant sector. Two common examples of asymptotically stagnant products are television broadcasting, whose main inputs are electronic equipment and live performance, and the use of computers in research, whose main inputs are sophisticated hardware and human labor devoted to software creation and data gathering.[3] Another suggestive example would be a consulting group that carries out consumer surveys that involve personal interviews of large samples of consumers. In analyzing their data, the consultants make extensive use of computer hardware that clearly is a product of the progressive sector and which continually grows cheaper and more powerful. But collecting the data through personal interviews is mostly a stagnant activity that offers little scope for cumulative labor-saving modifications.

Two things that behave more and more similarly as time passes are said to exhibit asymptotic behavior. Why, then, do we call these sectors asymptotically stagnant? Initially, the product's costs typically follow the behavior of its progressive input. Because the real cost of that input grows steadily cheaper, the asymptotically stagnant product also tends to grow less expensive. But precisely because the cost of the progressive input steadily declines, it accounts for an ever smaller share of the overall cost of producing the product. The stagnant input's share, conversely, keeps increasing. So, returning to our example of a consulting firm, the cost of computer hardware eventually becomes an insignificant part of the firm's overall outlays, and a steadily increasing portion of its operating budget is spent on interviewers and interview-related activities. Eventually this stagnant input will consume almost all of the firm's budget. The total budget must then closely follow the cost of the stagnant-sector input, which as we know is doomed to increase over time.[4]

The case of television broadcasting is highly suggestive. Consider a one-hour episode of a soap opera with ten performers. The cost of this broadcast is composed primarily of the wages of the actors, directors, camera operators, and other essential personnel, but it also includes the operation of the electronic equipment that transmits the performance to its audience. This equipment has improved substantially over the years, which materially reduces the cost of that portion of the broadcast. The performers' and production crew's salaries will then take up an increasing portion of the show's budget.

The asymptotically stagnant sector appears to include some high-tech industries. Perhaps the most noteworthy example is the R&D process itself, which plays a fundamental role in creating the productivity growth that fuels the cost disease. This means that over time some products will no longer offset rising real costs in stagnant-sector industries as effectively.

An Asymptotically Stagnant Activity

The cost trajectory of R&D has clear characteristics of an asymptotically stagnant activity. This is because R&D uses two types of input: mental labor (that is, human time) and technological equipment, such as computers. The cost of computer components and many of the other high-tech tools of research, as a fraction of the overall cost of R&D, is of course declining rapidly (for a computer of modestly rising quality and capacity). But the cost of the other input, the act of thinking, is very different. It is a crucial input for the research process, but there seems to be little reason to believe that we have become more proficient at this handicraft activity than Newton, Leibniz, or Huygens. Meanwhile, the cost of R&D labor activity continues to increase steadily.[5]

The effect of these rising labor costs upon the stagnant component of research—the sheer thinking activity of the researchers themselves (albeit unquantifiable)—may make the financing of innovation more difficult and thus serves as an impediment to innovation. For example, a firm facing high R&D labor costs that wants to increase its output may find it necessary to cancel plans for investment in the newer and more productive machines the R&D department has requested and instead to buy additional machines of the current (less expensive and less productive) type. This allows the firm to devote more of its R&D budget to researchers' salaries. Thus, the rising cost of innovation can lead to fiscal strategies that reduce investment in R&D, thereby further impairing R&D productivity. This, in turn, can impede overall productivity growth.

The Asymptotically Stagnant Sector and the General Welfare

Because so many products use inputs derived from both the progressive and stagnant sectors and thus are asymptotically stagnant, the scenario just described may be significant for the growth rate of the whole economy's productivity. But, again, such a slowdown in the volume of research is by no means inevitable. Although the rates of growth differ sharply, productivity in both the progressive and stagnant sectors generally is increasing. And as we have noted, an economy in which productivity in almost all outputs is increasing can afford more of everything. Thus, despite the appearance of rising costs in the stagnant and asymptotically stagnant sectors, there is no need for firms to cut back on R&D, just as consumers need not reduce their use of health-care or education services.

But although the output of a particular product *need not* be reduced when the cost disease relentlessly increases its real cost, it certainly remains possible that its output *will* be decreased. This decline may be due to a misunderstanding: the product's purchasers may assume that it is no longer affordable—a conclusion that we have seen to be untrue. Alternatively, output may fall because the product's rising price makes it more attractive for purchasers to direct their funds to items whose real prices are increasing more slowly or even declining.

If firms apply the latter strategy to their real outlays on R&D, for instance, then overall productivity growth—the source of the cost disease—will be reduced. Thus, the disease itself may rein in firms' R&D expenditures. In this way, the cost disease ultimately may undercut itself, like a parasite that devours its own host.

The cost disease does not affect every service, and its relationship to certain services is more complex and subtle. The interplay between the asymptotically stagnant sector and the cost disease substantially affects the pace of innovation and thus economic growth. Moreover, it is tempting to argue that a decline in productivity growth in innovation may substantially damage the general welfare. Because of compounding effects, even a minuscule decline in productivity growth, if it continues over decades, can add up to an enormous reduction in the economy's output and living standards. Material prosperity is still apt to grow but not at the unprecedented rates seen in recent centuries.

NINE

Productivity Growth, Employment Allocation, and the Special Case of Business Services

Lilian Gomory Wu and William J. Baumol

You could not step twice into the same rivers; for other waters are ever flowing on to you.

—HERACLITUS

Any index of the overall consumer price level is an average of the prices of all of the goods in the economy. It follows then that if the real (inflation-adjusted) prices of all commodities are not increasing at the same pace, some are rising at above-average rates—meaning that their real prices are increasing—while the real prices of others must be falling.[1] Thus, as we have seen, there are two sides to the cost disease story: one concerns products whose real prices are condemned to increase (that is, personal services in the stagnant sector), and the other concerns virtually all other products (notably, manufactured products in the progressive sector), whose real prices are fated to decrease.

As we saw in Chapter 2, the set of items whose real prices are rising remains roughly constant decade after decade, as does the set of items whose real prices are falling.[2] As we also saw, the items and services whose real prices are rising include a labor component in their production that is largely irreducible, either because of the nature of the product or because its quality requires direct human effort. In contrast, the products with falling real prices and costs are those whose production can be automated, thereby reducing their labor content even as their quality is unaffected—or improved—by automation. This chapter focuses on another group of commodities whose productivity is rising, which has been largely ignored in the cost disease literature.

Declining Real Costs in Agriculture

Although the declining-cost aspect of the cost disease largely has been overlooked, this does not mean that falling real prices in the progressive sector have gone unnoticed. The rapidly declining prices of computers and related equipment are perhaps the most obvious example. The falling-price pattern of telecommunications services and equipment is another. Equally important, but perhaps less obvious, is the decline in the real prices of kitchen equipment, television sets, and other household appliances. The prices of all of these essential components of our modern way of life have lagged considerably behind the rate of inflation.

Perhaps more surprisingly, costs in much of the agricultural sector have done the same. In most of Europe during the seventeenth and eighteenth centuries, well over half of the labor force was engaged in the production of crops and related activities.[3] (In the United States right after independence, the share was even higher.) Yet most Europeans lacked reliable access to food. In good years when growing conditions were favorable, they subsisted largely on grain supplemented by salted fish. Perhaps once a decade, the crop yield was sufficiently poor to cause famine and widespread death from starvation. Only a few nations, notably England and the United States, appear to have escaped this repeated catastrophe. There, too, the labor forces were heavily involved in agriculture.

Today, in contrast, agriculture in both Europe and the United States employs less than 3 percent of the labor forces.[4] Yet this minuscule labor outlay has led to a problem undreamed of in the past: chronic surpluses that, at times, have driven governments to pay farmers to reduce the amount they produce. Farms that are highly mechanized require fewer workers. The labor content of farm produce, and consequently its real cost, has fallen dramatically. This is yet another dramatic example of technical progress in the economy through the activities of entrepreneurs, who ensure that promising innovations are put to effective use.

In addition to government subsidies, the dramatic shift from food scarcity to surplus can be attributed to technical innovation and increased automation in farming. Agricultural equipment of fantastic power and capacity and advanced fertilizers and pesticides are now brought to bear on damage-resistant crop varieties to produce larger outputs with less labor. The changes underlying this agricultural revolution are thus very similar to those that affect the economy's manufacturing sector.

All this is important because growing productivity and the reduced prices and costs resulting from it ensure that most people's living standards can be improved. Formerly unattainable luxuries become affordable, particularly if consumers benefit from rising real wages as productivity grows. Thus, the conclusion reached in Chapter 4 that "we can afford it all" means that improved health care and education will remain affordable, perhaps even to the lower income members of society.

What the Cost Disease Analysis Reveals about the Progressive Sector

The cost disease analysis provides some suggestive observations about the consequences of such innovative developments in the progressive sector. Manufacturing, like agriculture, has seen its share of the American labor force decline steadily and dramatically, from almost 30 percent in 1959 to less than 10 percent in 2007.[5] The steadiness of this descent is shown in Figure 9.1.

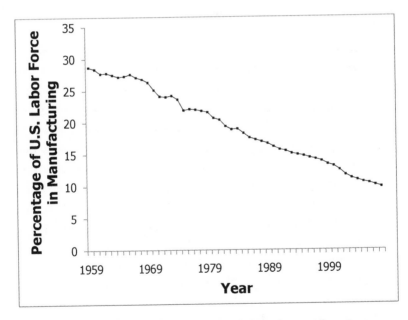

Figure 9.1. Percentage of U.S. labor force working in the manufacturing sector, 1959–2007. (Based on data from the U.S. Bureau of Labor Statistics.)

The conclusion commonly drawn from this decline in manufacturing employment is that countries such as China and Japan are stealing away our export capacity. But the issue is more complex. Both China and Japan also saw their manufacturing employment decline in recent decades—though in China this trend reversed in 2002.[6] In fact, America's loss of agricultural and manufacturing jobs is a cost disease phenomenon—one that is potentially benign if properly dealt with. These falling real prices entail very different threats that are widely overlooked. Finally, we must not overlook the problem of markets lost to outsourcing, which continues to be serious.

Productivity Growth and the Unique Case of Business Services

The cost disease also has some noteworthy implications for the overall rate of productivity growth. In our early writings on the cost disease,[7] one of us argued that it tended to slow down the overall growth rate of productivity in an economy. The reason for this is simple, as we will see next, but this argument is not nearly as conclusive as was once thought. First, the result depends on how we average the growth rates of the progressive and stagnant sectors, and as we saw in Chapter 6, there is no conclusively superior way to carry out the addition of apples and oranges that such a calculation requires. Second, not all the products of the services sector go directly to consumers. Some stagnant services, such as consulting advice, are purchased by business firms. Even though productivity growth also tends to be slow in services provided to businesses, for reasons we will see, an increase in these services' share of total output may actually enhance the overall growth rate of productivity—at least for a time.[8]

Indeed, there is an increasingly important set of services that are not used directly by consumers but rather are used by business firms in their production process. A prime example is a piece of software used by a business enterprise. The main distinguishing feature of such a service is that it can, and often does, undergo productivity growth not just once but twice in succession. The first increase comes when the service itself is being produced, and the second occurs when the service is then put to use by a manufacturing firm in its production. Each increase may be relatively modest, yet they may add up to a substantial improvement in productivity.

Consider a highly simplified example that involves a single final manufactured product and only two inputs, software and labor. The manufacturer, Firm A, outsources its software preparation to a specialized supplier, Firm B. By getting better computers and software for itself, Firm B may become faster in preparing new software, increasing its productivity by, say, 1 percent each year on average. But Firm A, also driven by competition to improve its use of inputs, increases its productivity by, say, an average of 3 percent per year. Thus (as in real life), the business services firm experiences much slower productivity growth than the manufacturer. The software produced by the business services firm, however, leads to two rounds of productivity improvements—1 percent per year during its creation, and 3 percent each year during its utilization—and thereby a total of well above 3 percent annual productivity growth is contributed to the final product.

Nicholas Oulton, who first made this observation, takes the story one step farther, arguing that the cost disease–induced transfer of more of the economy's labor force out of fast-growth manufacturing and into slow-growth business services actually speeds up the economy's overall productivity growth.[9] To understand why this is true, again imagine an economy in which total production consists of just two items: manufactured goods and software, produced by separate firms. Suppose manufacturing uses two inputs, software and labor, while software creation uses only labor. Suppose also that half of the labor force initially goes to manufacturing and the other half to software creation. And, as in the prior example, suppose the productivity of software creation expands by 1 percent per year, while that of manufacturing labor grows by 3 percent per year. Meanwhile, the software labor's combined two stages of productivity receive the doubled growth impetus just described so that even though software creation is an industry with slow productivity growth, its products allow overall productivity to grow by 4 percent each year, steadily outpacing the 3 percent annual productivity growth of the manufacturing labor.

Now consider what happens if there is a shift of employees from manufacturing to software creation so that only one quarter of the labor force works in manufacturing, while the remainder produces software. The punch line should be obvious. If we transfer workers from the fast-growth industry to the slow-growth industry, rather than reducing the overall productivity growth of the labor force as a whole, the average growth rate will increase from 3.5 percent to 3.75 percent: $(0.5)3 + (0.5)4 = 3.5$ to $(0.25)3 + (0.75)4 = 3.75$, respectively. This increase may seem small, but compounded over time it will result in enormous overall growth.

Not All Services Are Stagnant

It is tempting to relegate business-to-business services, like other services, to the stagnant sector of the economy, where productivity growth rates are lower than those typical in manufacturing. But, as we will see here, business services counteract the erroneous impression, often repeated in the literature, that *all or most services* are victims of the cost disease. Nicholas Oulton has pointed out that the growth performance of business services is very different from that of stagnant-sector consumer services because the former are used as *inputs* to other products or services and typically bring two or more rounds of productivity improvement.[10]

This implies that expansion of business services' share of total output can (and apparently does) increase the rate of overall productivity growth in the economy as a whole, even though the work involved in the creation of these services may resist substantial labor-saving developments. The production of business services is carried out in the slow-growth stagnant sector, but when these services are put to use by other firms they result in costs that grow more slowly than the average for the economy. Thus, business services, despite their creation in the stagnant sector, can and do escape the rising costs imposed by the cost disease.

On the Expanding Business Services Sector

Services supplied to firms from outside are hardly a new phenomenon. Even the largest enterprises have long obtained their banking and accounting services from others.[11] "Make-or-buy" decisions—the choice between internal supply or outside purchase of goods—were common even in the American colonies, when items such as the clocks used by businesses were purchased from Great Britain.

What is new, however, is the rapid expansion in the quantity of such interfirm purchases that consist of services, their role in the employment of entire economies, and their increasing influence on those economies' productivity growth. Computers and the Internet, in particular, have played a central role in these developments. Even the largest manufacturing firms now need specialized expertise in installing, maintaining, and updating the computer equipment that has enabled their productivity growth in recent decades. Moreover, the Internet now makes it possible to obtain such services from distant locations where far lower wages materially reduce the home company's costs.

The American business services sector employs almost 17 million people—roughly 12 percent of the country's employed labor force.[12] Between 1979 and 2009, the number of people working in business services rose by almost 130 percent, or just over 9 million jobs—an increase that accounted for almost one quarter of all employment growth during that period.[13]

In Europe, business services also constitute one of the fastest-growing sectors of the economy. One study reported that, between 1979 and 2001, business services accounted for 54 percent of employment growth and 18 percent of income growth.[14] In 2003, the sector employed more than 19 million workers, produced 1 trillion euros, and accounted for 11 percent of the euro zone's gross domestic product (GDP). The sector's employment growth, at 4.4 percent per year, led all sectors of the economy. Still, as the study's authors noted, business services firms in Europe are often small—probably below the size required for maximal efficiency, and competition among firms within the sector is relatively undeveloped because of "market segmentation and lack of market transparency."[15] All this implies that we can expect further expansion of these services as entrepreneurs grow more experienced and their efficiency improves.

Progressive-Sector Business Services

Because it is sometimes difficult to achieve any significant reduction in their labor content, business services are often assigned to the stagnant sector of the economy. But, as we have seen, the *use* of many of these services brings cumulative productivity growth, which takes them well into the progressive sector. Moreover, in instances where technology has replaced human labor, the activity of producing and supplying some business services may see rapid productivity growth. Telecommunications offers perhaps the best example of this. We can best grasp the astonishing magnitude of productivity growth in this industry by comparing today's inexpensive and virtually instantaneous global communication capabilities with past methods. A major turning point of the American Revolutionary War, for example, came when British General John Burgoyne surrendered at Saratoga on October 17, 1777. Unfortunately, news of the victory did not reach Benjamin Franklin in Paris, where he was soliciting French support for the American war effort, until December 6—well over a month after the event.

The range of such progressive-sector business services is remarkably broad and includes items as diverse as business strategy and business operations consulting, statistical and risk calculation, data management and analytics, and even the computer tools used for animated film production.[16] All of these activities have seen dramatic productivity growth that can be attributed to the sophisticated technology employed in their production. They are all services that belong to the progressive sector.

Thus, the notion that all services are victims of the cost disease is a misunderstanding. There are many exceptions that have great importance for the economy. We next present some noteworthy examples, in which the process of producing, delivering, and using a business service entails several cumulative steps—each of which contributes to overall productivity growth. Taken together, these limited contributions may entail productivity growth that equals or even exceeds that of progressive-sector industries.

Here we look first at some information technology business services supplied by IBM[17] to Avnet Technology Solutions, a global technology distributor that serves large technology manufacturers (such as Cisco, HP, IBM, and Oracle) and the many resellers that bring these manufacturers' products to market. To highlight the diverse settings in which business services can be applied, we also provide a case study that looks at business services used by Sun World, a California-based food grower, to increase the productivity of its agricultural operations.

Case Study 1: Using Business Services to Improve Communications and Efficiency among Avnet's Technology Industry Clients

In their simplest form, technology distributors like Avnet provide Internet commerce Web sites that allow resellers to research and purchase products from many different manufacturers via a convenient online portal. These distributors also provide more complex services, acting in effect as business consultants who help resellers manage their inventory and finances, secure loans to pay for orders, and find other ways to run their businesses more efficiently. Some of these business services are provided in person. In other instances, however, distributors employ computer systems that not only facilitate ordering and communication between manufacturers and resellers but also store information about past transactions where resellers and manufacturers can access it to make business decisions.

Resellers use Avnet's Channel Connection Web portal to obtain information easily and quickly on available products and their estimated shipping times, alternative products that may be more cost-effective or that may have shorter delivery cycles, information about their credit status, the status of orders already being processed, methods to maximize rebates and other incentives from manufacturers, and even information on the marketplace such as the adoption rate of a particular technology. The portal also enables manufacturers to obtain real-time information on the flow of assets (for example, on-time delivery rates, shipping costs, and warehouse inventories) and financial matters (for example, outstanding purchase orders) as well as resellers' evaluations of their performance relative to those of their competitors—information that helps manufacturers make better decisions for the long run.

Avnet's services are provided via a specialized Web portal (Channel Connection) that makes it possible for manufacturers and resellers to obtain personalized information about their orders in real time. The technology underlying this portal underwent gains in productivity at IBM, where it was created. Although these gains may be limited, at least in principle, they enabled IBM to constrain the cost of designing and building the technology used to create Avnet's Web portal. However, instead of going to consumers, this technology is then transferred to Avnet, where it is used as an input that enhances the productivity of Avnet's own activities via its use of the Web portal. Finally, the portal allows buyers and sellers—Avnet's customers—to run their businesses more efficiently, which directly increases their productivity. The essential point is that, unlike services provided directly to consumers, there are three rounds of productivity growth associated with Avnet's Web portal, and together they yield a substantial reduction in costs.

Using the Channel Connection portal, both manufacturers and resellers can process orders more quickly, reducing fulfillment time by as much as 80 percent. The Web portal also has raised the productivity of Avnet's own operations. With the launch of Channel Connection in 2002, Avnet's sales operations staff increased their productivity by more than one-third, and the company reduced its associated information technology costs by 20 percent, including a reduction in the costs associated with maintenance and modification of software applications of more than $1 million. In the portal's first year of use alone, Avnet reaped an estimated 360 percent return on its investment in the Channel Connection system. These productivity gains, however, were preceded by advances in productivity at IBM, where Channel Connection was designed and constructed in collaboration with Avnet.

The productivity enhancements provided by Avnet's Channel Connection portal thus illustrate the multiple rounds of productivity growth associated with business services. In this example, Channel Connection is a piece of technology developed by IBM that provides productivity-enhancing business services to both Avnet and Avnet's customers. Channel Connection thus provides not two but three rounds of productivity increases: those at IBM in creating the Web portal, those at Avnet in its initial utilization of the portal, and those at Avnet's customers when they use the portal to improve their own efficiency.

Case Study 2: Using Business Services and Data Analytics to Increase Agricultural Productivity

The California-based company Sun World grows fruits and vegetables for worldwide distribution and has long used data and analytics to run its farming operations. For more than a decade, it has employed data on crop yields, consumer trends, weather, labor, fuel costs, and water management in its financial analyses and planning. But Sun World mainly relied on manual data collection and analytical methods. This slow method of collecting and analyzing operations data often entailed months of work, which meant that the results could not be applied until the next growing season.[18]

In 2006, the grower hired IBM and Applied Analytix to help it use data analytics business services to analyze crop yields, farm labor costs, water usage, growing patterns, and a wide range of sales and distribution processes in nearly real time and then make immediate adjustments where appropriate. Experts from both companies collaborated to design a computer system with real-time data analytics tools that monitor and analyze the data Sun World collected about its operations in order to help the grower identify problems and quickly find solutions.

For instance, the number of boxes of grapes harvested per hour by each crew in each of Sun World's vineyards is now monitored continuously and integrated every five minutes into an analytics engine that allows the grower to compare the productivity of different equipment and harvesting teams and then determine which methods produce the best results. The system also enables Sun World to analyze data on root stock, timing, location, irrigation, crop type, and other factors in order to predict what combination produces the best yield at the lowest cost.

The new technology has increased Sun World's crop yields, reduced its waste, and significantly improved its overall productivity. For instance, by evaluating the effect of different irrigation systems on crop yields, Sun World has decreased its overall water usage by 8.5 percent since 2006. It also decreased its fuel consumption by 20 percent during the same period simply by better matching farming equipment to specific harvesting tasks. Tracking the number of boxes per hour harvested by each crew has increased the company's labor efficiency by 8 percent and decreased its labor and distribution costs by 10 to 15 percent.

Timely data collection and improved analytical capabilities clearly are helping Sun World increase its overall productivity, a result that exemplifies the second round of productivity growth that characterizes business services. In this example, the first round of growth occurred at IBM and Applied Analytix, which use data analytics to improve the productivity of their *own* operations, including the business services they offer to clients.

The examples provided here should make clear the diverse uses typical of business services and the multiplicity of stages entailed in the design, production, and use of such services. At each of these stages in the evolution and deployment of a business service, some additional productivity growth can be expected to occur. Even if productivity enhancement is relatively modest at each stage, taken together these individual increases add up to create substantial productivity growth overall.

Business Services That Increase Productivity by Facilitating Innovation

Other business services focus on the innovation process itself, helping to increase firms' productivity by improving the way they innovate.[19] This often results in multiple stages of productivity growth. An obvious example is the creation of novel software that makes it easier for others to put the ideas of inventors to use, with productivity enhancement occurring in both the design of the software and its utilization.

The importance of such services should be obvious, given the significant role innovation plays in stimulating growth within firms and in the larger economy. But as one recent report makes clear, bringing a new idea to market is not a simple process.[20] There is no one-size-fits-all innovation roadmap to follow, though we do know that collaboration among key players—for instance, via industry committees and conferences—is one of the essential components that facilitate and increase the productivity of the innovation process. Two minds are often better than one, especially when several types of specialized knowledge are needed.

The Rise of Collaborative Innovation

Today, the companies that are best at innovation are also apt to be the best collaborators, both internally and externally. When dealing with a complex problem or complex technology, different individuals, different divisions within a firm, or different collaborating firms may vary in their ability to deal with different portions of the requisite technology. By sharing ideas, these collaborators can emerge with new business models, better designed processes, and novel technology—and do so more quickly, as each collaborator contributes what it does best.

For example, IBM, Sony, and Toshiba worked together to develop the Cell Broadband Engine chip that is used in Sony's PlayStation game console. IBM also provides computer chips used in other game systems, such as Microsoft's Xbox 360 and Nintendo's Wii. Such collaboration clearly speeds and enhances productivity.

In the case studies that follow, we will see how one company, IBM, has used innovation-focused services to increase productivity in its innovation processes by facilitating communication among collaborating employees. The examples described here are particularly noteworthy because they are "mega-innovative innovations"—that is, innovations that serve as inputs, which facilitate the creation of other innovations. Because IBM makes these services available to other firms, they are considered business services.

The first two case studies describe business services that enhance productivity in the process of generating and analyzing new ideas. The third focuses on business services that spur productivity growth in the process IBM uses to refine and launch new technology.

Case Study 3: "Jams"—a Crowdsourcing Model for Business Innovation

Based on the premise that the best ideas can come from anywhere, IBM "Jams" constitute a new crowdsourcing-inspired[21] approach to enhancing business innovation.[22] Jams are moderated online discussions that focus on a specific topic, with hundreds or even hundreds of thousands of people coming together as equals to generate new ideas—a select few of which are then cultivated and developed. Jam sessions bring together people who normally would not have the chance to meet and exchange ideas.

For instance, IBM's 2006 Global Innovation Jam[23] brought together more than 150,000 people from 104 countries and 67 organizations and universities—IBM employees and their family members, university students and faculty, and IBM clients and business partners—to review new technology emerging from IBM research and its possible applications. Ideas generated during that Jam led to the launch of ten new IBM products, services, and start-up businesses with seed investments totaling $100 million. Two years later, many of these new products, services, and start-ups were fully operational and were already achieving impressive results.[24] Since then, several of these business units have become core IBM products and services.

IBM's Jams, and the technology that facilitates them, also have been made available to other firms, thereby spurring a second round of productivity growth. In 2007, IBM and the Original Equipment Suppliers Association, an industry group that represents American automotive parts suppliers, hosted the Automotive Suppliers Jam, which brought together 2,000 CEOs, business unit executives, middle managers, and engineers from hundreds of organizations in the automotive industry to identify the key challenges facing the North American automotive parts supplier industry and to collaborate on solutions.[25] That Jam made it possible for people from different management levels and functions, who never would have been able to gather at one time and place in the purely physical world, to share ideas democratically.

The Jams approach to collaboration is not restricted to business. In 2005, for instance, IBM, the Government of Canada, and UN-HABITAT—the United Nations' human settlements program—hosted Habitat Jam.[26] Thousands of people from more than 150 countries, including urban-planning experts, government leaders, and residents of cities—even slum dwellers in makeshift Internet cafes, took part in the Jam, posting more than 15,000 ideas for improving the environment, health, safety, and quality of life in the world's major cities.

In general, Jams have proven to be a productive tool for the stimulation of grassroots innovation. This is because Jams allow large numbers of people who would not ordinarily collaborate to come together to discuss their experiences and generate a large number of ideas. Within IBM, for instance, Jams generated strong interest in soliciting breakthrough innovative ideas from nontraditional sources within the company, such as the sales force and the operations staff who handle the company's administrative work. As we will see in the next case study, IBM employs another innovation service that enables *all* employees to contribute ideas for innovations that can improve the company's productivity.

Case Study 4: ThinkPlace—Democratizing Incremental Innovation

ThinkPlace, based on the belief that every IBM employee has good ideas that can improve the company, encourages employees to generate and refine new ideas via open-ended online conversations.[27] This gives employees a means of sharing their ideas with others who may help to develop and deploy them.

Any employee can use ThinkPlace to suggest ideas, refine them, express support for them, or explain why they might not work. The system is designed to gather ideas driven by immediate customer needs and multidisciplinary business opportunities that otherwise might fall into the cracks between IBM's established business units.[28] As a result of ThinkPlace, the company can rapidly conceptualize, refine, assemble, and market new ideas generated by employees. This brings all employees into innovation and problem-solving efforts and allows new ideas and solutions to emerge at a faster clip.

So far, more than 150,000 IBM employees have participated in ThinkPlace, and more than 35,000 ideas have been submitted. One idea proposed and refined via ThinkPlace generated $1 million in cost savings for the company's Integrated Delivery Center in Dublin, Ireland, by replacing shipping paper with recyclable air-filled plastic cushions. Another ThinkPlace idea led to the creation of an automatic, Web-based method for customers to update firmware (that is, the internal software that runs a computer's hardware) on their IBM computer systems. Previously, technicians were needed to install firmware updates for customers, but the new method automatically updates a customer's firmware via Internet downloads, saving IBM an estimated $2 million each year. Between 2005 and 2009, ThinkPlace cost IBM $5.5 million but generated more than $110 million in savings for the company—a twenty times return on the investment.

Case Study 5: Using Early Adopter Communities to Develop Innovative Technology

In developing new products, IBM uses a formal, investment-oriented innovation process to lay out the initial concept for a new project, estimate return on investment, and assess the project's feasibility and usefulness.[29] This process ensures that new products are released continuously while keeping new ideas flowing from the company's research and development laboratories, but it also creates a dilemma: it is often too rigorous for emerging technologies, whose potential benefits are not always certain. As a consequence, emerging technology may not be able to obtain the funding necessary for testing, developing, and launching.

In order to encourage innovation, IBM established its Technology Adoption Program (TAP),[30] a less hierarchical, collaborative approach to the introduction and management of innovation projects.[31] TAP's community of 120,000 volunteer early adopters (more than one-quarter of IBM's workforce) consists of staff members who are interested in testing new technology and providing feedback on it. The program is administered via a companywide intranet on which innovators post descriptions and provide online access to their new technologies and applications.

As the following examples illustrate, TAP improves productivity in a number of important ways.[32]

1. *Faster development and release of new products and services.* TAP is credited with reducing the time required for the development and testing of new IBM software products. For instance, Lotus Sametime 7.5, an enterprise-scale instant messaging platform, was developed using feedback from TAP early adopters and was brought to market in only five months—a reduction of more than two-thirds from the traditional 18-month cycle time.

2. *Earlier cancellation of unpromising innovation projects.* Termination of innovation projects in response to feedback and evaluation from early adopters is quicker and less costly than the use of a formal pilot process—an unexpected source of productivity gains. This allows IBM to focus its resources on the development of projects that are likely to yield successful products.

3. *Accelerated innovation.* TAP helps to connect IBM employees with new projects that can benefit from a diverse array of expert feedback. This allows innovators at IBM to quickly form ad hoc multidisciplinary teams around new projects.

In short, when an IBM employee has a new idea or sees a market opportunity, new technology can be developed, tested, reworked, and brought to market quickly using TAP. This allows the company to respond with greater speed and agility to changing needs in the marketplace and increases the company's innovative output and the productivity gains that result from these innovations.

The innovation business services described in these last three case studies can be considered business services because they are ideas created by one firm and then provided to other firms. Those firms—in this case, IBM's clients—use these services to enhance their innovative processes, thereby increasing their overall productivity.

Although productivity growth may be relatively slow at every stage of creation and use of these innovation business services, their contributions do add up. As with business services in general, the business-to-business services discussed here are multistage processes that make substantial cumulative contributions to overall productivity growth in the economy. Such enhanced productivity growth is the source of the magic that can transform the slow productivity growth in the initial creation and supply of business services into a cumulative set of gains that enhances productivity and holds costs down. This, in turn, lends credence to a more sanguine view of the future—as far as rising costs in some portions of the services sector are concerned. After all, as Oulton pointed out, the role of business services in the economy is expanding.[33] The multiple contributions to productivity growth that characterize business services clearly make plausible the prospect of continuing productivity growth in the economy as a whole, with its contribution to living standards and elimination of poverty. However, this story cannot go on forever. As more of the labor force moves from manufacturing to business services, this source of further productivity growth must be used up, and its contribution must eventually decline over time.

As this discussion makes clear, the cost disease is considerably more complex than it at first seems. In addition to causing continual increases in the real prices and costs of stagnant-sector services, its consequences include persistent declines in the real costs of goods produced by the progressive sector. This is because the former costs will grow more rapidly than average for the economy, and the latter will grow more slowly than the average. (The average growth rate is, by definition, the rate of inflation in the economy.)

In addition to its substantial implications for the allocation of the economy's labor force, this can lead to a steady slowing of overall productivity growth, at least in terms of money value, thereby decreasing the progressive sector's share of outputs when measured as a portion of GDP. Finally, we have noted that although the stagnant sector normally shows modest productivity growth, expanding that sector by transferring more of the economy's labor force into business services paradoxically can enhance the economy's overall productivity growth.

Thus, we reiterate: from the point of view of the public interest, the rising costs associated with the cost disease are much less threatening than they appear. It is important to recall that the rising prices of stagnant-sector outputs do not prevent society from enjoying an increasing abundance of these products and services. Instead, as argued in Chapter 5, the cost disease's more profound threat to society—misguided government policies aside—stems from the declining-cost, progressive sector.

PART 3

Opportunities for Cutting Health-Care Costs

TEN

Business Services in Health Care

Lilian Gomory Wu

To kill an error is as good a service as, and sometimes even better
than, the establishing of a new truth or fact.
—CHARLES DARWIN

The fact that the level of health-care costs in many other relatively
prosperous countries continues to be far lower than that in the
United States, though they tread similar upward paths of growth,
means that there must be ways for us to obtain savings in our health-
care system. This chapter and the next are intended to give substance to this contention by illustrating a number of opportunities
for cost reduction.

This chapter applies business services, like those described in
the previous chapter, to the reduction of health-care costs. Hospitals
are predominantly nonprofit institutions and cannot be regarded
as business firms. However, they can benefit from the multistage

productivity growth resulting from business services, which lowers costs and improves outcomes for patients. The examples in this chapter and its appendix, which deals with other innovative methods of increasing health-care organizations' productivity, will bring this out. The clear implication is that the cost disease, unconquerable though it may be, is no excuse for inaction.

We already have examined in detail the ways in which business services can improve productivity in a variety of industries (see Chapter 9). The health-care industry is characterized by slow productivity growth (in the sense of labor-saving changes) and, consequently, cost increases that are larger than average. As we will see here, this can be offset by the time and labor savings in the activities of doctors, nurses, and other hospital personnel that result from the use of business services, which provide at least two rounds of productivity improvement during utilization by their purchasers.

For instance, in a health-care setting, labor time can be saved via the use of technologies that help doctors, nurses, and others communicate more efficiently about how best to care for each particular patient. In addition to any resulting time savings, these technologies help to increase productivity by reducing the mistakes—from administration of the wrong medication to infections acquired in hospitals—that may have horrifying consequences for patients' welfare and indirectly for hospitals' operating efficiency. Clearly, there is a critical place in the health-care industry for such business services that reduce the labor of personnel and the dramatic productivity losses and worse that result from medical mistakes. All of this can be improved by the business services that hospitals and other health-care institutions employ—though this benefit is usually insufficient to offset the steady rise in costs entailed in the provision of health care.

Business Services for Health Care: Error Reduction and Productivity Improvement

Hospitals are more than just medical facilities—they are extraordinarily complex ecosystems of people, processes, and technology governed by numerous regulations. Moreover, even though their medical specialists require and use the latest cutting-edge technologies (whether or not the resulting benefits are worth the required expenditure), hospitals often are characterized by antiquated and inefficient business processes.[1] In short, hospitals face many major operational challenges—all of which have cost and productivity implications.

Perhaps chief among these challenges is the prevention of errors. Large numbers of American hospital patients continue to die each year from medical mistakes.[2] The reduction of such errors goes hand in hand with the productivity improvements and cost reductions that help to decrease wasteful health-care spending. According to one estimate, such unnecessary expenditures account for almost half of all U.S. health-care spending—roughly $700 billion each year.[3] Such disturbing findings have led health-care organizations to look for innovative ways to enhance patient safety and operational efficiency, sometimes through the use of business services.

Vassar Brothers Medical Center in Poughkeepsie, New York, is one example. The hospital employs several business services related to innovation and information technology built around a wireless broadband system, with the aim of reducing hospital errors and improving its efficiency and productivity. The new technology enables hospital employees to communicate more efficiently using Voice-over-Internet Protocol technology, to quickly track and deliver movable equipment such as intravenous infusion pumps by use of radio frequency identification technology, to administer medications more accurately using bar code technology, and to gain access to information necessary for treating patients at any time or place in the hospital.

As we will see in the case studies that follow, these services have improved the overall productivity of Vassar's operations, thereby enhancing the care provided to patients. Moreover, like all business services, they have produced multiple rounds of productivity growth. A prime example of this is the hospital's medication bar coding system. First, there was productivity growth in the manufacture of the pertinent bar coding equipment, the system's information technology components, and the necessary wireless technology. As the manufacturing process improves over time, these products become less expensive, even as their information storage and communication capacities increase. Vassar can thus expect to purchase better and relatively less costly products as time passes. Second, while the bar coding equipment is employed at the hospital, the efficiency of its use can be expected to grow over time, as staff acquire more experience and proficiency with the system and as new and improved applications are developed and employed.

Case Study 1: Bar Coding Medicine for Greater Accuracy

At Vassar Brothers Medical Center, each patient is issued a unique bar-coded ID bracelet that is linked to that patient's electronic medical records, and each nurse has a bar-coded ID card. Medications are administered only after first scanning a nurse's ID card and then scanning a drug's bar code and checking it against the patient's medical records by scanning the patient's bar code bracelet. This process aims to improve patient safety by reducing medication errors, such as giving a patient the wrong drug because it has a name similar to that of the right drug, giving a child an adult dose of a drug, or giving a patient a duplicate dose of a drug.

When a nurse attempts to administer medication incorrectly, Vassar's bar coding system automatically responds with an alert. The nurse then can use the hospital's wireless voice communication system to call the patient's doctor for clarification without having to leave the patient's bedside. This capability is especially important for community hospitals such as Vassar where physicians spend most of their time in private offices away from the hospital. As such, Vassar's medication bar coding and wireless communications systems work in tandem to improve the accuracy and efficiency of medication distribution by the hospital's nurses. This enables the hospital's nurses to devote more time to other tasks, thereby increasing their overall productivity.

The U.S. Food and Drug Administration (FDA) estimates that such bar code systems will result in nearly 500,000 fewer medication errors over the next twenty years—a 50 percent reduction that brings with it improved health outcomes and an estimated total cost savings of $93 billion.[4] In addition to the obvious improvements that result from the introduction of bar coding in the distribution of medications, such systems may help U.S. hospitals reduce operating costs by avoiding litigation associated with medication errors and lowering malpractice insurance premiums as well as by improving the management of hospitals' medication inventories and increasing the accuracy of billing for medication administered to hospital patients.

At Vassar, the outcome associated with bar coding medication has been impressive. In 2006, the hospital administered more than 1 million medications, and during that first year of use the medication bar coding system issued more than 30,155 alerts and warnings and prevented a total of 5,331 medication errors.[5]

Case Study 2: Instant Mobile Communication via Voice-over-Internet Protocol

In addition to the introduction of bar-coded medication distribution, Vassar Brothers Medical Center installed a new Voice-over-Internet Protocol communication system that allows nurses to make phone calls within the hospital without having to stop what they are doing and dial a phone number. In the past, hospital staff wasted a significant amount of time (and thus money) on inefficient methods of communication. For instance, if a nurse had a question about a patient's medication, he had to walk back to the nursing station to find the phone number for the person who could answer the question and then make the phone call. In some cases, the nurse would then have to wait near the phone for the call to be returned to get an answer.

Using Vassar's new Voice-over-Internet Protocol system, any employee can communicate as needed without making unproductive trips around the hospital to access a phone.[6] Moreover, staff members no longer need to spend time looking up new numbers because the intelligent system can translate a spoken request to dial a specific phone number. For instance, a Vassar nurse can push a button on a portable phone from anywhere in the hospital and simply say, "Call the Head of Pharmacy."

At Vassar, the improvements in productivity attributed to the use of the Voice-over-Internet Protocol system have been dramatic. The new communication system saves an estimated eighty-five minutes per shift that nurses otherwise would lose to unnecessary "travel" to and from landline phones and phone directories. That alone translates into an annual cost savings of $995,000 for the hospital.

Case Study 3: Tracking Medical Equipment in Real Time via Radio Frequency Identification Technology

Vassar Brothers Medical Center initially had no structured process for managing the procurement, storage, and allocation of intravenous (IV) pumps throughout the hospital. A typical pump might start the day in the emergency room and find its way to intensive care by the end of the day. As a result, IV pumps were frequently "lost" somewhere in the hospital.[7] This ad hoc approach spawned a number of related problems. For instance, clinical staff members frequently were forced to go far out of their way to find IV pumps, leaving them with less time to care for patients. Moreover, there was no way to know exactly how many IV pumps the hospital actually needed. This problem was exacerbated by the understandable tendency for hospital staff to hoard IV pumps. As such, it was impossible for Vassar to determine rationally how many IV pumps should be purchased or how inventories of existing IV pumps should be allocated.

Tracking IV pumps in real time using radio frequency identification (RFID) technology offered Vassar a solution to this problem. The RFID technology uses radio waves to identify objects and collect data about them, which are automatically entered into the computer system. This technology comprises two components: an RFID tag attached to an object, animal, or person, and a reader. In a hospital, RFID technology can be used to track movable equipment such as IV pumps so that they can be located quickly when needed.[8] This technology also can be programmed to check a piece of equipment to ensure that it is working properly.

At Vassar, each IV pump was tagged with an RFID tag, and RFID readers were attached to the ceiling of each room and every major section of hallway throughout the hospital. Vassar first piloted an RFID system in one of its wings, using a simple process:

the central supply department collected IV pumps twice a day, and nurses called central supply when they needed a pump. During the pilot period, data on the movement of IV pumps were collected automatically by the RFID tracking system, and nurses recorded their time spent looking and waiting for pumps.

Before installation of the RFID tracking system, Vassar nurses typically spent between thirty minutes and one hour per shift searching for misplaced IV pumps. However, the tracking system made it possible for central supply staff to determine the location and status of all IV pumps immediately. The pilot system cut the time nurses spent searching for missing pumps in half—a reduction in wasted time that translated into $1.3 million in annual cost savings for the hospital.[9]

Budgetary pressures have prevented Vassar from installing the RFID system hospitalwide on a permanent basis. However, using data from the pilot project, Vassar was able to determine that a planned purchase of $456,000 worth of new IV pumps was not needed. In effect, the hospital increased the productivity of the pumps already in its possession by avoiding the cost of the previously planned purchase.

Business Services for Health Care: The Price versus the Payoff

Adoption of the business services described in the prior case studies was hardly free of cost for Vassar Brothers Medical Center. As such, it is important that hospitals make the best use of these services. In order to do that, hospital managers typically focus their use of business services on several key areas—improved patient safety, better intrahospital communication, and more efficient utilization of valuable resources (that is, staff and equipment)—to lead to significant overall productivity improvements in an organization's operations. Investments in business services that enhance efficiency in these areas promise to provide an immediate payback to hospitals in the form of improved patient care and reduced operating costs.

To ensure that real, repeatable change was achieved via the use of business services, Vassar used industrial management models to design and implement these business services. This led Vassar to examine its organizational culture and structure and the costs entailed in improving these via the use of business services. For instance, the hospital identified the principal components of the medication process as doctors (who order medications), the pharmacy (which processes them), and the nursing staff (who administer them).[10] Vassar then applied business services strategically to the parts of the medication process that were likely to benefit significantly from such changes: for example, reducing medication errors by introducing the bar coding system.

As we have demonstrated here and in Chapter 9, business services are not final products but rather are production inputs that serve consumers after being incorporated into other production processes. As such, they can provide multiple rounds of productivity growth—first when productivity increases in the activities of the firm that supplies the business services and then again when these business services are used as inputs that increase the efficiency of the organizations that purchase them. Although each round of business services-induced productivity growth usually is characterized by relatively small increases, the cumulative effect can contribute significantly to the economy's overall rate of productivity growth.

In the case of health care, however, the application of productivity-enhancing business services yields widely varying results from one medical problem to another and from one medical innovation to another. There are many circumstances in which the labor savings attributable to such services are substantial, and, as a consequence, *quality-unadjusted* labor productivity rises, and cost increases slow or perhaps even reverse.[11]

But even if the health-care industry experiences steady and continuing labor savings as a result of the use of business services, we surely have not yet reached a point where patients will be willing to give up the personal oversight of doctors and nurses for what amount to robotic substitutes. The fact that each patient requires the individual time and direct attention of a physician and other trained medical staff means that even the most remarkable productivity improvements in health care induced by business services confidently can be predicted to lag behind those in manufacturing and many other industries, as they have done consistently in the past. As we know from earlier chapters, where trends in productivity growth differ from one industry to another, the productivity of some industries must increase more rapidly than average (that is, the economy's overall rate of inflation), while that of others lags behind. As such, it is difficult to believe that the real cost of health care—that is, the cost of health care relative to the economy's overall rate of inflation—will *not* continue to rise cumulatively and without respite.

Appendix: Multistage Gains through Innovation and Collaboration in Health Care

The case studies provided earlier in this chapter show how information technology business services helped one particular hospital, Vassar Brothers Medical Center in Poughkeepsie, New York, increase its productivity by reducing errors and improving operations efficiency. However, there are other methods—also borrowed from business—that can help to increase productivity in health-care organizations. For instance, as we will see in the case study that follows, Tufts Medical Center in Boston has reduced preventable, hospital-acquired infections using Six Sigma, a method of reducing errors borrowed from the manufacturing industry.[12] Rather than using business services to implement the Six Sigma findings, Tufts joined the Massachusetts Hospital Association, a consortium of hospitals that work together to share ideas for reducing infections and implementing other productivity-enhancing innovations and discuss their experiences in carrying out these solutions.

In this instance, the consortium of hospitals functions *like* a business service, in that it makes possible multiple rounds of productivity improvements. First, an innovation lowers costs and increases productivity in one hospital; then the hospital shares its experience with using the innovation with others in the consortium, which leads other hospitals to use the innovation in their operations, thereby increasing their productivity.

Case Study: Reducing Errors and Increasing Hospital Productivity Using Six Sigma Principles and Interhospital Collaboration

According to the Centers for Disease Control and Prevention,[13] citing a report by Klevens et al.,[14] in 2002 an estimated 1.7 million U.S. patients developed infections during hospital stays—100,000 of whom died from their infections. Among hospital-acquired infections, those associated with central lines (catheters placed into the large blood vessels of a patient's neck, arms, or legs to administer medications, provide nutrition, and monitor a patient) were the most serious.[15] As early as the mid-2000s, Tufts Medical Center had identified hospital-acquired infections as a serious problem, but the hospital made little progress in reducing infection rates until 2008 when it began using Six Sigma techniques to reduce infections and improve productivity.[16] In manufacturing, Six Sigma typically involves creating a special team that investigates every defect to find its cause and then determines how to improve the production process to eliminate the problem. The team also ensures that the method of eliminating the problem is systematically implemented throughout the production process and monitors the results.[17]

At Tufts, a small task force of two doctors, two nurses, and an infectious disease expert was created to focus on reducing central line infections. Every time an infection occurred in a Tufts patient, the team identified its cause and developed new procedures to prevent that problem from causing infections in future patients. For example, the team discovered that one source of infection was the practice of storing each patient's washbasin with another smaller basin that is used to catch spit and vomit—and, therefore, is full of bacteria from each patient. When the larger washbasin was used to wash a patient before inserting a central line, the patient's skin was contaminated with bacteria from the smaller basin, sometimes resulting in infections. To fix this problem, the team recommended that a special antibacterial bathing cloth be used to clean patients before the insertion of a central line. Later, when the team discovered that not all staff members understood the instructions to cover a patient's whole body before inserting a central line, they added a color photo of a fully covered patient to the hospital's official central line instruction kit.

In addition, through a Massachusetts Hospital Association working group focusing on best practices for central lines, the Tufts team was able to recommend a number of other methods for reducing central line infections, including the use of impregnated/coated central line catheters, chlorhexidine patient bathing, new standards for blood culture drawing, and several methods of engaging staff in efforts to prevent infection.

The team also had to ensure that the improvements they created were systematically integrated into the hospital's official central line insertion procedures. In an academic hospital like Tufts, where medical students, residents, and interns are continually coming and going, it is particularly challenging to make systemwide changes. To carry out their recommended improvements in this difficult working environment, the Tufts team developed a checklist and a "central line kit," which allowed all improvements to central line procedures to be efficiently and systematically introduced hospitalwide. At the team's recommendation, Tufts also set up a simulation lab to train staff in best practices for central line insertion and required that all doctors and nurses receive training before being allowed to insert central lines in patients. Finally, the task force instituted a requirement that each central line insertion involve both a doctor and a nurse trained in infection-prevention techniques; the nurse ensures that the doctor understands the proper technique for inserting the line and follows the checklist procedures.

The results of the Tufts team's efforts have been impressive. Between 2008 and 2010, the hospital reduced its rate of central line infections by 50 percent, which saved an estimated $1.5 million in 2009 and 2010 combined. Records indicate that the new central line procedures and accompanying education program for all doctors and nurses may have saved the lives of seven Tufts patients during that time period. Moreover, following its success in reducing central line infections, Tufts decided to use a similar approach in seeking to eliminate other hospital-acquired infections (for example, urinary tract infections and bedsores) and injuries (for example, falls).[18]

These innovative efforts to improve patient safety have reduced errors and increased operations efficiency, thereby enhancing productivity in the hospital. Moreover, by sharing its methods of improving productivity with other hospitals via the Massachusetts Hospital Association consortiums, Tufts has stimulated productivity growth in other hospitals. As with business services, such collaborations have facilitated multiple rounds of productivity improvements in other hospitals.

ELEVEN

Yes, We Can Cut Health-Care Costs Even If We Cannot Reduce Their Growth Rate

Monte Malach and William J. Baumol

> I sometimes joke that if you come to our hospital missing a finger,
> no one will believe you until we can get a CAT scan, an MRI, and
> an orthopedic consult.
>
> —ABRAHAM VERGHESE

We have noted repeatedly that the cost of health care is not rising only in the United States. Other developed nations[1] as well as many emerging economies are seeing their costs rise at a disturbingly fast, seemingly unstoppable rate. The cost disease ensures that this process will continue inexorably.

But this does not mean that the *level* of costs cannot be brought down or that we cannot curb wasteful practices and inefficiencies in the way health care is provided. It is important to emphasize the distinction between the *current magnitude* of health costs and the *speed* with which those costs are rising. The United States currently is the world champion in the former—its current level of health-care spending leaves others in the dust. Other developed countries, on average, have health-care costs that are lower than ours but which are increasing at rates similar to ours.

Of these two attributes, cost levels and cost increases, the cost disease deals *only with the latter*. As we know from earlier chapters, the disease condemns the costs of health-care and other services to rise at a disturbingly rapid rate in *all* countries in which productivity is growing rapidly. As long as productivity growth continues, these growth rates will not slow down.

But although the growth rates are beyond our control, the data for the different affected countries do show that the level of health-care costs can be restrained. Many countries have costs much lower than ours, even if they are still increasing just as quickly. Certainly it would be a good thing if health-care spending in the United States could be reduced to much lower levels. This chapter describes some ways to accomplish that goal.

It is useful to recall past attempts to limit medical care costs. Despite their considerable promise, managed care and diagnosis-related groups in the 1970s and 1980s did not significantly reduce health-care costs. Countries in Europe and elsewhere that have radically modified their health-care systems have been no more successful. Similarly, we expect that these recommendations for improving the efficiency of medical care can contribute to reducing the current *level* of health-care spending but not the relentless and rapid *rate* by which these costs continue to rise. The savings promised by the opportunities described here can be substantial, though once they are achieved the costs will resume their upward march here and in other wealthy countries throughout the world.

More Accurate Evaluation of Medical Treatments

An explosion of medical technology has expanded doctors' diagnostic capabilities and armed them with many new treatment options, but the steady stream of new medical equipment has also added to the cost of medical care.[2] The safety and effectiveness of these new medical technologies has not always been properly assessed, leading to unnecessary expenditures and, occasionally, grave risks to patients.

Throughout much of history, the only evidence of the effectiveness of particular medical treatments came from conventional wisdom. Many widely accepted treatments were later shown to be ineffective or even harmful—sometimes after decades of widespread use. For instance, until the mid-1950s, conventional wisdom dictated several months of complete bed rest for a patient recovering from a heart attack. This was accompanied by a high mortality rate, as inactivity caused blood clots (that is, deep vein thrombosis) that often resulted in pulmonary embolism, a life-threatening condition that occurs when a clot travels from the leg and lodges in a lung artery. By the 1960s, hospitals were beginning to place these patients in coronary care units, which continuously monitored patients' vital signs, allowing for immediate response to potentially fatal events. Early recognition and treatment when abnormalities in heart rhythm and blood pressure occur can halt a serious or near-fatal cardiac event, eliminating many long-term health problems—and the related costs. Aware of the dangers of blood clots, researchers also began to encourage ambulation (that is, walking) within one day of a heart attack and began to discharge patients from the hospital within one to three days—a remarkable change in the standard treatment, which contributed both substantial cost savings and better results.[3]

More recent examples of conventional medical wisdom being overturned by rigorous scientific analyses are plentiful. For instance, researchers have determined that aprotinin, an anticoagulant routinely used to prevent blood clots during heart bypass surgery, actually resulted in a higher mortality rate and more kidney dysfunction than other anticoagulants used during bypass surgery.[4] Discontinuation of the use of aprotinin in bypass surgery has saved costs and improved outcomes.

At one time, implantation of a pacemaker in only the right ventricle of the heart was the standard treatment for patients with abnormally slow heart rates. Further observation revealed that pacemakers that simultaneously stimulate both the right and left ventricles produce better results.[5] Before this was recognized, right-ventricle-only pacemakers frequently had harmful consequences, requiring costly additional procedures for many patients.

Inadequate premarket testing of medical equipment has also led to significant medical expenditures with few accompanying benefits. For instance, three years after being approved for use, one of the electrical cables connecting a defibrillator or pacemaker to a patient's heart was found to be prone to fracturing, rendering the defibrillator or pacemaker useless and causing serious harm to patients. Subsequent investigation revealed that the defibrillator cables had not been rigorously tested, an oversight that generated unnecessary costs and caused at least thirteen deaths.[6]

If doctors seek out rigorous, statistically grounded analyses of the effectiveness of tests and therapies, they will be able to identify the safest and most effective new treatments and then concentrate health-care spending on these new medical developments. But research and statistical analysis have their own pitfalls.[7] For instance, the misinterpretation of mere correlation as evidence of causation can be a source of serious error.[8] Another key shortcoming is the common (though not universal) practice of testing a new medicine by comparing it with a placebo rather than with a substitute medication already in use. This approach prevents researchers from determining whether an existing, possibly less expensive medicine with similar treatment indications is just as good as, or even better than, the new drug.[9] The accuracy of drug testing is confounded further by the placebo effect—the curious fact that some patients appear to derive therapeutic benefits from sugar pills.[10]

Finally, sampling procedures used in clinical trials also may be prone to errors. For instance, one recent report of the results of the clinical trials of surgical procedures for cancers of the prostate, colon, lung, and breast was rendered questionable by the selection of participants.[11] Although 62 percent of these four cancers occur in people over age 65, only 27 percent of the study's participants were in that age group. In addition, the colon and lung cancer trial groups included very few female participants. The results of this study initially encouraged the use of these procedures, despite their significant costs and questionable benefits. However, concerns about improper sampling rightly have prompted researchers to reconsider this.

Avoidance of Harmful or Unnecessary Procedures and Treatments

One of the most promising opportunities for cost reduction occurs when an expensive procedure or medication is proven to be unnecessary or even dangerous. Here again it is essential to recognize that even the most careful medical studies later may prove to be flawed.

An important case in point is a major study, published in 1985 by three national medical organizations,[12] that established hormone replacement as a preventive treatment for coronary heart disease and osteoporosis in menopausal women, as well as a therapy for menopausal symptoms. By 2001, 15 million women had filled prescriptions for hormone replacement therapy. But the supplemental estrogens used in the therapy eventually were shown to be a health hazard. Women taking these hormones had an increased incidence of coronary heart disease, stroke, blood clots, and breast cancer after undergoing hormone replacement therapy.[13] Elimination of routine hormone replacement therapy has saved lives and reduced costs related to treating these serious medical conditions.

More recent examples of this phenomenon are all too common. For instance, a new study indicates that alendronate, an expensive and widely used osteoporosis drug, may increase patients' risk for cancer of the esophagus.[14] Long-term use may also result in femur and jaw fractures.[15] Calcium and vitamin D supplements are less expensive and safer alternatives, although they are not as effective in treating osteoporosis in the short term.

A study of hysterectomies showed that almost 20 percent were unnecessary.[16] Failure to properly evaluate the cause of uterine maladies resulted in needless surgeries rather than more appropriate and less costly medical treatments. More important than the financial costs are the negative health outcomes. New research indicates that women who keep their ovaries live longer and are less likely to die from cardiovascular disease and lung cancer.[17]

Similarly, high demand from patients, malpractice concerns on the part of doctors, and the growing prevalence of multiple births due to fertility treatments have increased the incidence of cesarean births in the United States—as of 2007, they accounted for almost one-third of all U.S. births.[18] Cesarean deliveries have both the high cost and serious risks of major surgery, often require expensive infant care in intensive care units, and place mothers at risk for serious complications in subsequent pregnancies. The costs associated with cesarean deliveries are estimated to be at least double those of normal vaginal deliveries. Efforts to reduce cesarean deliveries could lower obstetrical costs substantially.[19]

New research also emphasizes the advantages of treating one form of breast cancer, ductal carcinoma in situ (DCIS), via quadrantectomy—removal of one-quarter of the breast—rather than total mastectomy. Although many patients and doctors wrongly suggest that mastectomy offers a more thorough treatment of DCIS, quadrantectomy provides the same or better outcomes for patients, requires a shorter recovery period, and is less costly.[20]

Doctors have also begun to rethink the frequent use of computed tomography (CT) angiography, which produces a tomographic X-ray image of abnormalities within arteries that can be used to diagnose coronary heart disease. New concerns have emerged about the risk of cancer from radiation exposure associated with this procedure.[21] Moreover, one recent study found that CT angiography in patients who had reported chest pain revealed little or no obstructive coronary heart disease in one-third of participating patients.[22] This result has led many doctors to question whether the benefits of CT angiography outweigh the high cost of the test and associated risk of cancer.[23]

Efforts to reduce the radiation exposure required for CT angiography[24] lower the risk of cancer but do not change the test's high cost and dubious diagnostic value. At $1,000 to $3,000 per procedure, CT angiograms have not been shown to be any more effective than a standard coronary arteriogram, which costs much less and exposes the patient to far less radiation.[25]

As another illustration, in cases where a statin drug has been prescribed to lower cholesterol, it was once thought that the addition of ezetimibe, an expensive new drug that decreases the intestinal absorption of lipids, would enhance the statin's effect. More recent research, however, indicates that the addition of ezetimibe does not always achieve better results than a statin alone.[26] Lovastatin combined with an older and much less expensive alternative, niacin, has been shown to lower cholesterol more effectively.[27]

Moreover, niacin alone has been shown to raise high-density lipoprotein ("good" cholesterol) and reduce low-density lipoprotein ("bad" cholesterol).[28]

New research also indicates that excessive treatment of high blood pressure with medication may lower blood pressure too much, which can lead to heart attack or stroke due to decreased blood flow. This not only results in higher medical costs, but produces no better or even worse outcomes in patients.[29] Those who received less costly treatment, involving fewer drugs and less stringent medical supervision of their blood pressure, had better outcomes.

A recent study of type-2 diabetes patients showed that aggressive efforts to lower blood sugar levels resulted in increased deaths from coronary heart disease brought on by hypoglycemia (excessively low blood sugar).[30] Conventional wisdom calls for keeping blood sugar low in diabetic patients as this protects against kidney disease, blindness, and limb amputations. These results suggest that overtreatment of diabetes via the excessive use of medications to lower blood sugar is not only more expensive but may have life-threatening consequences.

Finally, a multiyear study of Medicare patients revealed that complex fusion procedures for spinal stenosis—a painful condition in which the spinal canal compresses the spinal cord and nerves—have increased while the use of two less-expensive options, decompression surgery and simple fusion procedures, have decreased.[31] Yet the complex fusion procedures had no better results and were associated with an increase in major complications, a higher thirty-day mortality rate, and significantly increased medical costs. Reducing the use of complex fusion procedures would reduce costs and produce better outcomes.

Use of Genetic Information to Guide Medication and Treatment

Medical costs may also be reduced by paying more careful attention to genetic differences among patients. Expensive treatments that may be effective for patients with a particular set of genetic attributes may be ineffective for those with different characteristics. In addition to cost savings, recognizing such distinctions and modifying treatments accordingly should result in improved care.

Researchers are increasingly able to link specific genes with increased risk for a number of serious diseases or adverse reactions to medical therapies. Because new technologies have significantly driven down the cost of genetic sequencing, it soon may be cost-effective to establish individual genetic risk profiles that would quantify a patient's risk for particular diseases and identify the most effective therapies for that patient.[32] This would permit early identification and more accurate and efficient treatment of some diseases, which could lead to both improved outcomes and decreased costs.

One dazzling new example of this, the field of epigenetics (the study of how epigenomes alter gene activity without changing the genetic code), could lead to huge cost savings through the identification and suppression of genes linked to cancer, diabetes, Alzheimer's disease, and other hereditary conditions.[33] A more specific example concerns muscle pain and inflammation resulting from the use of many cholesterol-lowering drugs, an effect that has been linked to a specific gene variant.[34] If doctors preemptively identify patients with that variant through genetic testing, they could prescribe a statin, pravastatin, that is metabolized differently in the body and does not cause the same symptoms. This approach avoids the additional costs of pain relief and treatment of muscle inflammation that otherwise accompany the use of statin drugs.[35]

Coronary heart disease provides another significant example of medical treatment guided by genetic information. Cardiologists have recently begun using genetic testing to predict the likelihood of coronary heart disease in patients and identify genes that will affect a patient's metabolism of relevant drugs. They then use this information to determine the most effective methods of treatment.[36] Early diagnosis and treatment of coronary heart disease may prevent subsequent heart attack or stroke and thus reduce costs in the long run while providing better outcomes and quality of life.

It is now commonly recognized that breast and ovarian cancer likely result from mutations of two specific genes, BRCA1 and BRCA2.[37] Hereditary nonpolyposis colon cancer has also been linked with a single gene variance.[38] Specific genetic variants have been linked to inherited coronary heart disease,[39] nonalcoholic fatty liver disease, insulin resistance, and Brugada syndrome, which causes severe abnormalities in the structure and rhythm of the heart that can lead to sudden death.[40] In these instances and many others, genetic testing could identify patients who are at risk for these diseases and allow doctors to provide preventive therapy or at the very least make earlier diagnoses, which usually lead to more successful and more cost-effective treatment.[41]

Three genetic variants have also been linked to Alzheimer's disease.[42] These analyses could allow for early diagnosis and possible genetic intervention, providing tremendous cost savings through early treatment of an increasingly common and costly disease.[43]

Identification of Less Expensive Treatments—Both New and Old

Some new medical therapies and technologies increase the cost of treatment without offering any significant offsetting benefits. Other novel procedures and medications—for example, a new cervical cancer vaccine[44] and a less expensive, less invasive, and less risky new method of repairing leaking mitral heart valves[45]—clearly do provide better outcomes and decrease overall medical costs.

The decrease in deaths from coronary heart disease in the United States and Canada, Europe, and South America from 1980 to 2000 can be attributed, at least in part, to the increased use of pharmaceutical therapies such as aspirin (which decreases blood clotting), beta blockers (which lower blood pressure and stabilize abnormal heart rhythms), angiotensin-converting enzyme inhibitors and angiotensin receptor blockers (which dilate blood vessels), and statins (which lower cholesterol and lipids). In some instances, these drugs are replacing far more expensive surgical procedures such as bypass surgery and angioplasty.[46]

New evidence indicates that heart attack patients who are asymptomatic after three days (that is, those who have no chest pain, shortness of breath, abnormal heart rhythm, or heart failure) may be better off if they do *not* undergo bypass surgery or other invasive interventions.[47] It may be safer and more cost-effective to allow the heart to stabilize itself naturally by rerouting blood flow through alternative blood vessels, thereby alleviating obstructed vessels.[48] Efforts to relieve coronary artery blockage via bypass surgery or angioplasty and stenting can lead to recurrent blockage, bleeding, or a repeat heart attack. Moreover, for asymptomatic patients with diffuse coronary heart disease, such invasive procedures may be less effective than other treatment options because they address only one local obstruction. In these cases especially, pharmaceutical therapies are a safer, more effective, and less expensive treatment option. (However, patients on pharmaceutical therapy may eventually require a more invasive procedure, such as stenting, bypass, or angioplasty, when coronary heart disease progresses.)

Similarly, for some people with persistent angina (severe chest pain caused by a lack of blood and oxygen in the heart), a new medication, ranolazine, may eliminate the need for expensive and invasive procedures to relieve the condition. Rather than affecting bodywide blood flow, ranolazine targets the specific area of the heart where blood flow is restricted. It increases blood flow, prevents blood clots, and relieves symptoms of angina.[49]

New research also indicates that atrial fibrillation (a heart condition involving fast, irregular beating of the heart's upper chambers, which can lead to pulmonary embolism, stroke, or heart failure) can be treated more effectively by rate control rather than rhythm control. Rate control, which uses drugs to slow the heart rate, carries less risk of harmful complications and is associated with better overall outcomes for patients.[50] It is considerably less expensive than rhythm control, an invasive procedure involving electric shocks delivered via a catheter inserted into the heart, which carries the risk of serious complications and recurrent atrial fibrillation.[51] Another recent study in patients receiving heart rate control for atrial fibrillation found that patients who received less frequent (and therefore less costly) medical care for their condition achieved slightly better results than those who received more intensive heart rate control therapy.[52] In this instance, less medical care was both cheaper and more effective.

For those patients with an implantable cardioverter-defibrillator (ICD),[53] who do require regular monitoring, electronic home monitoring devices that automatically transmit information about the patient's heart to a doctor are just as effective and less expensive than regular office or home visits. In one recent study, doctors were notified more quickly when patients with automatic remote home monitoring devices experienced abnormal heart rhythms, thereby allowing for early diagnosis and treatment, which can prevent serious and costly complications.[54]

Moving beyond cardiology, overtesting for and overtreatment of prostate cancer has become a significant source of medical costs.[55]

Although prostate cancer is one of the less deadly cancers, annual prostate-specific antigen (PSA) testing has created a culture of over-testing and overtreatment of prostate abnormalities. It has led to an increase in costly prostate biopsies, with their attendant health risks. More than 80 percent of patients with enlarged prostates and elevated PSA levels actually have benign prostate obstruction, inflammation or infection of the prostate, or prostate enlargement without cancer. The rush to do prostate biopsies based on elevated PSA levels or prostate enlargement alone is not only costly and risky but may not even be necessary. Administering dutasteride, a drug that shrinks enlarged prostates and lowers PSA levels if cancer is not present, is a less expensive method of diagnosis and treatment. If the enlarged prostate decreases in size and the patient's PSA levels fall after dutasteride administration, it is usually safe to assume the presence of a benign process and to forego prostate biopsy, unless PSA levels subsequently rise.

Finally, an interesting new idea suggested by a recent study could lead to substantial cost savings in the development of new drugs.[56] The study proposes that a new drug's likelihood of success be analyzed and forecast early in the research and development process. If the drug is not deemed to be promising, a company could halt its development early on and shift funds to another project with a greater likelihood of success, thereby diminishing the enormous cost of new drug development and marketing.

Cost Savings via Preventive Medicine

One of the most promising methods of containing medical costs and improving patient outcomes involves the *prevention* of disease.[57] Many of these preventive approaches employ pharmaceutical therapies that reduce the need for more costly and riskier treatments. For instance, valsartan, a commonly used blood pressure medication, has been shown to prevent type-2 diabetes.[58] This promising treatment could help to curtail a fast-growing and very costly disease that now affects at least 17 million Americans.[59] Similarly, the most commonly used antidiabetic medication, metformin, reportedly reduces the incidence of colon and lung cancer—with clear cost-saving implications.[60]

In the past, conventional wisdom did not call for the use of statins (cholesterol-lowering drugs) without the documented presence of coronary heart disease symptoms. But statins have become a key example of pharmaceutical-based preventive therapies—aimed specifically at preventing cardiovascular disease and the occurrence of heart attack and stroke. New findings suggest that prescribing the new statin drug rosuvastatin for patients with *risk factors* but no active symptoms of coronary heart disease (for example, angina or heart attack) may help prevent these symptoms from appearing.[61] In a study of almost 18,000 healthy individuals in twenty-six countries, those taking rosuvastatin were roughly half as likely as those who received the placebo to experience coronary events. In study participants with a family history or existing history of coronary heart disease, the prevention of coronary events was even greater (65 percent) for those receiving the medication. Similar results obtained for another statin, lovastatin, indicate that the combination of lifestyle changes and statin therapy substantially reduces the occurrence of coronary events—with attendant cost savings.[62]

Statins have become a primary means of preventing coronary heart disease, heart attack, and stroke.[63] In the United States, they have reduced the overall occurrence of cardiovascular events by an estimated 25 to 45 percent.[64] When prescribed in combination with niacin, they are even more successful in lowering low-density lipoprotein ("bad") cholesterol levels, raising high-density lipoprotein ("good") cholesterols,[65] and removing the build-up of cholesterol and other fatty materials on artery walls.[66] In addition, a large dose of a potent statin given one day prior to angioplasty has been found to significantly reduce the incidence of heart attack in patients undergoing this procedure.[67]

There also is increasing evidence that statins provide other important supplemental benefits beyond their standard cholesterol-lowering effects. They appear to increase contractile movement of the blood vessel lining, which prevents the vessel spasms, blood clots, and obstructions that cause strokes, heart attack, and heart failure.[68] Statins prescribed over the long term in patients with high blood pressure permit the condition to be controlled with smaller doses of blood pressure medication, reducing the side effects (and costs) associated with larger doses.[69] Statin therapy also is reported to prevent the formation of gall stones, which are composed primarily of cholesterol.[70]

In addition to statins, aspirin and clopidogrel can be used to prevent blood clots in patients with coronary heart disease. Progressive diabetic vascular disease, which often leads to coronary heart disease, also has been found to be curtailed in patients taking clopidogrel. Administering clopidogrel to heart attack and heart failure patients has been shown to decrease mortality and the incidence of subsequent heart attacks. The prevention of heart attacks and strokes caused by blood clots reduces future medical costs and improves outcomes for patients.

There is also evidence that regular aspirin use—among the least expensive drug therapies—may help prevent colon cancer, an effect attributed to aspirin's anti-inflammatory properties.[71] Aspirin and the anticoagulant warfarin have also shown impressive results in preventing blood clot-induced strokes in patients with a congenital patent foramen ovale, an opening between the right and left upper chambers of the heart that occurs in 25 percent of individuals, which otherwise may require closure via a costly surgical procedure.[72]

Better diagnosis and treatment of depression may also help prevent heart attacks. The relationship between depression and heart attack risk has not yet been defined adequately.[73] But depression is known to affect blood coagulation, the contractile activity of blood vessels, heart rate variability, and patients' compliance with medication and diet restrictions, among other risk factors for heart attack. Heart attack patients with depression usually have longer, more expensive hospital stays than other patients.

Recognition of disease comorbidity (the presence of multiple associated diseases) may also allow for earlier diagnosis and treatment and thus decreased long-term medical costs.[74] For instance, people with severe psoriasis (a chronic skin condition that covers the skin in thick scales) have a higher incidence of stroke, heart attack, and arthritis.[75] Diabetics are also likely to have diffuse vascular disease, which can lead to kidney failure, heart attack, blindness, and stroke. If a patient has a disease that is associated with other serious medical conditions, the doctor would do well to look for the early signs of those related conditions.

Increasing the number of geriatricians, who specialize in providing care for elderly patients, also could help to save health-care costs. Currently, there are far too few trained and certified geriatricians. One likely reason is that compensation for these physicians, who perform very few reimbursable procedures, is among the lowest of all medical specialties.[76]

Finally, eliminating medical errors in hospitals could prevent an estimated 180,000 deaths per year and save approximately $4.4 billion annually among Medicare patients alone.[77] The commonest of these errors, unintentional drug poisoning, with its serious consequences for patients and attendant costs, has increased considerably in the United States in recent decades.[78] Administering the incorrect medicine to patients can result in disastrous and very costly consequences. The use of barcode-based medication administration systems can significantly reduce these errors, with obvious implications for improving the quality of patient care and reducing medical costs.[79]

Cost Savings via Lifestyle Changes That Reduce Disease and Associated Costs

Lifestyle changes adopted without the assistance of a doctor may help to reduce the incidence of dementia, diabetes, cardiovascular disease, and particularly obesity,[80] among other serious and all too prevalent diseases—with enormous attendant cost savings. According to one recent report, the widespread adoption of general guidelines for healthy living could save more than $2 trillion in medical costs by 2023.[81] In a recent study of type-2 diabetes patients, those assigned to an intensive lifestyle interventions group reduced their medication and medical care costs by nearly 20 percent compared with those assigned only to a general support and education group, who lowered their costs by only 10 percent.[82] These studies indicate that lifestyle changes result in both better patient outcomes and lower medical costs.

Moreover, if such lifestyle changes are adopted early in life (along with pharmaceutical therapy, where relevant), they are an effective method of treating high cholesterol and obesity in children and teenagers.[83] As with many medical conditions, early treatment of obesity and high cholesterol produces better patient outcomes and reduces long-term medical costs.

A Mediterranean diet (increased consumption of vegetables, nuts, and fresh whole grains) has been shown to decrease mortality from all causes, including cardiovascular disease and cancer.[84] Certain foods by themselves also offer health benefits that translate into lower medical costs. One recent study found that people living in countries where fish is eaten at least twice a week have a significantly lower incidence of dementia.[85] Decreased breast cancer mortality and recurrence rates also have been reported in women who consume high soy protein diets,[86] and men who eat soy products report lower rates of prostate cancer.[87] Salt reduction has been shown to reduce the incidence of high blood pressure, stroke, and heart attack,[88] and pistachio nuts reportedly increase antioxidant levels in the blood and lower low-density lipoprotein cholesterol levels, decreasing the risk of serious cardiovascular events.[89] Another study of lifestyle habits and coronary heart disease found that heart attack patients who eat chocolate at least twice a week have significantly lower rates of subsequent mortality.[90] In two separate studies, chocolate consumption was found to lower blood pressure and reduce participants' risk of cardiovascular disease and heart failure.[91]

Resveratrol, a natural plant extract found in red wines, red grapes, and red grape juice, reportedly activates sirtuins, proteins in the body that reduce inflammation and strengthen resistance to diseases related to aging.[92] However, excessive consumption of alcohol may cause cardiomyopathy (heart muscle disease that can lead to heart failure), a leading cause of death among alcoholics.

Finally, a recent study indicates that vitamin D may help prevent hypertension, cardiovascular disease, depression, and cognitive disorders and may generally prolong life.[93]

Although the number of smokers in the United States has decreased in recent decades,[94] smoking, with its attendant health hazards, remains unacceptably common. In 2008, just over 20 percent of American adults were smokers—only a slight reduction from 1997, when almost 25 percent of American adults were smokers. The links between cigarette smoking and lung cancer and coronary heart disease are well established.[95] Moreover, according to one recent study, people who quit smoking after their first heart attack had much higher rates of long-term survival.[96] Smoking cessation remains a prime means of reducing health-care costs via disease prevention.

Finally, maintaining an active lifestyle that includes regular exercise (at least 30 minutes per day) and the enjoyment of hobbies has been shown to lower cholesterol,[97] improve outcomes in patients with early-stage arteriosclerosis (hardening of the arteries),[98] and decrease overall mortality rates.[99]

Cost Savings via Reform of the Medical Liability System

Although there are legitimate instances of malpractice, current malpractice law in the United States contributes significantly to the high cost of medical care, both through the exorbitant malpractice insurance premiums doctors are forced to pay and the ubiquitous practice of defensive medicine.[100] The recommendations that follow in this section certainly are no revelation. America's dysfunctional medical liability system and its relation to high medical costs have been widely noted, so far to little effect.

Few medical procedures are completely without risk to the patient, though the dangers often are remote and minimal. Given this, all doctors should be required to explain the odds of success to each patient before undertaking a risky procedure or prescribing certain medications, to acknowledge the possibility of unanticipated permanent injury or death, and to obtain the patient's written informed consent. The absence of a document verifying informed consent for a medication or procedure is in itself the basis for many malpractice claims.

In California, Texas, and Georgia, where pain and suffering awards are now limited by law, malpractice insurance premiums have been reduced by almost one-half, which lowers doctors' overhead costs. Attempts to limit these awards via national legislation have not yet been successful. Of course, there are occasions when physicians do commit malpractice, for which they should be held liable. However, tort reform—reforms to the rules governing the legal liabilities of doctors—appears to be a promising way of reducing malpractice insurance costs for doctors as well as decreasing the costs incurred by unnecessary tests and medications prescribed by doctors purely as a means of protecting themselves against possible lawsuits.

A doctor's decision to prescribe medication is subject to two types of error. One involves prescribing a new drug before it has been tested adequately.[101] The other entails failing to adopt a superior new medication that has been tested to a reasonable extent but whose usefulness and safety have not yet been widely established. Physicians worried about lawsuits may be unwilling to prescribe a new medication because the tests already conducted have not convinced them of its safety. Other physicians may rush to prescribe a new medication—whether or not it has been sufficiently tested—because its benefits have been publicized widely and the drug is being requested by patients. In both instances, doctors must make a preliminary evaluation of a medication's long-term safety and effectiveness without knowledge of possible subsequent negative findings and *with* the threat of lawsuits attending any incorrect conjectures.

Cost Savings via Changes in Medical Education

Current medical training methods contribute indirectly to rising medical care costs. For one thing, the cost of medical training has increased dramatically, which ultimately is reflected in the cost of health care.[102] In 1949, when one of the authors was appointed as an intern in internal medicine at Beth Israel Hospital in Boston, he received no salary but was given free room and board. By 2009, the same hospital had about fifty internal medicine interns, each with an annual salary of $53,000 (without room and board). The enormous increase in both the number of interns Beth Israel hires and the pay they receive is not an isolated phenomenon.[103] Furthermore, as a consequence of the Libby Zion malpractice lawsuit in the 1980s, hospitals are now required to limit residents' and interns' hours allegedly in order to reduce medical mistakes resulting from exhaustion.[104] As a result, hospitals must hire more residents and interns, which increases hospitals' operating costs. These examples illuminate just two of the many reasons why the cost of educating American doctors has increased dramatically in recent decades.

Another problem with current methods of educating doctors has to do with medical schools' reliance on teaching by specialists and subspecialists rather than by broad-based internists and family physicians, who make up only a small fraction of the medical school teaching faculty. Changing the focus of medical training away from its current emphasis on specialization could reduce the overuse of specialized tests and unnecessary referrals to specialists or subspecialists, who charge much higher fees than internists and family physicians.

In addition to reducing medical costs, returning the emphasis of medical education (and, by extension, practice) to training in family practice and broad-based internal medicine would benefit patients, who then would receive treatment encompassing all (or most) of their diagnostic and therapeutic needs from a *single* doctor who is familiar with their entire medical history. Instead, the current system often requires patients to see four or five specialists regularly, each with an isolated focus on one ailment or body system.[105] This often results in discontinuity of care and excess cost—for instance, when multiple specialists order the same test or when multiple similar medications are prescribed to treat the same condition. The hospitalist movement,[106] which separates hospitalized patients from their primary care physicians, has exacerbated this problem by relieving doctors of both the responsibility and compensation for treating their hospitalized patients.[107]

The noted cardiologist Eugene Braunwald has written that effective medical care requires a single overseer—just as an orchestra requires a conductor.[108] Specialists and subspecialists are needed only for certain aspects of care—just as orchestral virtuosi perform only occasional solos. Coronary heart disease, for instance, is part of diffuse vascular disease (that is, any number of health conditions that affect the body's blood vessels) that also may involve arteries in the brain, the kidneys, the intestines, and the legs. Although specialists may be necessary for some procedures, the family practice doctor or broad-based internist are best positioned to recommend appropriate medical care for the whole patient.

During medical school and residency, future physicians are not instructed adequately about medical liability and cost consciousness in patient care. Some medical schools and residency programs are beginning to address this subject,[109] and the larger American health system will benefit if such training becomes a standard and ubiquitous part of medical training.

Cost Savings via Changes in Health Insurance Practices

Conventional wisdom holds that two-thirds of all diagnoses can be made simply by taking a patient's comprehensive medical history and conducting a thorough physical examination—this is especially true when a physician has several years of practice and can make these diagnoses based on accumulated knowledge and experience.[110] This process may be more accurate and more cost-effective than expensive, high-tech testing procedures, but it is also time-consuming and is not covered by most American insurance plans. Instead, as a timesaving device for doctors, many patients commonly are asked to fill out medical history forms. This practice is far less productive than a direct, face-to-face interview with the patient, where a hesitant answer or confusion may help a doctor identify a possible problem that a patient may not be aware of or may wish to conceal.

Abandoning medical history forms in favor of more thorough and focused questioning of patients also allows doctors to more accurately assess patients' risks for common diseases[111] and has been found to inspire and motivate patient lifestyle changes, improve individual decision making by doctors in training and in practice, and generally improve outcomes for patients.[112] Despite the obvious benefits, however, it will not be possible to make in-depth, face-to-face medical history interviews and physical examinations a routine feature of medical practice without making significant changes to standard health insurance coverage in the United States in order to reimburse doctors for the time they spend obtaining detailed patient histories and performing thorough physical examinations.

Finally, although it is an elusive goal, measurement of physicians' quality of care and performance also could help to improve the American health-care system.[113] The current pay-per-procedure system could be refashioned to link doctors' compensation with the quality and cost-effectiveness of the care they provide to patients. It must be acknowledged, however, that the documentation involved in the evaluation of physician performance may be so diffuse and unwieldy as to negate any cost benefits resulting from this new system, as doctors will be forced to spend time that could be used for patient care completing forms and documenting procedures.

Announcements of new information about diseases and new methods of diagnosis and treatment arrive with increasing frequency.

Indeed, as we revised this chapter over several months, we were tempted almost every week to insert another comment about some medical innovation that had just been announced in the medical journals and the press. Some of these do provide cost savings, and many promise benefits that may justify their startling prices. All of them indicate that rapid and impressive change, and the costs this entails, are part of the evolving science of health-care delivery.

The effectiveness, safety, and cost of these new medical techniques, however, are generally determined only after the new discoveries are already in use. Over time, many of these new techniques may prove inadequate. As this occurs and better approaches and procedures are recognized, doctors must be ready to abandon the methods that are no longer effective—especially those that come at great expense with little or no benefit to patients.

There are many changes in medical practice and our larger health-care system that would both reduce expenditures and improve the quality of care. Prevention of disease is one primary means of reducing medical costs. The introduction of incentives for physicians to discontinue costly procedures that have only marginal benefits may be another. It may be necessary to subsidize or regulate the cost of expensive new medical equipment, which may be used more often than is absolutely necessary by doctors who have no other means of recouping its cost. The elimination of waste in health-care expenditures—via more accurate evaluation of new and existing medical treatments, eradication of unnecessary or harmful procedures, identification of less expensive treatments, discouraging patient demands for unnecessary tests and treatments, and reform of the medical liability and medical insurance systems—is another method of reducing overall health-care costs. If we are to train future doctors to prefer diagnostic and treatment options that provide both cost savings and improved medical care to patients, we also must consider amending medical school curricula and recruiting more instructors with training in the provision of broad-based medical care. Paradoxically the most promising route to effective cost containment may *not* be through reducing payment to doctors—an option that remains perennially popular. Rather, as the noted health-care economist Uwe Reinhardt has observed, "Physicians are the central decision makers in health care. A superior strategy might be to pay them very well for helping us reduce unwarranted health spending."[114]

Though it is still too early to evaluate the Patient Protection and Affordable Care Act, signed into law in early 2010, there is reason to believe that these reforms will not produce substantial reductions in overall health-care expenditures, despite the inclusion of cost-saving measures. The law misses two important opportunities. First, by failing to mandate an increase in the number of broad-based internists and family physicians, it misses the opportunity to reduce Americans' reliance on costly medical specialists and eliminate the inevitable wasteful spending that occurs when a patient receives medical care from more than one doctor. This omission, coupled with the influx of millions of newly insured patients, may result in an immediate shortage of primary care physicians. Second, the law could have restructured the way doctors are paid, doing away with the pay-per-procedure system that reimburses doctors only when medical procedures are carried out. The current system does not reward doctors for the use of less costly methods of diagnosis (for example, physical examinations and in-depth, face-to-face medical history interviews) and treatment (such as pharmaceutical therapies and lifestyle changes), and therefore may actually discourage their use. Thus, the law's provisions can be expected to contribute to reducing the current *level* of health-care spending but not the relentless and rapid *rate* at which these costs continue to rise.

Short of a major change in the fortunes of the global economy, the cost disease that afflicts health care can be expected to persist. If we take all possible steps to reconsider and reshape the art of medical practice, we should be able to lower the level of expenditures and improve the quality of care delivered by our health-care systems, perhaps substantially. Yet, as we have noted, no matter what measures we take to improve efficiency and reduce waste in health care, we can expect medical care expenditures to continue to rise rapidly, as the cost disease mechanism grinds on.

Conclusions

Where Are We Headed and What Should We Do?

The future lies ahead!
—MORT SAHL

The picture that emerges is not so daunting. We can have it all: better health care, good education, and even more orchestral performances. In exchange, we will not have to surrender food, clothing, shelter, or even less essential commodities such as comfortable vacations, unrestricted travel, and readily available entertainment. This is not merely naïve optimism but something we have already experienced. The exploding cost of hospital care and galloping college tuition increases since World War II have not prevented Americans from consuming these and other services and goods. Indeed, we now live longer than ever, and a continually rising share of the population attends college. Instead, the true threat to this desirable future is foolish public policy.

Let us consider two alternative scenarios. In the first, overall productivity continues to expand, as it has done in recent centuries in many parts of the world. Of course, there is no guarantee that this will happen, but it is what I expect will occur in societies with competitive economies. In this scenario, we will be able to afford ever more of what society desires. Even if health care and education keep getting more expensive, our earnings will grow fast enough to make these services affordable.

This scenario was first called to my attention by the economist Joan Robinson, who pointed out that if productivity is rising everywhere—even if it is slower in some industries than in others—then by definition the same or even fewer hours of labor will produce more of all goods and services than before. That is essentially what happened in the United States during the twentieth century. As a result, we now can afford more of everything—all the ingredients that make for an improving standard of living—for virtually all members of society (except, of course, during periods of recession). This does not mean that our economic problems have been solved. The poor will still be with us, and some of the funding for health care and other services affected by the cost disease will probably have to be channeled through government agencies, with all the political problems that entails.

But suppose the future does not bring ever growing productivity. Suppose innovation grinds to a halt, we run out of natural resources, and average income levels cease their steady rise. Then what? As we saw in Chapter 8, the cost disease, too, will terminate because it stems from unequal rates of productivity growth in different sectors of the economy. If productivity growth is zero in all areas of the economy, these inequalities will disappear. The cost disease would no longer be any part of the problem, but that's the only good news: our problems—particularly poverty—would be far worse.

This second, dismal scenario is not about to play out. Even if innovation were slowing down, as some observers claim, the productivity growth driven by innovation would still be far from zero. Consider the miracle of the Internet, where innovation begets further innovation. Although we are currently in the midst of one of history's periodic eras of slower-than-normal economic growth, it seems clearly appropriate to aim for a future of continued productivity growth, with prosperity reaching previously unachieved heights.

Given this, it is clear that if improvements to health care and education are hindered by the illusion that we cannot afford them, we will all be forced to suffer from self-inflicted wounds. The very definition of rising productivity ensures that the future will offer us a cornucopia of desirable services and abundant products. The main threat to this happy prospect is the illusion that society cannot afford them, with resulting political developments—such as calls for reduced governmental revenues entwined with demands that budgets always be in balance—that deny these benefits to our descendants.

Notes

Introduction

1. Here, the term "personal services" refers to services in which the labor of the provider of the service is difficult to reduce and is provided directly to the user, as in a doctor's medical examination or the services of nurse practitioners.

2. Baumol and Bowen 1966.

3. Nordhaus 2008, p. 21. Nordhaus also noted that "industries with relatively low productivity growth ('stagnant industries') show a percentage-point for percentage-point higher growth in relative prices. . . . Moreover, differences in productivity over the long term of a half-century explain around 85 percent of the variance in relative price movements for well-measured industries" (2008, p. 21).

4. However, the cost disease did draw some attention during the attempt to pass health-care legislation in the United States in the 1990s under the leadership of Hilary Clinton.

ONE
Why Health-Care Costs Keep Rising

Epigraph. Arnold, "The Scholar-Gypsy," 1919, line 203.

1. National Center for Education Statistics 2010.

2. Taylor 2010.

3. According to Prestowitz (2010), life expectancy in the United States (78.11 years) ranks fiftieth among all nations—just ahead of Albania and Taiwan, while the infant mortality rate in the United States (6.26 per 1,000 births) is ranked forty-sixth internationally—just behind Cuba and Guam. Meanwhile, the United States spends roughly 17 percent of its gross domestic product (GDP) on medical care, while Singapore and France—where infant mortality, for instance, is much lower—spend just 3 percent and 8 percent of GDP on medical care, respectively. Prestowitz concludes that "even though they are less likely to survive as infants and even though they die earlier, Americans pay twice or more as much as other leading countries for their medical care" (p. 25).

4. Immerwahr and Johnson 2009.

5. National Center for Public Policy and Higher Education 2008, p. 8, fig. 5.

6. Throughout this book, we refer mostly to costs, but occasionally we refer to *both* prices and costs because the data that are readily available are expressed in terms of prices. We then infer the behavior of costs from those price data. However, it is important to remember because prices are driven by costs, the explanation for price movements must focus on costs.

7. Here it is important to note that statistics for such a multicountry comparison are surprisingly difficult to obtain. In part, this is attributable to measurement problems. There are a number of services in each sector—those provided by governments, for instance—whose outputs are very hard to measure or even to define and observe. Moreover, because health care and education are so heterogeneous, the statistics are exceedingly difficult to compare from one country to another.

TWO

What Causes the Cost Disease, and Will It Persist?

Portions of this chapter, including Figure 2.2, are based on materials in my book *The Microtheory of Innovative Entrepreneurship* (Princeton, N.J.: Princeton University Press, 2010).

Epigraph. Baumol, "Fourth Tautology" (unpublished).

1. Of course, there must be such products because if there are items whose costs rise faster than the average, then there also must be others whose rate of cost increase is below the average.

2. For more on health-care costs associated with aging populations, see Hartman et al. (2008), Chernichovsky and Markowitz (2004), and Newhouse (1992). For more on health-care costs associated with drug costs, see Catlin et al. (2008).

3. National Practitioner Data Bank 2006, p. 26.

4. Ibid., pp. 62–70.

5. Organisation for Economic Co-operation and Development 2009.

6. Association of American Medical Colleges 2008, p. 3, chart 3: "U.S. Medical School Applicants and Matriculants 1982–83 to 2007–08." Note that competition among doctors is not expected to decline any time soon in the United States. For the first time since the 1970s, a substantial number of new medical schools are opening in the United States, with the aim of increasing medical school enrollment by about 30 percent, or 5,000 students, per year (Devi 2010).

7. U.S. Bureau of Labor Statistics 2009d. Note that "medical workers" include all those employed in physicians' offices.

8. U.S. Bureau of Labor Statistics 2009f.

9. Snyder, Dillow, and Hoffman 2009, p. 57, fig. 6. Note that this decline in pupils per teacher is due, in part, to smaller class sizes.

10. A noted composer once confided to me that, in his view, attending a live musical performance is much like reading a novel in a crowded, overheated room with the words of the book projected on a dimly lit screen.

11. Uchitelle 2009.

12. Of course, increased productivity is not the only influence leading to declining employment in the manufacturing sector. Notably, outsourcing to lower-wage countries has played some part in this.

13. Uchitelle 2009.

14. However, overall inflation in a country's economy affects the costs of *all* goods and services and, therefore, contributes an additional monetary cost increase on top of stagnant services' innate cost increases.

15. The advent of mass media has contributed spectacularly to productivity in musical performance, enormously increasing the number of listeners reached by a given performance. Yet this has not solved the problem. The costs of television broadcasting, for example, are increasing at a compounded rate very similar to those of live performance. This is due to rapid growth of productivity in the high-tech portion of broadcasting, which has made the cost of television transmission an ever-declining portion of the total budget of broadcasting activity. As such, the live performance component constitutes a constantly rising share of broadcasting costs. For a full discussion with statistical evidence, see Baumol, Batey Blackman, and Wolff (1989, chapter 6).

16. U.S. Bureau of Labor Statistics 2009a.

17. Ibid.

18. U.S. Bureau of Labor Statistics 2009c.

19. U.S. Bureau of Labor Statistics 2009b.

20. U.S. Bureau of Labor Statistics 2009f.

21. Note, however, that in the sixteenth and seventeenth centuries, there was no *unified* Italy, nor any *United* Kingdom.

THREE

The Future Has Arrived

Epigraph. Martin Luther King Jr., "I See the Promised Land," April 3, 1968. King 1986, p. 286.

1. This, of course, is because steadily increasing wages for the workers who clean the streets, drive subway trains, deliver mail, answer phones, and prepare food in restaurants drive up the overall cost of providing these services. To keep up with these rising costs, businesses and governments that provide these services must find ways to lower their own expenses—frequently by reducing the number of workers they employ. Those reductions—not the rising costs associated with the cost disease itself—cause the quality and quantity of these services to decline.

2. Here, it is important to clarify that this is the foreseeable fate of those services for which demand rises, even as their costs increase. However, others, such as the services of maids and butlers, can be expected to be met by declining demand as their costs increase. Many of these have all but disappeared.

Of course, the supply of labor also is pertinent to this. A rapid rise in population can expand the labor supply, which, in turn, reduces wages and slows the cost increases stemming from the cost disease. But happily, in much of the world, exploding productivity is expanding real (inflation-adjusted) wages. As one recent author put it, "It is a cliché, but nonetheless true . . . that a middle-class family living in a developed, twenty-first century country enjoys a life filled with luxuries that a king could barely afford two centuries ago" (Rosen 2010, p. xviii).

3. Note that this change has not yet occurred in the developing world, where wages have remained low. In India, for instance, middle-class and lower-middle-class families still can afford to (and typically do) hire maids, cooks, and drivers.

4. Stallybrass 2006.

5. Ibid., p. 558.

6. I had surmised earlier that the cost of auto repair would rise at a rate consistently exceeding inflation, but that expectation was not confirmed by the data. The pattern of cost changes for auto repair today apparently resembles that of manufacturing and testing, partly because auto mechanics now use computers to more quickly identify which component of a car is not working.

7. Veblen 1899, p. 176.

8. Satava 2003.

9. In Chapter 4, I provide further details that bolster this point. Chapter 5 of *The Microtheory of Innovative Entrepreneurship* (Baumol 2010) also addresses this issue.

10. See Chapter 1 of this book for more details and data on rising health-care and education costs in other industrialized nations; see Chapter 7 for analysis of health-care costs in low- and middle-income countries.

11. That is, these services are what economists call "price inelastic" (and "income elastic"), which means that demand for these commodities is not reduced much by rising prices but can be raised substantially by growth in purchasing power.

FOUR
Yes, We Can Afford It

Portions of this chapter, including Figure 4.1, are based on materials in my book *The Microtheory of Innovative Entrepreneurship* (Princeton, N.J.: Princeton University Press, 2010).

Epigraph. Baumol, "Sixth Tautology" (unpublished).

1. Bradford 1969.

2. This book, with its multiplicity of authors, is evidently not the place to enter the political debate over the ideal variant of health-care reform. None of this is intended as a political statement but rather as an illumination of what services our society can afford and what it will have to pay for those services that are deemed to be indispensable.

3. China's gross domestic product (GDP) per capita grew by an astonishing average of just over 9 percent each year between 1990 and 2006 (Organisation for Economic Co-operation and Development, and Korea Policy Centre 2009).

4. Maddison 2001, p. 264, table B-21.

5. Cox and Alm 1997, p. 5.

6. Ibid.

7. Ibid., p. 8.

8. Ibid., p. 11.

9. Federal Reserve Bank of Dallas, 1997, p. 19.

10. Halfhill 2006; Warren et al., 1997.

11. Letter of 28 September 1790 (Anderson 1990).

12. Of course, as we have noted, economists are not always very good at foreseeing the distant future. The discussion that follows is intended only to indicate what will happen to growth and costs during the twenty-first century if the growth performance of the twentieth century is replicated—a possibility that we have no basis to reject, though the global recession of the first decade of the twenty-first century, taken as a portent, may not be encouraging.

13. We calculated current productivity growth using GDP per capita data for the United States during the half-century between 1950 and 2001 (Maddison 2003, p. 262). We used this average annual growth rate of 2.13 percent to calculate projected U.S. GDP per capita for 2105. In turn, we used health-care expenditure data for the United States for 1995 and 2005 (Organisation for Economic

Co-operation and Development 2007, pp. 8–9) to calculate the average annual increase in health-care spending in the United States as a percentage of U.S. GDP during that ten-year period (1.41 percent). That growth rate of 1.41 percent was used to calculate projected U.S. health-care spending as a percentage of U.S. GDP in 2105. In selecting the data to use for these calculations, we opted to use the Maddison's GDP per capita data because calculations using this data produced the most moderate results, falling between extremely low and extremely high growth rates calculated using real GDP per capita data for the United States from the OECD and the 2006 *Economic Report of the President*, respectively.

Some readers may object (understandably) that these projections are distorted by the differing time periods of the data we used to calculate the growth rates for GDP per capita (1950–2001) and health-care spending (1995–2005). First, we point out that because we do not consider our calculations to be actual forecasts but rather projections, this is not a serious matter. No matter what quantitative methods we employ here, we surely cannot claim to foresee what the numbers really will be one century from now. Our calculations are meant only to illustrate the logic of this issue. Second, when we calculated the average annual growth rate for GDP per capita using data for 1995 and 2005 in order to match the time period for our health-care data, we obtained an even higher growth rate (2.27 percent) than the more conservative average annual growth rate of 2.13 percent, which we used to calculate projected U.S. GDP per capita for 2105. As already noted, we prefer to use the data that yield the most moderate results. (Similarly, one can substitute nonlinear relationships for the linear form we used to calculate our projections, but it is doubtful that this will add materially to our clairvoyant powers.) In sum, it is safe to conclude that no matter which of the acceptable growth rates we select for the calculation of these projections, the quotation at the head of this chapter remains true: if productivity rises in almost every part of the economy, the public can have more of *every* commodity.

14. Of course, so long as some members of society earn their living by working in activities other than health care, by definition, the cost of health care can never rise to account for 100 percent of GDP.

15. Baumol 2002.

16. Ibid., especially chapter 3.

17. Schumpeter, 1936.

18. Carroll 1902, p. 38.

19. This section summarizes material discussed at far greater length in Baumol 2010.

20. Of course, many of these individuals have gone on, like Bill Gates, to found gigantic enterprises of their own. But the members of this group have all

started off as lone workers or as members of a small group of founders of a fledgling company.

21. Baumol 2002, chapter 5.

22. The role of institutions in influencing the supply of productive entrepreneurs is, of course, not new and has been emphasized by a number of authors, notably Douglass C. North (see North and Thomas 1973; North 1990). What is new, however, is the assertion that institutional changes do not induce the creation of a body of new entrepreneurs where there were few before, but rather entice enterprising individuals away from their previously *unproductive* activities and lead them to transfer to *productive* undertakings. In a recent personal communication, Professor Richard Sylla of New York University's Stern School of Business offered a striking example of this critical conclusion: "[In] Meiji Japan . . . reformers commuted peasant rice payments to Samurai into government bonds, giving the Samurai government bonds and taxing the peasants in money to pay interest on the bonds. The Samurai were encouraged to become investors . . . and bankers . . . and Japan with a modern financial system suddenly left the rest of Asia in the dust and caught up with the West." The Samurai's transition from fighting to banking surely must be a classic example of an institutional change prompting unproductive entrepreneurs to transfer their efforts to productive activities.

23. Himmelstein et al., 2005, pp. w5–w63.

24. Anstett 2009; Hawke 2005. In the interest of fairness, it is also important to note an earlier study of Canadians' use of U.S. medical services, which reported that "results . . . do not support the widespread perception that Canadian residents seek care extensively in the United States. Indeed, the numbers found are so small as to be barely detectible relative to the use of care by Canadians at home" (Katz et al., 2002, p. 20).

25. Foubister et al., 2006, p. xv, table 1: "Subscriber numbers and people covered, as a percentage of the United Kingdom population, 1997–2003."

26. An exceptionally sophisticated empirical study of public spending on higher education (Ryan 1992) provides evidence that shortchanging those services affected by the cost disease is common. The study concludes, albeit subject to a number of caveats, that "under allocation of resources to higher education may have become wide-spread, with the most acute difficulties occurring in countries showing the greatest fiscal restriction, i.e., Denmark, New Zealand and the U.K." (p. 261).

27. Similar phenomena can be expected in other industrialized countries.

28. By "planned economies," we refer to the former Soviet Union as well as a number of other countries that have experimented with extensive government intervention in the operation of their economies—generally with unsatisfactory consequences.

29. The paradox of our analysis is that the one way that the cost disease can be cured is to bring productivity to a halt. If labor-saving improvements are zero across all industries, including manufacturing, then neither health care nor education possibly can fall behind, and their relative costs will cease to rise. However, this surely is a solution to be avoided studiously.

30. "Editorial opinion: Bridgeport goes bankrupt," 1991, p. A20.

31. Moynihan 1993, p. xxv.

FIVE

Dark Sides of the Disease

Epigraph. Kahaner 2008, p. 2.

1. As the noted British economist Lionel Robbins once remarked, the twentieth century's many wars and acts of organized genocide make it, perhaps, the most horrible in history. Unfortunately, the incredible pace of technological progress now under way may give the twenty-first century the means to outdo the twentieth.

2. The cost of the latest fighter jet may inch ever higher, and the military budgets of the world's major powers surely will continue to impose damaging deficits upon their governments, but bargain-basement military equipment remains plentiful, as the quotation at the head of this chapter emphasizes.

It is also important to note that manufacturing costs are not the only influence affecting prices in the weapons markets. For example, the magnitude of military activity in a particular geographic area and the resulting scale of demand are clearly pertinent. But such influences surely do not negate the role of production costs in determining the prices of weapons.

3. The *New York Times* reported that North Korea's successful atomic test in 2006 "brought to nine the number of nations believed to have nuclear arms. But atomic officials estimate that as many as 40 more countries have the technical skill, and in some cases the required material, to build a bomb" (Broad and Sanger 2006).

4. For an illuminating discussion of environmental catastrophes, see Posner (2004) and the lengthy review of that book by Parson (2007). For more on the root causes of environmental deterioration in particular, see the stimulating book by Speth (2008).

5. See, for example, Speth 2008, chapter 4.

6. The cost disease does not make *all* services progressively more expensive, as explained in Chapter 2. Telecommunications services, for instance, have grown ever cheaper as a result of technical progress. However, such productivity-progressive services are generally produced with the aid of substantial quantities of equipment and energy. This is no coincidence, for the cost of producing these ser-

vices can be more easily reduced precisely because their labor component is relatively small and more easily decreased by the substitution of equipment. As such, increased output of these services will do little to protect the environment.

7. For this purpose, economists also favor market-driven substitutes for tax increases. For example, rather than taxing all polluting emissions, many economists advocate a "cap and trade" arrangement, under which a polluter must purchase permits that specify the maximum amount of emissions that the holder of the permits will be permitted to release. These permits can be sold by one firm to another in a market. The underlying idea is that the demand for permits will drive up their price, making the permits as expensive to the polluter as a tax on emissions.

8. It is important to note that economists are not alone in urging a revision of the entire tax system. One leading proponent of this approach to taxation is William Drayton, founder and CEO of Ashoka, an organization that carries out invaluable work in the field of social entrepreneurship. This approach to policy related to containment of environmental damage stems from the work of British economist A. C. Pigou. His monumental volume (1912) initiated a new branch of economics, the field of "welfare" economics, which encompasses environmental policy as one of its subjects.

SIX

Common Misunderstandings of the Cost Disease

Epigraph 1. National Heart, Lung, and Blood Institute 2007, p. 31, chart 3-22.
Epigraph 2. Healthcare Cost and Utilization Project 2007, p. 41.

1. Note that a constant level of inefficiency or larceny would not explain the cost disease because the crucial point is not that costs in the affected industries are high but that they are *rising rapidly, year after year.*

2. For an excellent, albeit no longer current, analysis of the service and manufacturing sectors' share of GDP, see Summers (1985). More recent data from the World Bank indicate that the percentage of total world GDP accounted for by industry (including manufacturing, mining, construction, water, electricity, and gas) declined by roughly one quarter during the last forty years—from nearly 40 percent in 1970 to just under 30 percent in 2006.

3. The output proportions of the stagnant and progressive sectors depend on, among other things, consumers' reactions to the falling prices of the progressive-sector products, the rising prices of the stagnant-sector products, and the rising incomes of employees—which result from the continuing growth of productivity in the economy, among a miscellany of other influences. Given this, we should not jump to the conclusion that the output proportions of these two sectors will

remain unchanging, even approximately. But as an assumption adopted to make this analysis a bit more straightforward, it certainly is legitimate—so long as we keep in mind its questionable status as a depiction of reality.

4. From a practical perspective, it should be noted that it is difficult to measure quality improvement. After all, how does one definitively quantify changes of a relatively subjective nature? For this reason, the methods that are used to quantify changes in quality are hardly straightforward and often are considered questionable. As a result, many researchers who work with productivity figures simply do not attempt an adjustment for quality improvement, but do so with apology.

5. This is particularly true in health care, where we know that quality-unadjusted productivity is hardly rising, if at all. At the same time, however, seemingly miraculous improvements in medical technology more than offset that rise in cost and ensure that quality-adjusted productivity is rising.

6. The observations in this section were provided by my knowledgeable coauthor, Dr. Monte Malach, to whom I am grateful.

7. As of 2010, the list of robotic surgeries being performed includes kidney transplants, bladder and urinary tract stone removal, gall bladder surgery, coronary artery bypass grafts, cardiac arrhythmia treatment, gynecologic surgery, uterine and ovarian surgery, pancreatic surgery, liver resection and transplantation, bariatric (weight loss) surgery, hip and knee replacement, hernia repair, radio surgery for various tumors, and childhood congenital tracheoesophageal fistula repair.

8. There is no question about the benefits of robotic surgery, but it is important to note that there are many naysayers who argue that individual medical expertise obtained over time is equally accurate and far less costly than robotic surgery.

9. Prewitt et al., 2008.

10. Ibid.

11. Ibid.

12. U.S. Renal Data System 2011, "Table Kb: Medicare Payments per Person per Year by Claim Type."

13. MacReady 2009. Note that as of 2009 more than 360,000 people in the United States were undergoing kidney dialysis (ibid.).

SEVEN

The Cost Disease and Global Health

Epigraph. Bacon 1605, p. 71.

1. Newhouse (1977), Abel-Smith (1967), and Kleiman (1974), among others, showed this proportional relationship using data for Organisation for Economic Co-operation and Development (OECD) countries.

2. World Health Organization (2001); other scholars have obtained similar findings for countries in Europe (Murilo, Piatecki, and Saez 1993) and for developing countries (Murray, Govindaraj, and Musgrove 1994).

3. Cross-country regressions of total health spending per capita on GDP per capita yield a positive correlation, R^2, of approximately 0.94.

4. Van der Gaag and Štimac 2008b.

5. Van der Gaag and Štimac 2008a.

6. Ibid.

7. World Health Organization 2010b.

8. Baumol 1988.

9. Van der Gaag and Štimac 2008a.

10. Lu et al., 2010.

11. Van der Gaag and Štimac 2008a.

12. Baumol 1988.

13. Schellekens et al., 2007.

14. Musgrove, Zeramdini, and Carrin 2002.

15. Narayan 2007.

16. Morgan, Ferris, and Lee 2008; Emanuel and Fuchs 2008.

17. Constant et al., 2011; Hartman et al., 2008; Chernichovsky and Markowitz 2004.

18. Newhouse 1992; Catlin et al., 2008.

19. Thomas, Ziller, and Thayer 2010.

20. For a more detailed discussion of the many factors that contribute to rising health-care costs, see Chapter 11 in this book.

21. Baumol 1993.

22. See Chapters 2 to 4 of this book for a complete explanation of the cost disease.

23. Chernew, Hirth, and Cutler 2009.

24. See Chapter 1 of this book for these data. Recent macroeconomic analysis yields robust evidence in support of the cost disease in developed countries (Hartwig 2008) and the United States (Nordhaus 2008; Flanagan 2012).

25. Truffer et al., 2010.

26. Orszag and Ellis 2007.

27. Maddison 2007.

28. Gurría 2009.

29. O'Neill et al., 2005; World Economic Outlook 2009.

30. Notestein 1945.

31. Omran 1971.

32. Fries 1980.

33. Lu et al., 2010.

34. United Nations Health Partners Group in China 2005; Wang, Xu, and Xu 2007.

35. World Health Organization 2010a.

36. Anderson and Chalkidou 2008; Fowler et al., 2008.

37. Collier 2007; Commission on Growth and Development 2008.

38. United Nations General Assembly 2010.

39. Van der Gaag and Štimac 2008b; and Lu et al., 2010.

40. Abel-Smith 1991.

41. Krishna 2010.

42. Xu et al., 2007.

43. World Health Organization 2010a.

44. Garrett, Chowdhury, and Pablos-Méndez 2009.

45. Escobar, Griffin, and Shaw 2011.

46. Bleich et al., 2007.

47. Frenk et al., 2006; Gottret, Schieber, and Waters 2008.

48. Hsiao and Heller 2007.

49. Lagomarsino et al., 2009.

50. Sources for the Ghana case study are McKinsey and Company (2010) and the Joint Learning Network for Universal Health Coverage (2011).

51. World Health Organization 2010b.

52. International Monetary Fund, and the International Development Association 2008.

53. Garrett, Chowdhury, and Pablos-Méndez 2009.

54. Reddy et al., 2011.

55. Hu et al., 2008.

56. A note regarding sources and limitations of the data given in Table 7.1: the World Health Organization (WHO) provides time series, standardized national health account data for its member states for the years 1995 through 2005. Since 2000, approximately sixty low-income and middle-income countries have created national health accounts (Hjortsberg 2001). Prior to 2000, there are limited data available for some developing countries. In Table 7.1, we use nominal (unadjusted for inflation) total health spending data from 2007 (World Health Organization 2009).

The methods used to analyze national health account data integrate different sources of data (government budgets, household surveys, etc.) and exclude family home care (Rannan-Eliya 2008). Not surprisingly, different countries and organizations vary slightly in the way they calculate and report a given statistic. The resulting imprecision implies that the key association between GDP per capita and total health spending per capita is even greater than that reported in this chapter.

Also because the International Monetary Fund (2008) does not have GDP per capita data for the following WHO member states, they are not included in the analysis presented in this chapter: Andorra, Cook Islands, Cuba, Democratic People's Republic of Korea, Iraq, Marshall Islands, Micronesia (Federated States of), Monaco, Montenegro, Nauru, Niue, Palau, San Marino, Somalia, and Tuvalu.

The International Labor Organization (ILO) measures formal health coverage "in terms of the population formally covered by social health protection, for example, under legislation, without reference being made to effective access to health services, quality of services or other dimensions of coverage." Here it is important to emphasize that collecting data on formal health coverage is difficult, and that the ILO dataset was chosen because it covers the largest number of countries available at this time. However, the data are not without limitations. For example, the data consider only one aspect of coverage, the number of people covered, and do not take into account *what* is covered and *how fully* the services are covered for payment purposes. For instance, the United States is listed as having 100 percent health coverage, which certainly is not the case, while Sri Lanka's coverage is listed as 0.1 percent, which is greatly underestimated.

57. Bump 2010.
58. Bloom and Canning 2000; Hughes et al., 2011.
59. Chernew, Hirth, and Cutler 2009.
60. Abel-Smith 1967.

EIGHT

Hybrid Industries and the Cost Disease

Portions of this chapter are based on materials in my books *The Free-Market Innovation Machine* (2002, chapter 15) and *Productivity and American Leadership* (1989, chapter 6).

Epigraph. Emerson 1914.
1. The discussion in this chapter is simplified by assuming that when the unit cost of a commodity changes substantially and persistently, its market price generally will be forced to move in the same direction. Thus, in this chapter if we speak of falling costs or falling prices, for instance, we are implying, in either case, that costs and prices are generally *both* declining.
2. Baumol, Batey Blackman, and Wolff 1989.
3. However, as has been shown in an article by François Horn (2002) of the Université Charles de Gaulle in Lille, productivity in software creation has been rising rapidly, though not as quickly as it has in hardware. Thus, it is surely

incorrect to characterize all nonhardware inputs into the computation process as stagnant in terms of productivity growth.

4. For more on this, see Baumol, Blackman, and Wolff 1989, chapter 6.

5. The productivity of labor, along with workers' earnings, has risen rapidly since the onset of the Industrial Revolution. A reasonable (if very rough) estimate is that the real product of an hour of labor since that time has risen, at least in the progressive sector, by something on the order of 2,000 percent. If the market value of research and development labor activity has risen at anywhere near that pace, this implies that the cost of this activity must indeed be growing substantially.

NINE

Productivity Growth, Employment Allocation, and the Special Case of Business Services

Epigraph. Bartlett 1992, p. 62.

1. Throughout this chapter, we have simplified the discussion by assuming that when the unit cost of a commodity changes substantially and persistently, its market price generally will be forced to move in the same direction. Thus, in this chapter we will sometimes speak of falling costs, sometimes of falling prices—in either case, we are implying that costs and prices are generally *both* declining.

2. Of course, one cannot preclude the possibility that at some future date a technological breakthrough will move an item from the rising-cost category to the declining-cost category. But such a relocation is neither certain nor easy. If an item's real cost is on either a rising-cost or declining-cost trajectory, one can be reasonably confident that it will continue to follow that path for a substantial period of time.

3. In the Middle Ages, approximately 90 percent of the European labor force was involved in agriculture, according to Fagan (2001).

4. Food and Agriculture Organization of the United Nations 2006; U.S. Bureau of Labor Statistics 2008a, Occupational Employment Statistics Survey. For the United States, this percentage was calculated using national employment estimates for the following occupations, as classified by the U.S. Bureau of Labor Statistics: First-Line Supervisors/Managers of Farming, Fishing, and Forestry Workers; Farm Labor Contractors; Agricultural Inspectors; Animal Breeders; Graders and Sorters, Agricultural Products; Agricultural Equipment Operators; Farmworkers and Laborers, Crop, Nursery, and Greenhouse; Farmworkers, Farm and Ranch Animals; and Agricultural Workers, All Others.

5. U.S. Bureau of Labor Statistics 2008b, Current Employment Statistics.

6. In China, total manufacturing employment increased at an uneven pace until 1995, when employment in that sector began to decline—a trend that continued through 2002. However, between 2002 and 2008, employment in China's

manufacturing sector *grew* from 83 million people in 2002 to 104 million people in 2008 (National Bureau of Statistics of China, 1978–2002, 2008). Meanwhile, in Japan, employment in the manufacturing sector increased steadily until 1992 and then decreased dramatically, even as overall employment continued to increase (Banister 2005).

7. Baumol and Bowen 1966.

8. Oulton 2001.

9. For a fuller and more formal discussion of the impact of the business services sector on productivity growth, with references to the literature, see Sasaki (2007).

10. Oulton 2001.

11. The material in this section is based, in great part, on Rubalcaba and Kox (2007).

12. U.S. Bureau of Labor Statistics 1979–2009a.

13. U.S. Bureau of Labor Statistics 1979–2009a; U.S. Bureau of Labor Statistics 1979-2009b.

14. Rubalcaba and Kox 2007.

15. Ibid., p. 8.

16. For instance, a new animation technique known as motion capture, where the movements of live actors are captured by sensors and converted to three-dimensional digital files in real time, allows animators to work with characters and animation as if they were directing a live-action movie. At Threshold Animation Studies, the adoption of this real-time animation process reduced the average production time for each film by 30 to 50 percent. Moreover, Threshold has found that some scenes that once required six months to produce using traditional digital animation practices can be completed in just 15 minutes (!) using real-time animation motion capture techniques.

17. We are fortunate that the principal author of this chapter, Dr. Lilian Gomory Wu, is the Global University Programs Executive at IBM. Our ease of access to IBM materials led us to focus our discussion of business services on examples from IBM.

18. IBM Corporation 2010.

19. Economists use the term "innovation" to refer to the entire process of inventing a new product, modifying it to appeal to consumer tastes, and then manufacturing and marketing it.

20. Confederation of Indian Industry 2007.

21. Catone 2007.

22. IBM Corporation 2007a.

23. IBM Corporation 2006.

24. For complete details, see Bjelland and Wood 2008.

25. Original Equipment Suppliers Association 2007.

26. IBM Corporation 2005; Global Dialogue Center 2006.

27. Note that, as of 2010, ThinkPlace had evolved into Innovation Hubs, which apply the ThinkPlace model to smaller communities within IBM. For example, all IBM employees involved in procurement now have their own Innovation Hub, just as employees in research, sales, and other departments each have dedicated Innovation Hubs to generate new ideas specific to their areas of work.

28. Rummler and Brache 1995.

29. This section is based on a paper by Chow et al. (2007) and an IBM red paper, "Supporting Innovators and Early Adopters: A Technology Adoption Program Cookbook" (Alkalay et al., 2007).

30. Sanford 2005.

31. Alkalay et al., 2007.

32. Ibid.

33. Oulton 2001.

TEN

Business Services in Health Care

Epigraph. Letter to A. Stephen Wilson, March 5, 1879. Darwin and Seward 1903, p. 422.

1. For further discussion of the costs versus quality improvements stemming from health-care innovations, see Chapter 6.

2. An authoritative and widely recognized Institute of Medicine report released a decade ago (Kohn, Corrigan, and Donaldson 2000) put the number, at that time, at 98,000 deaths per year. A more recent study (HealthGrades 2004) using Medicare patient data estimated that 195,000 people die each year in U.S. hospitals because of preventable errors, including mistakes in diagnosis, poor or unnecessary performance of an operation or procedure, failure to prevent injury, or errors in the use of a drug. A still more recent study that focused on medication errors in U.S. hospitals (Aspden et al., 2006) concluded that, on average, "a typical patient would be subject to one administration medication error per day" (p. 111). In all, the most current estimates indicate that more than 3 million "preventable adverse events," such as medication errors and infections acquired in-hospital, occur each year in U.S. hospitals (Yong and Olsen 2010, p. 17).

3. Kelley and Fabius 2010.

4. Traynor 2004.

5. Of these 5,331 medication errors, 2,067 would have been category C errors (errors that reach the patient but do not cause harm), 832 would have been category D errors (errors that reach the patient and require monitoring to confirm that no

harm is done and no intervention is required), and 14 would have resulted in serious harm to the patient.

6. A recent study determined that nurses walk up to five miles a day—mostly to deal with nonclinical issues such as answering phone calls at nursing stations (Welton et al., 2006).

Vassar's new Voice-over-Internet Protocol communication system also reduces the time nurses otherwise would spend waiting for doctors to answer their pages. This amounts to significant time savings, as the average Vassar nurse spends about fifty minutes each day communicating with physicians by phone.

7. The discussion in this section is based on an IBM case study (IBM Corporation 2007b).

8. Bendavid and Adams 2009.

9. Results in this section are based on Kehoe (2007), who described Vassar's intravenous pump real-time tracking project.

10. Roughly 56 percent of preventable medication errors in hospitals can be attributed to mistakes made by physicians when prescribing a drug, and another 34 percent are attributed to mistakes made by nurses in administering a drug. Errors made by unit secretaries account for an additional 6 percent of medication errors, and another 4 percent of all errors can be attributed to pharmacy staff (Kimmel and Sensmeier 2002).

11. For more on quality-unadjusted versus quality-adjusted productivity growth, see Chapter 6.

12. Six Sigma techniques were pioneered by Motorola in the 1980s as a means of removing defects from business and manufacturing processes. Subsequently, this method has spread from manufacturing and has been adopted by many other industries.

In addition to using Six Sigma methods, Tufts has borrowed "crew resource management" techniques from commercial aviation to build communication skills among employees. As part of this, clear safety standards are established, and every employee is empowered to "stop the manufacturing line" if a serious problem is spotted. Staff members who work in high-risk areas at Tufts (for example, mobile intensive care, surgery, and interventional radiology) are trained to use checklists to maintain safety standards and stop any procedure if they see a problem.

13. Centers for Disease Control and Prevention 2010a.

14. Klevens et al., 2007.

15. In the mid-2000s, the central line infection rate was estimated at 5.3 infections per 1,000 catheter days in intensive care units, with an associated mortality rate of 85 percent—which translates into 14,000 deaths per year (Levinson 2008). The Centers for Disease Control and Prevention (CDC) (2005) also estimated that each year 250,000 cases of bloodstream infections associated with central lines

occurred in hospitals in the United States, with 12 percent of these infections (or 30,000 cases) resulting in death. According to the CDC, the marginal cost of each central line infection is approximately $25,000.

16. In the mid-2000s, Tufts convened a group of more than forty experts to study and recommend how to reduce the rate of central line infections. The group consisted of Tufts doctors and nurses as well as experts in infectious disease prevention. They studied the literature to identify best practices and combined these with their knowledge of the Tufts working environment to develop new procedures for inserting central lines in Tufts patients. Unfortunately, these new practices did not reduce the hospital's overall infection rates.

17. This daunting challenge is described especially well by Kim and Rosenberg (2011) in their recent editorial on reducing blood culture contamination, in which they note that "no single intervention will solve the problem of blood culture contamination, but meticulous attention to each and every step in the process can reduce contamination to acceptable levels" (p. 203).

18. Hospital-acquired urinary tract infections are the most frequent infection associated with health care; an estimated 500,000 cases occurred in 2002, with 13,000 associated deaths (Klevens, et al., 2007). In addition, patient falls are the leading cause of injury-related death for individuals age 65 and older (Centers for Disease Control and Prevention 2010b), and according to the Agency for Healthcare Research and Quality there were more than 500,000 hospitalizations related to bedsores in 2006—an increase of nearly 80 percent since 1993 (Agency for Healthcare Research and Quality 2008).

ELEVEN
Yes, We Can Cut Health-Care Costs Even If We Cannot Reduce Their Growth Rate

This chapter is based on our article "Further Opportunities for Cost Reduction of Medical Care," (*Journal of Community Health*, 2010).

Epigraph. Knox 2010.

1. Baumol 1993.

2. Physicians who purchase and use new equipment may be enticed, wittingly or unwittingly, into using it more than they should in order to cover the cost of the equipment. As we will see in this chapter, more medical care is often worse care, and the overuse of expensive new medical technology is no exception.

3. In addition to reducing the overall cost of care for heart attack patients, coronary care units have improved patient outcomes dramatically. In one particular New York City hospital, for example, in-hospital mortality rates among heart

attack patients dropped from 47 percent in 1954, before the introduction of specialized coronary care units (Malach and Rosenberg 1958), to 22 percent in 1967 after the adoption of continuous monitoring of patients via coronary care units (Killip and Kimball 1967). Since then, the overall in-hospital mortality rate for heart attack patients in the United States has continued to drop. As of 2002, that mortality rate had fallen to approximately 10 percent. More current mortality rates are estimated to be in the 5 to 10 percent range (Ting et al., 2007; Ford et al., 2007; Malach and Imperato 2006).

4. Schneeweiss et al., 2008; Shaw et al., 2008.

5. Yu et al., 2009.

6. Meier 2009.

7. Indeed, even the U.S. Food and Drug Administration (FDA) premarket approval process has been accused of shortcomings in rigor and susceptibility to bias (Dhruva, Bero, and Redberg 2009). For instance, although the antidiabetes drug rosiglitazone received FDA approval, it recently was found to increase the risk of heart attack in patients (Bakalar 2010). This raises the question of the adequacy and the safety of the FDA process for drug approval and of pharmaceutical companies' possible influence on this.

In addition, for an illuminating and amusing compendium of widespread misunderstandings in the field of economics resulting from careless statistical reasoning, see *Freakonomics* (Levitt and Dubner 2005).

8. For instance, although we know that wet streets are correlated with rainfall, it does not follow that wet ground proves that it has been raining. In the field of medical research, similarly flawed conclusions regarding causation may result in much unnecessary spending on ineffective and even harmful medical treatments.

9. Incidentally, the Drug Effectiveness and Review Project (Hoadley et al., 2006), which compares the safety and effectiveness of new drugs with older medications, found that newer medicines are not always better than older alternatives, though they are almost always more expensive.

10. Oken 2008.

11. Stewart et al., 2007.

12. Stampfer et al., 1985.

13. Rossouw et al., 2002.

14. Cardwell et al., 2010.

15. Favus 2010.

16. Brownlee 2007.

17. Parker et al., 2009.

18. Menacker and Hamilton 2010.

19. One method of reducing cesarean deliveries is proposed by new guidelines put forth by the American College of Obstetrics and Gynecology. Despite the risks

for uterine rupture and other complications resulting from vaginal delivery after a prior cesarean delivery, the guidelines recommend that doctors first attempt vaginal delivery, keeping cesarean delivery as an emergency alternative only.

20. Saul 2010. It also is important to note that DCIS is reportedly misdiagnosed in seven to 20 percent of all cases (ibid.). As such, even the less invasive quadrantectomy procedure may be completely unnecessary.

21. Bogdanich 2010.

22. Patel et al., 2010.

23. This question is valid not only for patients who undergo CT angiography but for all patients who undergo any kind of medical imaging procedure. For instance, although magnetic resonance imaging (MRI) is performed three times as often, per capita, in the United States as it is in Canada—at great cost, there is no evidence that better patient outcomes are attained in the United States (Fuchs 2009). This suggests that such overutilization is a waste of health-care resources (Emanuel and Fuchs 2008). Similarly, the Centers for Medicare and Medicaid Services in the United States have declared that there is insufficient evidence that CT colonography is any more effective in diagnosing colon cancer than the colonoscopy test (Knudsen et al., 2010), which is significantly less expensive and involves no radiation exposure.

24. The American Board of Radiology Foundation has developed new guidelines designed to curb overuse of all forms of medical imaging (Hendee et al., 2010).

25. Fazel et al., 2009.

26. Taylor et al., 2009.

27. However, in larger doses niacin has troublesome side effects, due to its blood vessel dilating effect, which causes uncomfortable hot flashes and skin flushing.

28. Lee et al., 2009.

29. Ginsberg and Cushman 2010; Ernst and Moser 2009.

30. Ray et al., 2009.

31. Dayo et al., 2010; Canagee 2010.

32. Lifton 2010.

33. Epigenomes, which sit on the outside top of each gene, promote or quiet the expression of that particular gene. Environmental forces such as starvation or overeating can cause epigenomes to enhance or suppress a particular gene in a mother or father's genetic material, thereby passing on a new trait to the next generation. This could explain some genetic mysteries, such as why only one member of a set of identical twins may develop asthma or bipolar disorder (Cloud 2010).

34. Voora et al., 2009.

35. In some instances, a lower dose of a statin (simvastatin) may remove the syndrome of painful skeletal muscles. The addition of COQ10 also alleviates this condition.

36. Damani and Topol 2007.
37. National Cancer Institute 2009.
38. Markowitz and Bertagnolli 2009.
39. McPherson 2010.
40. London et al., 2007.
41. Indeed, such efforts already are under way. A recent study of women with BRCA1 and BRCA2 mutations reported that those women who had their breasts or ovaries removed as a means of preventing breast or ovarian cancer had fewer instances of cancer and lower overall mortality rates (Domchek et al., 2010). However, it is important to note that this is not yet a standard therapy.
42. Seshadri et al., 2010.
43. Daviglus et al., 2010.
44. American College of Obstetricians and Gynecologists 2010.
45. Feldman et al., 2011.
46. Partnership for Prevention 2007.
47. Hochman et al., 2006; Boden et al., 2009.
48. When a heart attack occurs, the heart automatically attempts to reroute blood flow through other, unblocked vessels in the heart that otherwise are not normally used for major blood supply.
49. Stone et al., 2010; Boden 2010.
50. Talajic et al., 2010. However, patients receiving rate control are still in danger of developing blood clots due to persistent atrial fibrillation. This risk must be mitigated via the use of anticoagulant drugs. Because anticoagulants may result in serious bleeding or stroke, patients taking these drugs require careful monitoring.
51. Mayo Clinic 2010.
52. Van Gelder et al., 2010.
53. An implantable cardioverter-defibrillator monitors a patient's heart rhythm and automatically restores normal rhythm if abnormalities occur.
54. Varma et al., 2010.
55. Andriole et al., 2010; Shao et al., 2010.
56. Singer 2009.
57. Partnership for Prevention 2007.
58. Califf et al., 2010.
59. Centers for Disease Control and Prevention 2009.
60. Pollak 2010.
61. Ridker et al., 2008.
62. Downs et al., 1998.
63. Indeed, a somewhat tongue-in-cheek contribution to the *American Journal of Cardiology* proposes a new concept: "Macstatin." This would entail distribution of a standard cholesterol-lowering drug along with ketchup when restaurant-goers

order French fries and hamburgers, in an effort to neutralize the high cholesterol content of fast food (Ferenczi et al., 2010).

64. Blumenthal and Michos 2009; Rodés-Cabau et al., 2009.

65. Elevation of high-density lipoprotein cholesterol levels tends to lower low-density lipoprotein levels reciprocally.

66. Taylor et al., 2009.

67. Tsimikas 2009.

68. Blumenthal and Michos 2009; Rodés-Cabau et al., 2009; Amarenco and Labreuche 2009.

69. Ernst and Moser 2009; Kostis 2007.

70. Hubbard 2010.

71. Flossman and Rothwell 2007.

72. Mattle, Meier, and Nedelichav 2010; Kronzon and Ruiz 2010.

73. Malach and Imperato 2004.

74. Parekh and Barton 2010.

75. Prodanovich et al., 2009.

76. Freudenheim 2010.

77. Wilson 2010.

78. Stetka 2010.

79. Poon, Keohane, and Yoon 2010.

80. In particular, the failure to address the problem of obesity in the United States, where 72.5 million adults are obese and more than 26 percent of all people report that they are obese (though the true percentage is almost certainly higher), has led to significant increases in medical costs (Centers for Disease Control and Prevention, 2010c). Serious and very costly health conditions, such as diabetes, heart disease, high cholesterol, high blood pressure, and stroke, are significantly more common among the obese (Bhattacharya and Sood 2004). In 2006 alone, medical costs associated with obesity were estimated to be $147 billion, and the average annual cost of treating a single obese person was almost $1,500 greater than the cost of treatment for an individual of normal weight (Centers for Disease Control and Prevention 2010c).

81. DeVol and Bedroussian 2007.

82. Redman et al., 2010.

83. Pletcher et al., 2010; Berenson and Srinivasan 2010.

84. Mitrou et al., 2007; Feart, Samieri, and Barberger-Gateau 2010; Büchner et al., 2010.

85. Albanese et al., 2009.

86. Shu et al., 2009.

87. Yan and Spitznagel 2009.

88. Smith-Spangler et al., 2010.

89. Kay et al., 2010.

90. Janszky et al., 2009.

91. Buijsse et al., 2010; Mostofsky et al., 2010.

92. Bertelli and Das 2009. Researchers have found that sirtuins also reduce lung and colon cancer, type-2 diabetes, and cardiovascular and Alzheimer's disease *in mice.*

93. Barnard and Colón-Emeric 2010; Kennel, Drake, and Hurley 2010.

94. Centers for Disease Control and Prevention 2008.

95. Stueve and O'Donnell 2007.

96. Gerber et al., 2009.

97. Kokkinos et al., 2010; Kelly 2010.

98. Saihara et al., 2010.

99. Manini et al., 2006.

100. Rodwin, Chang, and Clausen 2006. Defensive medicine—the method by which doctors seek to safeguard against malpractice lawsuits by ordering otherwise unnecessary diagnostic or therapeutic procedures—is commonly thought to account for no less than 25 percent of all medical costs in the United States. (However, it is impossible to quantify these costs.)

It is also important to note that patients' demands for unnecessary tests or treatments may contribute to the growing prevalence of defensive medicine. Unnecessary medical care is not only dangerous for patients, but also contributes significantly to medical costs.

101. This does not include off-label prescriptions, which are problematic due to malpractice concerns.

102. In recent decades, the real cost of attending medical school in the United States has increased by an average of 50 percent at private schools and by 150 percent on average at public schools (Jolly 2004). Accordingly the average amount of debt carried by graduating medical students has increased significantly. As of 2008 medical school graduates surveyed by the American Association of Medical Colleges had an average debt load of almost $142,000, with almost 20 percent of students surveyed reporting educational loans totaling $200,000 or more (Harris 2008). The huge (and steadily increasing) debt associated with medical education in the United States often requires doctors to focus their attention on amassing significant earnings in order to pay off their student loans. This leads many new doctors to enter subspecialties of medicine where higher earnings are common.

103. At most teaching hospitals the salaries of interns and residents are subsidized by the federal government.

104. For the details of the Libby Zion case, see Lerner 2006. For an analysis of the subsequent medical education reforms, see Laine, et al., 1993.

105. Beckman 2010.

106. Hospitals are now training and hiring their own in-house physicians, known as "hospitalists," who deliver day-to-day care to hospital patients and effectively replace a patient's private physician during a hospital stay.

107. Editors of the *Annals of Internal Medicine* 2010.

108. Braunwald 2009.

109. Okie 2010.

110. Cohen, Neumann, and Weinstein 2008; Phillips and Andrieni 2007; Horowitz 2008.

111. Wilson et al., 2009.

112. Berg et al., 2009.

113. Berwick 2009.

114. Reinhardt 2007.

References

Abel-Smith, B. 1967. *An International Study of Health Expenditure.* Public Health Papers No. 32. Geneva: World Health Organization.

———. 1991. Financing health for all. *World Health Forum* 12: 191–200.

Agency for Healthcare Research and Quality. 2008. Pressure ulcers increasing among hospital patients. *AHRQ News and Numbers*, December 3, 2008. http://www.ahrq.gov/news/nn/nn120308.htm.

Albanese, E., A. D. Dangour, R. Uauy, et al. 2009. Dietary fish and meat intake and dementia in Latin America, China, and India: A 10/66 Dementia Research Group population-based study. *American Journal of Clinical Nutrition* 90:392–400.

Alkalay, A., C. Almond, J. Bloom, et al. 2007. *Supporting innovators and early adopters: A technology adoption program cookbook.* IBM Redbooks. Poughkeepsie, N.Y.: IBM International Technical Support Organization. http://www.redbooks.ibm.com/redpapers /pdfs/redp4374.pdf.

Amarenco, P., and J. Labreuche. 2009. Lipid management in the prevention of stroke: Review and updated meta-analysis of statins for stroke prevention. *Lancet* 8:453–463.

American College of Obstetricians and Gynecologists. 2010. Committee opinion: Human papillomavirus vaccination. *Journal of Obstetrics and Gynecology* 116:800–803.

Anderson, E., ed. and trans. 1990. *The letters of Mozart and his family.* New York: Norton.

Anderson, G., and K. Chalkidou. 2008. Spending on medical care: More is better? *Journal of the American Medical Association* 299:2444–2445.

Andriole, G. L., D. G. Bostwick, O. W. Brawley, et al. 2010. Effect of dutasteride on the risk of prostate cancer. *New England Journal of Medicine* 362:1192–1202.

Anstett, P. 2009. Canadians visit U.S. to get health care. *Detroit Free Press,* August 20, 2009. http://freep.com/article/20090820/BUSI NESS06/908200420/1319/.

Arnold, M. 1919. The scholar-gypsy. In *The Oxford book of English verse, 1250–1900,* ed. A. T. Quiller-Couch. Oxford: Clarendon.

Aspden, P., J. Wolcott, J. Bootman, and L. Cronenwett. 2006. *Preventing medication errors.* Washington, D.C.: National Academies Press. http://books.nap.edu/openbook.php?record_id=11623.

Association of American Medical Colleges. 2008. *U.S. Medical School Applicants and Students 1982–83 to 2007–08.* http://www.aamc.org /data/facts/charts1982to2007.pdf.

Bacon, F. 1605. *The advancement of learning.* London: Macmillan, 1873.

Bakalar, N. 2010. Analysis finds slant in articles on a diabetes drug, Avandia. *New York Times,* April 13, 2010, D5.

Banister, J. 2005. Manufacturing employment in China. *Bureau of Labor Statistics Monthly Labor Review* 128, no. 7:12–13.

Barnard, K., and C. Colón-Emeric. 2010. Extraskeletal effects of vitamin D in older adults: Cardiovascular disease, mortality, mood, and cognition. *American Journal of Geriatric Pharmacotherapy* 8:4–33.

Bartlett, J. 1992. *Bartlett's familiar quotations*, 16th ed. New York: Little, Brown.

Baumol, W. 1988. Price controls for medical services and the medical needs of the nation's elderly: Parts I and II. *Connecticut Medicine* 52:485–494, 542–551.

———. 1993. Social wants and dismal science: The curious case of the climbing costs of health and teaching. *Proceedings of the American Philosophical Society* 137:612–637.

———. 2002. *The free-market innovation machine: Analyzing the growth miracle of capitalism.* Princeton, N.J.: Princeton University Press.

———. 2010. *The microtheory of innovative entrepreneurship.* Princeton, N.J.: Princeton University Press.

Baumol, W., S. Batey Blackman, and E. Wolff. 1989. *Productivity and American leadership: The long view.* Cambridge, Mass.: MIT Press.

Baumol, W., and W. Bowen. 1966. *Performing arts: The economic dilemma.* New York: Twentieth Century Fund.

Beckman, H. 2010. Three degrees of separation. *Annals of Internal Medicine* 151:890–891.

Bendavid, Y., and J. Adams. 2009. "Asset Management" in Healthcare. *RFID Radio*, October 2009, episode 018. Academia RFID Center of Excellence. http://www.rfidradio.com/?p=29.

Berenson, G., and W. Srinivasan. 2010. Cardiovascular risk in young persons: Secondary or primordial prevention. *Annals of Internal Medicine* 153:202–203.

Berg, A. O., M. A. Baird, J. R. Botkin, 2009. National Institutes of Health State-of-the-Science Conference Statement: Family history and improving health. *Annals of Internal Medicine* 151:872–877.

Bertelli, A., and D. Das. 2009. Grapes, wines, resveratrol and heart health. *Journal of Cardiovascular Pharmacology* 54:468–476.

References

Berwick, D. 2009. Measuring physicians' quality and performance. *Journal of the American Medical Association* 302:2485–2486.

Bhattacharya, J., and N. Sood. 2004. Health insurance, obesity, and its economic costs. In *The economics of obesity: A report on the workshop held at USDA's Economic Research Service*, 21–24. Washington, D.C.: United States Department of Agriculture. http://www.ers.usda.gov/publications/efan04004/efan04004g.pdf.

Bjelland, O., and R. Wood. 2008. An inside view of IBM's "Innovation Jam." *MIT Sloan Management Review* 50:32–40.

Bleich, S., D. Cutler, A. Adams, et al. 2007. Impact of insurance and supply of health professionals on coverage of treatment for hypertension in Mexico: Population based study. *British Medical Journal* 335:875.

Bloom, D., and D. Canning. 2000. The health and wealth of nations. *Science* 287:1207.

Blumenthal, R., and E. Michos. 2009. The HALTS trial—halting atherosclerosis or halted too early? *New England Journal of Medicine* 361:2178–2180.

Boden, W. E. 2010. Ranolazine and its anti-ischemic effects: Revisiting an old mechanistic paradigm anew? *Journal of the American College of Cardiology* 56:943–945.

Boden, W. E., R. A. O'Rourke, K. K. Teo, et al. 2009. Impact of optimal medical therapy with or without percutaneous coronary intervention on long-term cardiovascular end points in patients with stable coronary artery disease (from the COURAGE Trial). *American Journal of Cardiology* 104:1–4.

Bogdanich, W. 2010. F.D.A. toughens process for radiation equipment. *New York Times*, April 8, 2010. http://www.nytimes.com/2010/04/09/health/policy/09radiation.html.

Bradford, D. 1969. Balance on unbalanced growth. *Zeitschrift fur Nationaliikonomie* 29:291–304.

Braunwald, E. 2009. Cardiology as a profession in 2020 and beyond. *ACCEL* (American College of Cardiology) 41-11, disc 2: track 1.

Broad, W., and D. Sanger. 2006. Restraints fray and risks grow as nuclear club gains members. *New York Times*, October 15, 2006. http://www.nytimes.com/2006/10/15/world/asia/15nuke.html.

Brownlee, S. 2007. *Overtreated: Why too much medicine is making us sicker and poorer.* New York: Bloomsbury.

Büchner, F. L., H. B. Beuno-de-Mesquita, M. M. Ros, et al. 2010. Variety in fruit and vegetable consumption and the risk of lung cancer in the European prospective investigation into cancer and nutrition. *Cancer, Epidemiology, Biomarkers, and Prevention* 19:2278–2286.

Buijsse, B., C. Weikert, D. Drogan, et al. 2010. Chocolate consumption in relation to blood pressure and risk of cardiovascular disease in German adults. *European Heart Journal* 31:1616–1623.

Bump, J. 2010. *The long road to universal health coverage: A century of lessons for development strategy.* http://www.rockefellerfoundation.org/uploads/files/23e4426f-cc44-4d98-ae81-ffa71c38e073-jesse.pdf.

Califf, R. M., R. A. Holman, J. J. McMurray, and S. M. Haffner. 2010. The nateglinide and valsartan in impaired glucose tolerance outcome research (NAVIGATOR) trial. Special topic presentation at the 59th annual scientific session of the American College of Cardiologists, Atlanta, March 14–16, 2010.

Canagee, E. J. 2010. Increasing morbidity of elective spinal stenosis surgery. *Journal of the American Medical Association* 303:1309–1310.

Cardwell, C., C. C. Abnet, M. M. Cantwell, and L. J. Murray. 2010. Exposure to oral bisphosphonates and risk of esophageal cancer. *Journal of the American Medical Association* 304:657–663.

Carroll, L. 1902. *Through the looking glass.* New York: Harper and Brothers.

Catlin, A., C. Cowan, M. Hartman, S. Heffler, National Health Expenditure Accounts Team. 2008. National health spending in 2006: A year of change for prescription drugs. *Health Affairs* 27:14–29.

Catone, J. 2007. Crowdsourcing: A million heads is better than one. *ReadWriteWeb*, March 22. http://www.readwriteweb.com/archives /crowdsourcing_million_heads.php.

Centers for Disease Control and Prevention. 2005. Reduction in central line-associated bloodstream infections among patients in intensive care units: Pennsylvania, April 2001–March 2005. *Morbidity and Mortality Weekly Report* 54:1013–1016.

———. 2008. Figure 8.1: Prevalence of Current Smoking among Adults Aged 18 Years and Over: United States, 1997–June 2008. *January-June 2008 National Health Interview Survey.* http://www .cdc.gov/nchs/data/nhis/earlyrelease/200812_08.pdf.

———. 2009. Number (in millions) of civilian/noninstitutionalized persons with diagnosed diabetes, United States, 1980–2007. *Diabetes Data and Trends.* http://www.cdc.gov/diabetes/statistics /prev/national/figpersons.htm.

———. 2010a. *Healthcare-associated infections: The burden.* http://www .cdc.gov/HAI/burden.html.

———. 2010b. Leading causes of death reports, 1999–2007. National Center for Injury Prevention and Control Web-Based Injury Statistics Query and Reporting System. http://webappa.cdc.gov /sasweb/ncipc/leadcaus10.html.

———. 2010c. Vital signs: State-specific obesity prevalence among adults—United States, 2009. *Morbidity and Mortality Weekly Report* 59. http://www.cdc.gov/mmwr/pdf/wk/mm59e0803.pdf.

Chernew, M., R. Hirth, and D. Cutler. 2009. Increased spending on health care: Long-term implications for the nation: projections show ever more personal income and economic resources shifting to health care. *Health Affairs* (Millwood) 28:1253–1255.

Chernichovsky, D., and S. Markowitz. 2004. Aging and aggregate costs of medical care: Conceptual and policy issues. *Health Economics* 13:543–562.

Chow, A., B. Goodman, J. Rooney, and C. Wyble. 2007. Engaging a corporate community to manage technology and embrace innovation. *IBM Systems Journal* 46, no. 4. http://www.research.ibm.com /journal/sj/464/chow.html.

Cloud, J. 2010. Why your DNA isn't your destiny. *Time* 175:49–53.

Cohen, J., P. Neumann, and M. Weinstein. 2008. Does preventive care save money? Health economics and the presidential candidates. *New England Journal of Medicine* 358:661–663.

Collier, P. 2007. *The bottom billion: Why the poorest countries are failing and what can be done about it.* Oxford: Oxford University Press.

Commission on Growth and Development. 2008. *The growth report: Strategies for sustained growth and inclusive development.* http://cgd.s3 .amazonaws.com/GrowthReportComplete.pdf.

Confederation of Indian Industry. 2007. *Innovate India: National innovation mission.* New Delhi: Confederation of Indian Industry and the India Development Foundation. http://business.outlook india.com/pdf/InnovateIndiaReportl.pdf.

Constant, A., S. Petersen, C. Mallory, and J. Major. 2011. *Research synthesis on cost drivers in the health sector and proposed policy options.* Ottawa: Canadian Health Services Research Foundation.

Cox, W. M., and R. Alm. 1997. Time well spent: The declining *real* cost of living in America. In *Time Well Spent: 1997 Annual Report,* 5–17. Dallas: Federal Reserve Bank of Dallas. http://dallasfed.org /fed/annual/1999p/ar97.pdf.

Damani, S., and E. Topol. 2007. Future use of genomics in coronary artery disease. *Journal of American College of Cardiology* 50:1933–1940.

Darwin, F., and A. Seward, eds. 1903. Letter 752, to A. Stephen Wilson, Down, March 5, 1879. In *More letters of Charles Darwin.* Vol. 2. London: John Murray.

Daviglus, M., C. C. Bell, W. Berrettini, et al. 2010. National Institutes of Health State of the Science Conference Statement: Preventing Alzheimer's disease and cognitive decline. *Annals of Internal Medicine* 153:176–181.

References

Dayo, R. A., S. K. Mirza, B. I. Martin, et al. 2010. Trends, major medical complications associated with surgery for lumbar spinal stenosis in older adults. *Journal of the American Medical Association* 303:1259–1265.

Devi, S. 2010. U.S. plans to boost number of medical schools. *Lancet* 375:792–793.

DeVol, R., and A. Bedroussian. 2007. *An unhealthy America: The economic burden of chronic disease—charting a new course to save lives and increase productivity and economic growth.* Santa Monica, Calif.: Milken Institute.

Dhruva, S., L. Bero, and R. Redberg. 2009. Strength of study evidence examined by the FDA in premarket approval of cardio-vascular devices. *Journal of the American Medical Association* 302:2679–2685.

Domcheck, S., T. M. Friebel, C. F. Singer, et al. 2010. Association of risk-reducing surgery in BRCA1 or BRCA2 mutation carriers with cancer risk and mortality. *Journal of the American Medical Association* 304:967–975.

Downs, J. R., M. Clearfield, S. Weis, et al. 1998. Primary prevention of acute coronary events with lovastatin in men and women with average cholesterol levels: Results of AFCAPS/TexCAPS (Air Force/Texas Coronary Atherosclerosis Prevention Study). *Journal of the American Medical Association* 279:1615–1622.

Editorial opinion: Bridgeport goes bankrupt. 1991. *Washington Post,* June 11, 1991, A20.

Editors of the *Annals of Internal Medicine.* 2010. Frustrations with hospitalist care: Need to improve transitions and communication. *Annals of Internal Medicine* 152:469.

Emanuel, E., and V. Fuchs. 2008. The perfect storm of overutilization. *Journal of the American Medical Association* 299:2789–2791.

Emerson, R. 1914. Uses of great men. In *The Oxford book of American essays,* ed. B. Matthews, no. ix. New York: Oxford University Press.

Ernst, M., and M. Moser. 2009. Use of diuretics in patients with hypertension. *New England Journal of Medicine* 361:2153–2164.

Escobar M., C. Griffin, and R. Shaw, eds. 2011. *The impact of health insurance on low- and middle-income countries.* Washington, D.C.: Brookings Institution Press.

Fagan, B. 2001. *The little ice age: How climate made history, 1300–1850.* New York: Basic Books.

Favus, M. 2010. Bisphosphonates for osteoporosis. *New England Journal of Medicine* 363:2027–2035.

Fazel, R., H. M. Krumholz, Y. Wang, et al. 2009. Exposure to low-dose ionizing radiation from medical imaging procedures. *New England Journal of Medicine* 361:849–857.

Feart, C., L. Samieri, and P. Barberger-Gateau. 2010. Mediterranean diet and cognitive function in older adults. *Clinical Nutrition and Metabolic Care* 13:14–18.

Federal Reserve Bank of Dallas. 1997. *Time Well Spent: 1997 Annual Report.* Dallas: Federal Reserve Bank of Dallas. http://dallasfed .org/fed/annual/1999p/ar97.pdf.

Feldman, T., E. Foster, D. D. Glower, et al. 2011. Percutaneous repair or surgery for mitral regurgitation. *New England Journal of Medicine* 364:1395–1406.

Ferenczi, E., P. Asaria, A. D. Hughes, et al. 2010. Can a statin neutralize the cardiovascular risk of unhealthy dietary choices? *American Journal of Cardiology* 106:587–592.

Flanagan, R. 2012. *The perilous life of symphony orchestras.* New Haven, Conn.: Yale University Press.

Flossmann, E., and P. Rothwell. 2007. Effect of aspirin on long-term risk of colorectal cancer: Consistent evidence from randomized and observational studies (British Doctors Aspirin Trial and the UK-TIA Aspirin Trial). *Lancet* 369:1603–1613.

Food and Agriculture Organization of the United Nations. 2006. FAOSTAT Online Statistical Service. Rome: Food and Agriculture Organization. http://faostat.fao.org.

Ford, E. S., U. A. Ajani, J. B. Croft, et al. 2007. Explaining the decrease in U.S. deaths from coronary disease, 1980–2000. *New England Journal of Medicine* 356:2388–2398.

Foubister, T., S. Thomson, E. Mossialos, and A. McGuire. 2006. *Private Medical Insurance in the United Kingdom.* Copenhagen: World Health Organization and European Observatory on Health Systems and Policies.

Fowler, F., P. Gallagher, D. Anthony, et al. 2008. Relationship between regional per capita medicare expenditures and patient perceptions of quality of care. *Journal of the American Medical Association* 299:2406–2412.

Frenk, J., E. González-Pier, O. Gómez-Dantés, et al. 2006. Health system reform in Mexico 1: Comprehensive reform to improve health system performance in Mexico. *Lancet* 368:1524–1534.

Freudenheim, M. 2010. The new landscape: Preparing more care of elderly. *New York Times*, June 28, 2010. http://www.nytimes.com /2010/06/29/health/29geri.html.

Fries, J. 1980. Aging, natural death, and the compression of morbidity. *New England Journal of Medicine* 303:130–135.

Fuchs, V. 2009. Eliminating "waste" in health care. *Journal of the American Medical Association* 302:2481–2482.

Garrett, L., M. Chowdhury, and A. Pablos-Méndez. 2009. All for universal health coverage. *Lancet* 374:1294–1299.

Gerber, Y., L. J. Rosen, U. Goldbourt, et al. 2009. Smoking status and long-term survival after first acute myocardial infarction. *Journal of the American College of Cardiology* 54:2382–2387.

Ginsberg, H., and N. Cushman. 2010. Effects of combination lipid therapy on cardiovascular events in type 2 diabetes mellitus; Effects of intensive blood pressure control on cardiovascular events in type 2 diabetes mellitus: The Action to Control Cardiovascular Risk in Diabetes (ACCORD) blood pressure trial. Special topic presentation at the 59th annual scientific session of the American College of Cardiologists, Atlanta, March 14–16, 2010.

Global Dialogue Center. 2006. Habitat Jam Exhibit. Global Dialogue Center Knowledge Gallery. http://www.globaldialoguecenter.com /exhibits/backbone/index.shtml.

Gottret, P., G. Schieber, and H. Waters, eds. 2008. *Good practices in health financing: Lessons from reforms in low- and middle-income countries.* Washington, D.C.: World Bank.

Gurría, A. 2009. Secretary-General speech for the launch of the Economic Outlook No. 86. November 19, 2009. Paris: Organisation for Economic Co-operation and Development. http://www.oecd .org/document/33/0,3343,en_2649_34109_44096033_1_1_1_1,00 .html.

Halfhill, T. 2006. Ambric's new parallel processor. *Microprocessor Report*, October 10. http://www.ambric.info/pdf/MPR_Ambric _Article_10-06_204101.pdf.

Harris, S. 2008. Graduates report higher debt, primary care interest. *AAMC Reporter*, December. https://www.aamc.org/newsroom /reporter/dec08/78966/dec08_graduates.html.

Hartman, M., A. Catlin, D. Lassman, et al. 2008. U.S. health spending by age, selected years through 2004. *Health Affairs* 27:w1–w12.

Hartwig, J. 2008. What drives health care expenditure? Baumol's model of "unbalanced growth" revisited. *Journal of Health Economics* 27:603–623.

Hawke, C. 2005. Canadian health care in crisis. *CBS News*, March 20, 2005. http://www.cbsnews.com/stories/2005/03/20/health /main681801.shtml.

Healthcare Cost and Utilization Project. 2007. *Healthcare cost and utilization project facts and figures: Statistics on hospital-based care in the United States, 2007.* Rockville, Md.: Agency for Healthcare Research and Quality.

HealthGrades. 2004. *Patient safety in American hospitals.* Denver, Colo.: HealthGrades. http://www.healthgrades.com/media /english/pdf/HG_Patient_Safety_Study_Final.pdf.

References

Hendee, W R., G. J. Becker, J. P. Borgstede, et al. 2010. Addressing overutilization in medical imaging. *Radiology* 257:240–245.

Himmelstein, D. U., E. Warren, E. Thorne, and S. Woolhandler. 2005. Illness and injury as contributors to bankruptcy. *Health Affairs*, February 2. http://content.healthaffairs.org/cgi/reprint/hlthaff.w5.63v1.

Hjortsberg, C. 2001. *National health accounts: Where are we today?* Stockholm: Swedish International Development Cooperation Agency. http://www.who.int/nha/docs/en/NHA_where_are_we_today.pdf.

Hoadley, J., J. Crowley, D. Bergman, and N. Kaye. 2006. *Understanding key features of the Drug Effectiveness Review Project (DERP) and lessons for state policy makers.* Portland, Maine: National Academy for State Health Policy. http://www.nashp.org/sites/default/files/medicaid_DERP.pdf.

Hochman, J., G. A. Lamas, C. E. Buller, et al. 2006. Coronary intervention for persistent occlusion after myocardial infarction (Occluded Artery Trial). *New England Journal of Medicine* 355:2395–2407.

Horn, F. 2002. Les paradoxes de la productivité dans la production des logiciels. In *Nouvelle économie des services et innovation*, ed. F. Djellal and F. Gallouj, 69–99. Paris: L'Harmattan.

Horowitz, H. 2008. The interpreter of facts. *Journal of the American Medical Association* 299:497–498.

Hsiao, W., and P. Heller. 2007. *What should macroeconomists know about health care policy? A primer.* IMF Working Paper WP/07/13. Washington, D.C.: International Monetary Fund.

Hu, S., C. Tang, Y. Liu, et al. 2008. Reform of how health care is paid for in China: Challenges and opportunities. *Lancet* 372:1846–1853.

Hubbard, S. 2010. Statins reduce gall stone risk. *Newsmax*, February 22.

Hughes, B., R. Kuhn, C. Mosca Peterson, et al. 2011. *Patterns of potential human progress: Improving global health: Forecasting the next 50 years.* Vol. 3. Boulder, Colo.: Paradigm.

IBM Corporation. 2005. HabitatJam. http://www.ibm.com/ibm /ideasfromibm/us/government/apr10/habitatjam.html.

———. 2006. InnovationJam. January 2006. http://www-03.ibm.com /press/us/en/pressrelease/20605.wss.

———. 2007a. The changing role of the CIO: From technology manager to chief innovator. http://www.ibm.com/ibm/ideas fromibm/us/cio/081307/index1.shtml.

———. 2007b. Vassar Brothers Medical Center adapts to healthcare challenges through mobile processes. February 20. ftp://ftp.soft-ware.ibm.com/software/solutions/pdfs/ODC00283-USEN-00.pdf.

———. 2010. Smarter farming: California's Sun World transforms produce business with IBM Technology. July 21. http://www-03 .ibm.com/press/us/en/pressrelease/32159.wss.

Immerwahr, J., and J. Johnson. 2009. *Squeeze play 2009: The public's views on college costs today.* San Jose, Calif.: National Center for Public Policy and Higher Education. http://www.highereducation .org/reports/squeeze_play_09/index.shtml.

International Labor Organization, Social Security Department. 2008. *Paper 1—Social health protection: An ILO strategy towards universal access to health care.* Geneva: International Labor Organization. http://www.ilo.org/public/english/protection/secsoc /downloads/policy/policy1e.pdf.

International Monetary Fund. 2008. World Economic Outlook Database. http://www.imf.org/external/pubs/ft/weo/2008/01 /weodata/index.aspx.

International Monetary Fund, and International Development Association. 2008. *Ghana: Joint IMF and World Bank debt sustainability analysis.* http://www.imf.org/external/pubs/ft/dsa/pdf /dsacr08344.pdf.

Janszky, I., K. J. Mukamal, R. Ljung, et al. 2009. Chocolate consumption and mortality following a first acute myocardial infarction: The Stockholm Heart Epidemiology Program. *Journal of International Medicine* 266:248–257.

References

Joint Learning Network for Universal Health Coverage. 2011. *Ghana: National health insurance scheme.* http://www.jointlearning network.org/content/national-health-insurance-scheme-nhis.

Jolly, P. 2004. Medical school tuition and young physician indebtedness. Washington, D.C.: Association of American Medical Colleges. https://services.aamc.org/publications/showfile.cfm ?file=version21.pdf&prd_id=102&prv_id=113&pdf_id=21.

Kahaner, L. 2008. *AK-47: The weapon that changed the face of war.* Hoboken, N.J.: John Wiley and Sons.

Katz, S., K. Cardiff, M. Pascali, et al. 2002. Phantoms in the snow: Canadians' use of health care services in the United States. *Health Affairs* 21, no. 3:19–31.

Kay, C. D., S. K. Gebauer, S. G. West, and P. M. Kris-Etherton. 2010. Pistachios increase serum antioxidants and lower serum oxidized-LDL in hypercholesterolemic adults. *Journal of Nutrition* 140:1093–1098.

Kehoe, B. 2007. Tracking IV pumps in real time. *Materials Management in Health Care* 16, no. 7:20–24.

Kelley, B., and R. Fabius. 2010. *A path to eliminating $3.6 trillion in wasteful healthcare spending.* Thomson Reuters White Paper. http://factsforhealthcare.com/reduce/.

Kelly, R. 2010. Diet and exercise in the management of hyperlipidemia. *American Family Physician* 81:1097–1102.

Kennel, K., M. Drake, and D. Hurley. 2010. Vitamin D deficiency in adults: When to test and how to treat. *Mayo Clinic Proceedings* 85:752–758.

Killip, T., and J. Kimball. 1967. Treatment of myocardial infarction in a coronary care unit: A two-year experience with 250 patients. *American Journal of Cardiology* 20:457–464.

Kim, J., and E. Rosenberg. 2011. The sum of the parts is greater than the whole: Reducing blood culture contamination. *Annals of Internal Medicine* 154:202–203.

Kimmel, K. C., and J. Sensmeier. 2002. *A technological approach to enhancing patient safety.* Healthcare Information and Management Systems Society White Paper. http://www.himss.org/content/files /whitepapers/patient_safety.pdf.

King, M. L., Jr. 1986. I see the promised land. In *A testament of hope: The essential writings and speeches of Martin Luther King Jr.*, ed. J. Washington, 279–286. New York: HarperCollins.

Kleiman, E. 1974. The determinants of national outlay on health. In *The economics of health and medical care*, ed. M. Perlman, 66–81. London: Macmillan.

Klevens, R. M., J. R. Edwards, C. L. Richards Jr., et al. 2007. Estimating health care-associated infections and deaths in U.S. hospitals, 2002. *Public Health Reports* 122:160–166.

Knox, R. 2010. The fading art of the physical exam. *NPR Morning Edition*, September 20. http://www.npr.org/templates/story/story .php?storyId=129931999.

Knudsen, A. B., I. Lansdorp-Vogelaar, C. M. Rutter, et al. 2010. Cost-effectiveness of computed tomographic colonography screening for colorectal cancer in the Medicare population. *Journal of the National Cancer Institute* 102:1238–1252.

Kohn, L., J. Corrigan, and M. Donaldson, eds. 2000. *To err is human: Building a safer health system.* Washington, D.C.: National Academies Press.

Kokkinos, P., J. Myers, C. Faselis, et al. 2010. Exercise capacity and mortality in older men: A 20-year follow-up study. *Circulation* 122:790–797.

Kostis, J. 2007. A new approach to primary prevention of cardiovascular disease. *American Journal of Medicine* 120:746–747.

Krishna, A. 2010. Who became poor, who escaped poverty, and why? Developing and using a retrospective methodology in five countries. *Journal of Policy Analysis and Management* 29: 351–372.

References

Kronzon, I., and C. Ruiz. 2010. Diagnosing patent foramen ovale: Too little or too much. *Journal of the American College of Cardiology—Cardiovascular Imaging* 3:349–350.

Lagomarsino, G., D. de Ferranti, A. Pablos-Méndez, et al. 2009. Public stewardship of mixed health systems. *Lancet* 374:1577–1578.

Laine, C., L. Goldman, J. Soukup, et al. 1993. The impact of a regulation restricting medical house staff working hours on the quality of patient care. *Journal of the American Medical Association* 269:374–378.

Lee, J. M., M. D. Robson, L. M. Yu, et al. 2009. Effects of high-dose modified-release nicotinic acid on atherosclerosis and vascular function: A randomized, placebo-controlled, magnetic resonance imaging study. *Journal of the American College of Cardiology* 54:1795–1796.

Lerner, B. 2006. A case that shook medicine. *Washington Post*, November 28. http://www.washingtonpost.com/wp-dyn/content/article/2006/11/24/AR2006112400985.html

Levinson, D. 2008. *Adverse events in hospitals: State reporting systems.* Department of Health and Human Services, Office of Inspector General, OEI-06-07-00471. http://oig.hhs.gov/oei/reports/oei-06-07-00471.pdf.

Levitt, S., and S. Dubner. 2005. *Freakonomics.* New York: HarperCollins.

Lifton, R. 2010. Individual genomes on the horizon. *New England Journal of Medicine* 362:1235–1236.

London, B., M. Michalec, H. Mehdi, et al. 2007. Mutation in glycerol-3-phosphate dehydrogenase 1–like gene (*GPD1-L*) decreases cardiac Na$^+$ current and causes inherited arrhythmias. *Circulation* 116:2260–2268.

Lu, C., M. Schneider, P. Gubbins, et al. 2010. Public financing of health in developing countries: A cross-national systematic analysis. *Lancet* 375:1375–1387.

MacReady, N. 2009. Skyrocketing costs of dialysis may require difficult decisions. *Medscape Medical News*, November 9. http://www.medscape.com/viewarticle/712019.

Maddison, A. 2001. *The world economy: A millennial perspective*. Paris: Organisation for Economic Co-operation and Development.

———. 2003. Table 8C: World Per Capita GDP, 20 Countries and Regional Averages, 1–2001 AD. *The world economy: Historical statistics*. Paris: Organisation for Economic Co-operation and Development.

———. 2007. *Contours of the world economy, 1–2030 A.D.* New York: Oxford University Press.

Malach, M., and Baumol, W. J. 2009. Opportunities for the cost reduction of medical care. *Journal of Community Health* 34:255–261.

———. 2010. Further opportunities for cost reduction of medical care. *Journal of Community Health* 35:561–571.

Malach, M., and P. Imperato. 2004. Depression and acute myocardial infarction. *Preventive Cardiology* 7, no. 2:83–90.

———. 2006. Acute myocardial infarction and acute coronary syndrome: Then and now (1950–2005). *Preventive Cardiology* 9:228–234.

Malach, M., and B. Rosenberg. 1958. Acute myocardial infarction in a city hospital: Clinical review of 264 cases. *American Journal of Cardiology* 1:682–693.

Manini, T. M., J. E. Everhart, K. V. Patel, et al. 2006. Daily activity energy expenditure and mortality among older adults. *Journal of the American Medical Association* 296:171–179.

Markowitz, S., and M. Bertagnolli. 2009. Molecular basis of colorectal cancer. *New England Journal of Medicine* 361:2449–2460.

Mattle, H., B. Meier, and R. Nedelichav. 2010. Prevention of stroke in patients with patent foramen ovale. *International Journal of Stroke* 5:92–102.

Mayo Clinic. 2010. Atrial fibrillation. *Bulletin of the Mayo Clinic*, May 7. http://www.mayoclinic.com/health/atrial-fibrillation/DS00291.

References

McKinsey and Company. 2010. *Catalyzing change: The system reform costs of universal health coverage.* New York: Rockefeller Foundation.

McPherson, R. 2010. Chromosome 9p21 and coronary artery disease. *New England Journal of Medicine* 362:1736–1737.

Meier, B. 2009. Medtronic links device for heart to 13 deaths. *New York Times,* March 13, 2009. http://www.nytimes.com/2009/03/14 /business/14device.html.

Menacker, F., and B. Hamilton. 2010. Recent trends in cesarean delivery in the United States. National Center for Health Statistics Data Brief 35. http://www.cdc.gov/nchs/data/databriefs/db35.pdf.

Mitrou, P. N., V. Kipnis, A. C. Thiébaut, et al. 2007. Mediterranean dietary pattern and prediction of all-cause mortality in a U.S. population: Results from the NIH-AARP Diet and Health Study. *Archives of Internal Medicine* 167:2461–2468.

Morgan, J., T. Ferris, and T. Lee. 2008. Options for slowing the growth of health care costs. *New England Journal of Medicine* 358:1509–1514.

Mostofsky, E., E. B. Levitan, A. Wolk, and M. A. Mittleman. 2010. Chocolate intake and incidence of heart failure: A population-based prospective study of middle-aged and elderly women. *Circulation: Heart Failure* 3:612–616.

Moynihan, D. P. 1993. *Baumol's disease: New York state and the federal FISC: XVII—fiscal year 1992.* Cambridge, Mass.: Traubman Center for State and Local Government, John F. Kennedy School of Government, Harvard University.

Murilo, C., C. Piatecki, and M. Saez. 1993. Health care expenditure and income in Europe. *Econometrics and Health Economics* 2:127–138.

Murray, C., R. Govindaraj, and P. Musgrove. 1994. National health expenditures: A global analysis. *Bulletin of the World Health Organization* 72:623–637.

Musgrove, P., R. Zeramdini, and G. Carrin. 2002. Basic patterns in national health expenditure. *Bulletin of the World Health Organization* 80:134–142.

References

Narayan, P. 2007. Do health expenditures catch up? Evidence from OECD countries. *Health Economics* 16:993–1008.

National Bureau of Statistics of China. 1978–2002. 4-5: Number of employed persons at year-end by sector. In *China statistical yearbook 2008*. http://www.stats.gov.cn/tjsj/ndsj/2008/indexeh.htm.

——. 2008. Table 6: Number of employed persons in units by sector. *Communiqué on Major Data of the Second National Economic Census (No. 1)*, December 25. http://www.stats.gov.cn/was40/gjtjj_en_detail.jsp?searchword=10433.1&channelid=9528&record=1.

National Cancer Institute. 2009. BRCA1 and BRCA2: Cancer risk and genetic testing. *NCI Fact Sheet*, May 29. http://www.cancer.gov/cancertopics/factsheet/Risk/BRCA.

National Center for Education Statistics. 2010. Total tuition, room and board rates charged for full-time students in degree-granting institutions, by type and control of institution: Selected years, 1980–81 to 2008–09. In *Digest of education statistics, 2009*. Washington, D.C.: U.S. Department of Education. http://nces.ed.gov/fastfacts/display.asp?id=76.

National Center for Public Policy and Higher Education. 2008. *Measuring up 2008: The national report card on higher education*. San Jose, Calif.: National Center for Public Policy and Higher Education. http://measuringup2008.highereducation.org/print/NCP-PHEMUNationalRpt.pdf.

National Heart, Lung, and Blood Institute. 2007. *Morbidity and mortality: 2007 chart book on cardiovascular, lung, and blood diseases.* Bethesda, Md.: National Institutes of Health. http://www.nhlbi.nih.gov/resources/ docs/07-chtbk.pdf.

National Practitioner Data Bank. 2006. *2006 annual report*. http://www.npdb-hipdb.hrsa.gov/pubs/stats/2006_NPDB_Annual_Report.pdf.

Newhouse, J. 1977. Medical care expenditure: A cross-national survey. *Journal of Human Resources* 12:115–125.

———. 1992. Medical care costs: How much welfare loss? *Journal of Economic Perspectives* 6:3–21.

Nordhaus, W. 2008. Baumol's diseases: A macroeconomic perspective. *B. E. Journal of Macroeconomics* 8: article 9.

North, D. 1990. *Institutions, institutional change and economic performance.* Cambridge, U.K.: Cambridge University Press.

North, D., and R. Thomas. 1973. *The rise of the Western world: A new economic history.* Cambridge, U.K.: Cambridge University Press.

Notestein, F. 1945. Population: The long view. In *Food for the world*, ed. T. Schultz, 37–57. Chicago: University of Chicago Press.

Oken, B. 2008. Placebo effects: Clinical aspects and neurobiology. *Brain* 131:2812–2823.

Okie, S. 2010. Teaching physicians the price of care. *New York Times*, May 4, 2010, D5.

Omran, A. 1971. The epidemiologic transition: A theory of the epidemiology of population change. *Milbank Memorial Fund Quarterly* 29:509–538. http://www2.goldmansachs.com/ideas /brics/book/99-dreaming.pdf.

O'Neill, J., D. Wilson, R. Purushothaman, and A. Stupnytska. 2005. *How solid are the BRICs*, Appendix 4. The Goldman Sachs Group, Global Economics Paper 134. http://www2.goldmansachs.com /hkchina/insight/research/pdf/BRICs_3_12-1-05.pdf.

Organisation for Economic Co-operation and Development. 2007. Health spending and resources. In *OECD in figures 2007.* Paris: Organisation for Economic Co-operation and Development.

———. 2009. Practising physicians: Density per 1,000 population (United States, 1993–2007). In *Health care resources.* http://stats .oecd.org.

Organisation for Economic Co-operation and Development, and Korea Policy Centre. 2009. Key findings: China. In *Society at a glance—Asia/Pacific edition.* http://www.oecd.org/dataoecd/27/43 /43464649.pdf.

Original Equipment Suppliers Association. 2007. Automotive Supplier Jam. http://www.oesa.org/pdf/ASJFinalReport.pdf.

Orszag, P., and P. Ellis. 2007. The challenge of rising health costs: A view from the Congressional Budget Office. *New England Journal of Medicine* 357:1793–1795.

Oulton, N. 2001. Must the growth rate decline? Baumol's unbalanced growth revisited. *Oxford Economic Papers* 53:605–627.

Parekh, A., and Barton, M. 2010. The challenge of multiple comorbidity for the U.S. health care system. *Journal of the American Medical Association* 303:1303–1304.

Parker, W., M. S. Broder, E. Chang, et al. 2009. Ovarian conservation at the time of hysterectomy and long-term health outcomes in the Nurses' Health Study. *Obstetrics and Gynecology* 113:1027–1037.

Parson, E. 2007. The Big One: A review of Richard Posner's *Catastrophe: Risk and response*. *Journal of Economic Literature* 5:147–213.

Partnership for Prevention. 2007. *Preventive care: A national profile on use, disparities, and health benefits*. http://www.prevent.org /images/stories/2007/ncpp/ncpp%20preventive%20care%20report .pdf.

Patel, M., E. D. Peterson, D. Dai, et al. 2010. Low diagnostic yield of elective coronary angiography. *New England Journal of Medicine* 362:886–895.

Phillips, R., and J. Andrieni. 2007. Translational patient care: A new model for inpatient care in the twenty-first century. *Archives of Internal Medicine* 167:2025–2026.

Pigou, A. 1912. *The economics of welfare*. London: Macmillan.

Pletcher, M., K. Bibbins-Domingo, K. Liu, et al. 2010. Nonoptimal lipids commonly present in young adults and coronary calcium later in life: The CARDIA (Coronary Artery Risk Development in Young Adults) study. *Annals of Internal Medicine* 153:137–146.

Pollak, M. 2010. Metformin and other biguanides in oncology: Advancing the research agenda. *Cancer Prevention Research* 3:1060–1065.

Poon, E., C. Keohane, and C. Yoon. 2010. Effect of bar-code and electronic-medication on the safety of medication administration. *New England Journal of Medicine* 362:1698–1707.

Posner, R. 2004. *Catastrophe: Risk and response.* New York: Oxford University Press.

Prestowitz, C. 2010. *The betrayal of American prosperity.* New York: Free Press.

Prewitt, R., V. Bochkarev, C. McBride, et al. 2008. The patterns and costs of the Da Vinci Robotic Surgery System in a large academic institution. *Journal of Robotic Surgery* 2:17–20.

Prodanovich, S., R. S. Kirsner, J. D. Kravetz, et al. 2009. Association of psoriasis with coronary artery, cerebrovascular, and peripheral vascular diseases and mortality. *Archives of Dermatology* 145:700–703.

Rannan-Eliya, R. 2008. *National health accounts estimation methods: Household out-of-pocket spending in private expenditure.* Geneva: World Health Organisation/National Health Accounts Unit. http://www.who.int/nha/methods/oops_paper_ravi.pdf.

Ray, K. K., S. R. Seshasai, S. Wijesuriya, et al. 2009. Effects of intensive control of glucose on cardiovascular outcomes and in patients with diabetes mellitus. *Lancet* 373:1765–1772.

Reddy, S., V. Patel, P. Jha, et al. 2011. Towards achievement of universal health care in India by 2020: A call to action. *Lancet* 377:760–768.

Redman, J. B., A. G. Bertoni, S. Connelly, et al. 2010. Effect of the Look AHEAD study intervention on medication use and related cost to treat cardiovascular disease risk factors in individuals with type 2 diabetes. *Diabetes Care* 33:1153–1158.

Reinhardt, U. 2007. What doctors make and why. Letter to the editor. *New York Times*, August 5, 2007, 9.

Ridker, P. M., E. Danielson, F. A. Fonseca, et al. 2008. Rosuvastatin to prevent vascular events in men and women with an elevated C-reactive protein. *New England Journal of Medicine* 359:2195–2207.

Rodés-Cabau, J., J. C. Tardif, M. Cossette, et al. 2009. Acute effects of statin therapy on coronary atherosclerosis following an acute coronary syndrome. *American Journal of Cardiology* 104:750–757.

Rodwin, M., H. Chang, and J. Clausen. 2006. Malpractice premiums and physicians' income: Perceptions of a crisis conflict with empirical evidence. *Health Affairs* 25:750–758.

Rosen, W. 2010. *The most powerful idea in the world.* New York: Random House.

Rossouw, J. E., G. L. Anderson, R. L. Prentice, et al. 2002. Risks and benefits of estrogen plus progestin in healthy postmenopausal women: Principal results from the Women's Health Initiative randomized controlled trial. *Journal of the American Medical Association* 288:321–333.

Rubalcaba, L., and H. Kox. 2007. *Business services in European economic growth.* Houndmills, U.K.: Palgrave Macmillan.

Rummler, G., and A. Brache. 1995. *Improving performance: How to manage the white space in the organization chart.* San Francisco: Jossey-Bass.

Ryan, P. 1992. Unbalanced growth and fiscal restriction: Public spending on higher education in advanced economies since 1970. *Structural Change and Economic Dynamics* 3:261–288.

Saihara, K., S. Hamasaki, S. Ishida, et al. 2010. Enjoying hobbies is related to desirable cardiovascular effects. *Heart and Vessels* 25, no. 2:113–120.

Sanford, L. 2005. *Corporate culture is the key to unlocking innovation and growth.* IBM Corporate Responsibility Report: 1–2. IBM Corporation. http://www.ibm.com/ibm/environment/annual/ibm_crr _061505.pdf.

Sasaki, H. 2007. The rise of service employment and its impact on aggregate productivity growth. *Structural Change and Economic Dynamics* 18:438–459.

Satava, R. M. 2003. Biomedical, ethical, and moral issues being forced by advanced medical technologies. *Proceedings of the American Philosophical Society* 147:246–258.

Saul, S. 2010. Cancer errors may increase with early test. *New York Times*, July 20, 2010, A1, A10.

Schellekens, O., M. Lindner, J. Lange, and J. van der Gaag. 2007. *A new paradigm for increased access to healthcare in Africa.* Washington, D.C.: International Finance Corporation.

Schneeweiss, S., J. D. Seeger, J. Landon, and A. M. Walker. 2008. Aprotinin during coronary-artery bypass grafting and risk of death. *New England Journal of Medicine* 358:771–783.

Schumpeter, J. A. 1936. *The theory of economic development.* 1911. Trans. Redvers Opie. Cambridge: Harvard University Press.

Seshadri, S., A. L. Fitzpatrick, M. A. Ikram, et al. 2010. Genome-wide analysis of genetic loci associated with Alzheimer's disease. *New England Journal of Medicine* 303:1832–1840.

Shao, Y. H., P. C. Albertsen, C. B. Roberts, et al. 2010. Risk profiles and treatment patterns among men diagnosed as having prostate cancer and a prostate-specific antigen level below 4.0 ng/mL. *Archives of Internal Medicine* 170:1256–1261.

Shaw, A. D., M. Stafford-Smith, W. D. White, et al. 2008. The effect of aprotinin on outcome after coronary-artery bypass grafting. *New England Journal of Medicine* 358:784–793.

Shu, X. O., Y. Zheng, H. Cai, et al. 2009. Soy food intake and breast cancer survival. *Journal of the American Medical Association* 302:2437–2443.

Singer, N. 2009. Slipstream: Seeking a shorter path to new drugs. *New York Times*, November 14, 2009. http://www.nytimes.com/2009/11/15/business/15stream.html.

References

Smith-Spangler, C. M., J. L. Juusola, E. A. Enns, et al. 2010. Population strategies to decrease sodium intake and the burden of cardiovascular disease. *Annals of Internal Medicine* 152:481–487, W170–173.

Snyder, T., S. Dillow, and C. Hoffman. 2009. *Digest of Education Statistics 2008*. NCES 2009-020. Washington, D.C.: U.S. Department of Education, National Center for Education Statistics, Institute of Education Sciences.

Speth, J. 2008. *The bridge at the edge of the world: Capitalism, the environment, and crossing from crisis to sustainability*. New Haven, Conn.: Yale University Press.

Stallybrass, P. 2006. Benjamin Franklin: Printed corrections and erasable writing. *Proceedings of the American Philosophical Society* 150:553–567.

Stampfer, M. J., W. C. Willett, G. A. Colditz, et al. 1985. A prospective study of postmenopausal estrogen therapy and coronary heart disease. *New England Journal of Medicine* 313:1044–1049.

Stetka, B. 2010. Unintentional drug poisoning deaths: A national epidemic. *Medscape Psychiatry and Mental Health*, June 28, 2010. http://www.medscape.com/viewarticle/724186.

Stewart, J. H., A. G. Bertoni, J. L. Staten, et al. 2007. Participation in surgical oncology clinical trials: Gender-, race/ethnicity-, and age-based disparities. *Annals of Surgical Oncology* 14:3328–3334.

Stone, P., B. R. Chaitman, K. Stocke, et al. 2010. The anti-ischemic mechanism of action of Ranolazine in stable ischemic heart disease. *Journal of the American College of Cardiology* 56:934–942.

Stueve, A., and L. O'Donnell. 2007. Continued smoking and smoking cessation among urban young adult women: Findings from the Reach for Health Longitudinal Study. *American Journal of Public Health* 97:1408–1411.

Summers, R. 1985. Services in the international economy. In *Managing the service economy*, ed. R. P. Inman, 27–48. Cambridge, U.K.: Cambridge University Press.

References

Talajic, M., P. Khairy, S. Levesque, et al. 2010. Maintenance of sinus rhythm and survival in patients with heart failure and atrial fibrillation. *Journal of the American College of Cardiology* 55:1796–1802.

Taylor, A. J., T. C. Villines, E. J. Stanek, et al. 2009. Extended-release niacin or ezetimibe and carotid intima-media thickness. *New England Journal of Medicine* 361:2113–2122.

Taylor, M. C. 2010. Academic bankruptcy. *New York Times*, August 14, 2010. http://www.nytimes.com/2010/08/15/opinion/15taylor.html.

Thomas, J., E. Ziller, and D. Thayer. 2010. Low costs of defensive medicine, small savings from tort reform. *Health Affairs* (Millwood) 29:1578–1584.

Ting, P., T. S. Chua, A. Wong, et al. 2007. Trends in mortality from acute myocardial infarction in the coronary care unit. *Annals of the Academy of Medicine, Singapore* 36:974–979.

Traynor, K. 2004. FDA to require bar coding of most pharmaceuticals by mid-2006. *American Journal of Health-System Pharmacy* 61:644–645.

Triplett, J., and B. Bosworth. 2003. Productivity measurement issues in services industries: Baumol's disease has been cured. *Federal Reserve Bank of New York Economic Policy Review* 9, no. 3:23–33.

Truffer, C. J., S. Keehan, S. Smith, et al. 2010. Health spending projections through 2019: The recession's impact continues. *Health Affairs* 29:1–8.

Tsimikas, S. 2009. High-dose statins prior to percutaneous coronary intervention. *Journal of the American College of Cardiology* 54:2164–2166.

Uchitelle, L. 2009. When, oh when, will help be wanted? Jobs lost and gained during the recession: Percent employment change, Dec. 2007 through June 2009. *New York Times*, July 19, 2009. http://www.nytimes.com/2009/07/19/weekinreview/19uchitelle.html.

United Nations General Assembly. 2010. High level plenary meeting on MDGs outcome document. Resolution of the 65th Session of the General Assembly of the United Nations. October 19, 2010. http://www.un.org/en/mdg/summit2010/pdf/outcome_docu mentN1051260.pdf.

United Nations Health Partners Group in China. 2005. *A health situation assessment of the People's Republic of China.* 37: 42–43. Beijing: United Nations Health Partners Group in China.

U.S. Bureau of Labor Statistics. 1979–2009a. Labor force statistics. *Current Population Survey.* http://data.bls.gov:8080/PDQ/outside .jsp?survey=ln.

———. 1979–2009b. Workforce statistics. *Industries at a Glance: Professional and Business Services.* http://www.bls.gov/iag/tgs/iag60 .htm.

———. 2008a. Occupational Employment Statistics Survey. May 2008. http://data.bls.gov/oes/search.jsp.

———. 2008b. Table B-1: Employees on nonfarm payrolls by industry sector and selected industry detail (manufacturing industry). *Current Employment Statistics (National).* http://www.bls.gov/ webapps/legacy/cesbtab1.htm.

———. 2009a. Funeral expenses consumer price index. *All Urban Consumers (Current Series) Database.* http://data.bls.gov/PDQ /outside.jsp?survey=cu.

———. 2009b. Funeral homes and funeral services: All worker productivity index. *National Industry Productivity and Costs Database.* http://data.bls.gov/PDQ/outside.jsp?survey=ip.

———. 2009c. Legal services consumer price index. *All Urban Consumers (Current Series) Database.* http://data.bls.gov/PDQ /outside.jsp?survey=cu.

———. 2009d. Offices of physicians: Employment, hours, and earnings. *National Earnings Database: Current Employment Statistics Survey.* http://www.bls.gov/data/#wages.

———. 2009e. *Productivity change in the manufacturing sector, 1987–2008.* ftp://ftp.bls.gov/pub/special.requests/opt/lpr/mfgbar data.txt.

———. 2009f. *Productivity change in the nonfarm business sector, 1947–2008.* ftp://ftp.bls.gov/pub/special.requests/opt/lpr/mfgbar data.txt.

U.S. Renal Data System. 2011. *USRDS 2009 annual data report: Atlas of chronic kidney disease and end-stage renal disease in the United States.* Bethesda, Md.: National Institutes of Health, National Institute of Diabetes and Digestive and Kidney Diseases. http://www.usrds .org/reference.aspx.

Van der Gaag, J., and V. Štimac. 2008a. *Towards a new paradigm for health sector development.* Amsterdam Institute for International Development. http://www.rockefellerfoundation.org/uploads/files /9b109f8d-0509–49fc-9d0c-baa7ac0f9f84–3-van-der.pdf.

Van der Gaag, J., and V. Štimac. 2008b. *Towards a new paradigm for health sector reform: Results for development institute.* Mimeograph.

Van Gelder, I. C., H. F. Groenveld, H. J. Crijns, et al. 2010. Lenient versus strict rate control in patients with atrial fibrillation. *New England Journal of Medicine* 362:1363–1373.

Varma, N., A. E. Epstein, A. Irimpen, et al. 2010. Efficacy and safety of automatic remote monitoring for implantable cardioverter-defibrillator follow-up: The Lumos-T safely reduces routine office device follow-up (TRUST) trial. *Circulation* 122:325–332.

Veblen, T. 1899. *The theory of the leisure class: An economic study of institutions.* London: Allen and Unwin, 1924.

Voora, D., S. H. Shah, I. Spasojevic, et al. 2009. The SLCO1B1*5 genetic variant is associated with statin-induced side effects. *Journal of the American College of Cardiology* 54:1609–1616.

Wang, H., T. Xu, and J. Xu. 2007. Factors contributing to high costs and inequality in China's health care system. *Journal of the American Medical Association* 298:1928–1930.

Warren, M. S., J. K. Salmon, D. J. Becker, et al. 1997. Pentium Pro inside: I. A treecode at 430 gigaflops on ASCI red, II. Price/performance of $50/Mflop on Loki and Hyglac. International Conference for High Performance Computing Networking,

Storage, and Analysis, SC97 Technical Paper. http://loki-www.lanl
.gov/papers/sc97/.

Welton, J., M. Decker, J. Adam, and L. Zone-Smith. 2006. How far
do nurses walk? *Medsurg Nursing* 15:213–216.

Wilson, B., N. Quereshi, P. Santaguida, et al. 2009. Systematic
review: Family history in risk assessment for common diseases.
Annals of Internal Medicine 151:878–885.

Wilson, D. 2010. Mistakes chronicled on Medicare patients. *New
York Times*, November 16, 2010, B3.

World Economic Outlook. 2009. *Crisis and recovery*. Washington,
D.C.: International Monetary Fund.

World Health Organization. 2001. *National health accounts—Where
are we today?* Issue paper, document 6, WHO Health Division.
http://www.who.int/nha/docs/en/NHA_where_are_we_today.pdf.

———. 2009. World Health Organization Statistical Information
System. http://apps.who.int/whosis/database/core/core_select.cfm.

———. 2010a. *Health systems financing: The path to universal coverage.*
Geneva: WHO Press. http://www.who.int/whr/2010/whr10_en.pdf.

———. 2010b. *World health statistics 2010.* Geneva: WHO Press.
http://www.who.int/whosis/whostat/2010/en/index.html.

Xu, K., C. Evans, G. Carrin, et al. 2007. Protecting households from
catastrophic health spending. *Health Affairs* 26:972–983.

Yan, L., and E. Spitznagel. 2009. Soy consumption and prostate
cancer risk in men: A revisit of a meta-analysis. *American Journal of
Clinical Nutrition* 89:1–9.

Yong, P., and L. Olsen. 2010. The healthcare imperative: Lowering
costs and improving outcomes: Brief summary of a workshop.
Washington, D.C.: National Academies Press.

Yu, C. M., J. Y. Chan, Q. Zhang, et al. 2009. Biventricular pacing in
patients with bradycardia and normal ejection fraction. *New
England Journal of Medicine* 361:2123–2134.

About the Authors

WILLIAM J. BAUMOL (PH.D.) is the Harold Price Professor of Entrepreneurship and the academic director of the Berkley Center for Entrepreneurship and Innovation, New York University; and is a senior economist and professor emeritus at Princeton University.

DAVID DE FERRANTI (PH.D.) is the president and founder of the Results for Development Institute.

MONTE MALACH (M.D., M.A.C.P., F.A.C.C.) is a clinical professor of medicine at New York University's Langone Medical Center and School of Medicine; and a clinical professor of medicine at State University of New York Downstate Medical Center.

ARIEL PABLOS-MÉNDEZ (M.D., M.P.H.) is the assistant administrator for global health at the U.S. Agency for International Development. He was previously the managing director at the Rockefeller

Foundation and a professor of clinical medicine and clinical epidemiology at the College of Physicians and Surgeons and Mailman School of Public Health, Columbia University.

HILARY TABISH (M.P.H.) is an independent consultant working with the Rockefeller Foundation.

LILIAN GOMORY WU (PH.D.) is the global university programs executive at IBM.

Index

Abel-Smith, Brian, 108
Afghanistan, 71
Africa, 100, 102
aging populations, 98, 184n2
agriculture: declining real costs in, 117–119; increasing productivity in, 128–130
AK-47 rifles, 69, 70
alendronate, 159
Alzheimer's disease, 163
angina, 164–165
angioplasty, 168
animation technology, 197n16
anticoagulants, 203n50
aprotinin, 157
arms race, 55–56
Arnold, Matthew, 3
arteriosclerosis, 172
Asia, 102

aspirin, 168–169
assault rifles, 69, 70
asymptotically stagnant sector, 112–115
atrial fibrillation, 165, 203n50
automatic teller machines (ATMs), 39
automation, xvii, 23, 39–40
automobile industry, 20–21, 23–25, 72
automobile insurance, 38, 41
automobile repair, 37–38, 41, 186n6
Avnet, 126–128

Bacon, Francis, 94
bar code technology, 144–145
Baumol's disease. See cost disease
Belgium, 41

benefits, versus costs, 84–86, 91–93
Bosworth, Barry, 86
Bowen, William, xix, 112
Bowen's curse. *See* cost disease
brain drain, 107
Braunwald, Eugene, 175
Brazil, 100
breast cancer, 160, 163, 171, 203n41
BRIC nations, 100. *See also specific countries*
Brugada syndrome, 163
Burgoyne, John, 125
business services: case studies, 126–137; expansion of, 123–124; in health care, 141–153; innovation and, 130–137; productivity growth and, 120–137, 149–150; progressive-sector, 124–126
bypass surgery, 164

Canada, 11, 12, 62
cap and trade, 75, 191n7
cardiomyopathy, 171
catastrophic health expenditures, 107
Cell Broadband Engine chip, 131
central line infections, 151–153, 199n15, 200n16
cervical cancer vaccine, 163–164
cesarean births, 159, 201n19
Channel Connection Web portal, 126–128

China: GDP per capita, 29–30, 45–46, 187n3; health spending in, 100; innovation in ancient, 57; manufacturing in, 81, 120, 196n6; productivity growth in, 46; real GDP growth, 47; universal health coverage in, 104
chocolate, 171
cholesterol-lowering medications, 160–161, 167–168, 203n63
climate change, xx, 66, 71–73
clinical trials, 157–158
clopidogrel, 168
collaborative innovation, 130–131
colleges, employee wages in, 11, 13
college tuition: increases in, 3–9, 77–78
colon cancer, 163, 168
commodities: cost of producing, xviii, 14; declining labor costs of, 48–50; military, 69–71; prices of, 15, 19, 116–117, 196n1
comorbidity, 169
competition, oligopolistic, 55–56
computed tomography (CT) angiography, 160, 202n23
computers: business services and, 123; declining prices of, 19, 49–50, 117; used in research, 112, 114
conspicuous waste, 39

consumer price index (CPI), 6–9, 29, 38, 116

coronary care units, 156, 200n3

coronary heart disease, 163, 164, 167–168, 171–172, 175

cost controls, 62, 64–65

cost disease: causes of, 16–32; concept of, xvii–xix, 3; constraining, 73–76; declining-cost aspect of, 116–117, 137; evidence of, 28–29; explanation of, 19–22; future of, 31–32; global health and, 94–108; hybrid industries and, 111–115; impacts of, 43–44, 53, 59–66; labor allocation and, 80–83; misunderstandings concerning, 77–93; persistence of, 16, 22–24; productivity growth as source of, 5; threats from, 69–76

costs: versus benefits, 84–86, 91–93; calculating changes in real, 14–15; decreases in, 48–50, 70, 72; real versus nominal, 13–14

cost-saving productivity growth, 83

CPI. *See* consumer price index (CPI)

cross-country comparison: of educational costs, 9–10; of health-care costs, 9–12

crowdsourcing, 131–133

data analytics, 128–130

da Vinci Robotic System, 88–89

declining prices, xx, 48–50, 74, 82, 116–117

defensive medicine, 172, 205n100

dementia, 171

demographic changes, 100

Denmark, 9, 10

depression, 169

developing countries, health spending in, 100–104, 107, 194n56

diabetes, 161, 167, 169, 170

diagnostic procedures, 175–176

disease comorbidity, 169

disease prevention, 166–170, 177

disposable products, 36–38

doctors. *See* physicians

domestic help, 35, 42, 186n2, 186n3

Drayton, William, 191n8

drug errors, 169–170

drug testing, 157–158, 166, 201n7

drug therapies, 164–165

ductal carcinoma in situ (DCIS), 160

dutasteride, 166

early adopters, 134–136

economic growth, 45–47, 82–83, 99–100

economic transition of health, 99–108

education: access to, 42; affordability of, xviii–xx, 33, 42,
50–55, 67–68, 119, 181;
demand for, 42; global
comparison of costs, 9–10;
increasing costs of, xx, xxi,
3–9, 61; labor productivity in,
21; medical, 173–175, 177–178,
185n6, 205n102; percent
enrolled in postsecondary, 41;
quality versus costs in, 85;
spending on, 189n24
electronic products, declining
prices of, 49–50
elevator operators, 39
emerging economies,
102–104
emissions taxes, 75
entrepreneurship: in China, 46;
innovation and, 56–58;
institutions and, 189n22;
productivity growth and,
29–32
environmental destruction,
71–74
environmental policy, 74–75
epigenetics, 162; epigenomes,
162, 202n33
error reduction, in health care,
143–145
Europe: business services sector
in, 124; health-care systems
in, 155
exercise, 172
ezetimibe, 160

financial measures, of manufacturing output, 79–80, 92
first law of health economics,
95–100, 108
fish consumption, 171
Flanagan, Robert, 87
Food and Drug Administration
(FDA), 145, 201n7
food costs, 48
fossil fuels, 72
France, 41
Franklin, Benjamin, 125
free markets, 55, 58
funeral services, 28
future scenarios, 180–182

Galbraith, John Kenneth, 65
general welfare, 114–115
genetic information, 162–163
geriatricians, 169
Germany, 10, 11, 12, 41
Ghana, 103
global health, 94–108
Global Innovation Jam, 132
government intervention, 60–63,
180
government services: decline in
quality of, 33–34; funding of,
44; increase in, as percentage
of GDP, 63–64
Grant, Ulysses S., 71
Great Recession, 100
greenhouse gases, 72
gross domestic product (GDP):
health-care costs as percent-

age of, 51–52; health spending
and, 95–99, 108; manufacturing share of, 78; per capita,
29–30, 45–46, 52, 53, 100,
187n3, 188n13; public sector
share of, 63–64
growth rates: of cost increases,
5–6, 155; overall economy, 82;
real prices, 6

Habitat Jam, 132–133
health, economic transition of.
See economic transition of
health
health care: affordability of,
xviii–xxx, 33, 42, 50–55,
67–68, 119, 181; automation
in, 40; business services in,
141–153; cost controls in, 62;
demand for, 42, 98, 99; global,
94–108; inequities in, 101;
innovation in, 87–93, 144–153,
176–177; poor and uninsured
and, 59–60; productivity
growth in, 142, 149–153;
quality-adjusted productivity
in, 86–87; quality advances in,
87–93; quality and access to,
42; quality versus costs in, 85;
share of spending devoted to,
51–53
health-care costs: causes of
rising, 12, 17–18, 98–99;
efforts to contain, 66–67, 74;
global comparison of, 9–12;

increases in, xviii–xxi, 3–9,
19, 61, 66, 87, 92–93; misunderstandings concerning,
62–63; opportunities for
cutting, 92, 141–179; as
percentage of GDP, 51–52; in
U.S., 5–11, 99, 155
health-care workers, wages of,
10–11, 13, 18
health economics, first law of.
See first law of health economics
health insurance: national,
102–104; reform of, 175–179
health spending: in developing
countries, 100–104, 107,
194n56; drivers of rise of,
98–99; government, 97;
increasing, 100; per capita, 11,
12, 95–98, 108; private, 97–98,
102, 104; unnecessary, 143; in
U.S., 155, 184n3, 187n13
heart attack, 156, 164, 168, 169,
171, 172, 200n3, 203n48
high blood pressure, 161
higher education: increasing cost
of, 3–9, 77–78; spending,
189n24
high-income countries, 104,
107–108
hormone replacement therapy,
158–159
hospital-acquired infections,
151–153, 199n15, 200n16,
200n18

hospitalists, 206n106
hospitals: business services in, 141–153; consortium of, 151, 153
hospital services, increasing costs of, 7–8, 77–78
household appliances, 117
household tasks, 35, 42
hybrid industries, 111–115
hysterectomies, 159

IBM, 127–128, 131–136, 198n27
implantable cardioverter-defibrillator (ICD), 165, 203n53
income per capita, 41, 53
incremental innovation, 133–134
India, 71, 100, 104
Industrial Revolution, xvii, 5, 29–30, 31, 46
infant mortality, 184n3
inflation, xvii, xviii, 4; price, 6, 26; rate of, 19, 137
informed consent, 172
innovation: in agriculture, 118; business services and, 130–137; collaborative, 130–131; crowdsourcing model for, 131–133; decline in, 181–182; definition of, 197n19; early adopters and, 134–136; entrepreneurship and, 56–58; in health care, 87–93, 144–153, 176–177; incremental, 133–134; investment in,

55–56; labor-saving, 39–40; productivity growth and, 29–32, 46, 67; rising cost of, 114
Innovation Hubs, 198n27
institutions, 189n22
insulin resistance, 163
Internet, 123, 182
investment, in research and development, 55–56
Iran, 71
Iraq, 71
Italian Renaissance, 45–46
Italy: education spending, 10; GDP per capita, 29–30, 45–46; real GDP growth, 47

Jams, 131–133
Japan: education spending, 10; health spending per capita, 11, 12; manufacturing in, 81, 120
job losses, in manufacturing, 24, 81, 119–120

Kahaner, Larry, 69
kidney dialysis, 89–90
King, Martin Luther, Jr., 33

labor allocation, 80–83, 117–122, 137
labor costs, decreases in, 48–50
labor-intensive services. *See also* personal services; stagnant sector

labor productivity, 20–22, 28, 44–47, 80–81, 196n5. *See also* productivity growth
labor supply, 186n2
Lee, Robert E., 71
legal services, 22, 28–29
life expectancy, 184n3
lifestyle changes, 170–172
liver disease, 163
living standards: deterioration of, 17, 115; improvements in, xx, 5, 33, 53, 73, 118–119, 181; physical output and, 82–83
lovastatin, 167
lung cancer, 172

magnetic resonance imaging (MRI), 202n23
maintenance costs, 36–37
"make-or-buy" decisions, 123
malpractice lawsuits, 17–18, 159, 172–174
manufactured products: affordability of, xx; consumer spending on, 73; decreasing costs of, 61, 70, 72, 74, 79; output of, 79–80; repair of, 37; taxation of, 74–75
manufacturing: employment in, 24, 81, 119–122, 196n6; output, 78–80, 92; productivity growth in, xvii, 20–21, 28; share of GDP by, 78; shifting output away from, 72–73; standardization in, 23

Massachusetts Hospital Association, 151, 153
mass media, 185n15
medical diagnosis, 175–176
medical education, 173–175, 177–178, 185n6, 205n102
medical equipment: testing of, 157; tracking, 147–148
medical errors, 142–145, 151–153, 169–170, 198n2, 198n5, 199n10
medical history forms, 176
medical innovations, 87–93, 144–153, 176–177
medical liability reform, 172–173
medical profession, competition in, 18
medical specialization, 174–175, 178
medical tourism, 107
medical treatments: evaluation of, 156–158, 201n8; expensive, 177; genetic information to guide, 162–163; harmful or unnecessary, 158–161, 177; identification of less expensive, 163–166
medications: for disease prevention, 166–169; effectiveness of new, 157–158, 160–161, 201n9; errors, 144–145, 149, 169–170, 198n2; genetic information to guide, 162–163
Mediterranean diet, 170–171

mega-innovative innovations, 131
metformin, 167
middle-income countries, 102–104
military armaments, 69–71, 190n2
mismanagement, 66
mitral heart valves, 164
motion capture, 197n16
Moynihan, Daniel Patrick, 68
municipal services, 64

Netherlands, 9, 10, 11, 12, 41
newspaper production, 39–40
niacin, 160–161, 167
nominal costs, 13–15
Nordhaus, William, xix, 87, 183n3
North Korea, 71, 190n3
nuclear weapons, 71, 190n3

obesity, 170, 204n80
official development assistance, 97, 101–102
oligopolistic competition, 55–56
Organisation for Economic Co-operation and Development (OECD) countries, 104
Oulton, Nicholas, 121, 122–123, 136
out-of-pocket health expenditures, 97–98, 102, 104–106
outsourcing, 120, 185n12
ovarian cancer, 163, 203n41

pacemakers, 157
Pakistan, 71
Patient Protection and Affordable Care Act, 178
performing arts, 22, 25–26, 185n15
personal services, 20–21, 183n1; affordability of, 33, 41–42, 44, 50–55, 67–68, 93; costs of, xvii–xviii, 21–22, 44; decline in quality of, 33–34; future role of, 67; increasing costs of, 27–29, 66–68, 92–93; productivity growth in, 26–27
physical measures, of manufacturing output, 79–80, 92
physicians: incomes of, 18; measurement of performance of, 176; payment of, 178; per capita, 18; training of, 173–175, 177–178
physician services, increasing costs of, 6–7
Pigou, A. C., 191n8
pistachio nuts, 171
placebo effect, 158
planned economies, 189n28
police protection, 22, 26–27, 42
politics, health-care costs and, 4
pollution, 72
poor, 54, 55, 59–60
poor countries, 101–102
postal service, 22, 34
poverty: future, 17, 181; reduction in, 5, 73, 101

presidential election (2008), 4

preventive medicine, 166–170, 177

price inflation, 6, 26

private services, decline in quality of, 33–34

privatization, 64–65

production costs, 79–80, 92

productivity growth, xvii–xviii, xix–xx; affordability of services and, 44, 50–55; in agriculture, 128–130; business services and, 120–137, 149–150; continued increase in, 55–56, 67; cost decreases and, 48–50; cost increases and, xxi, 5, 44; cost-saving, 83; decline in, 115, 137, 181–182; definition of, xx; environmental impact of, 71–73; future, 181–182; in health-care industry, 142, 149–153; innovation, entrepreneurship and, 29–32, 46, 56–58, 67; labor allocation and, 80–83; lack of, in stagnant services, 22–24, 28; in manufacturing, 20–21; measures of, 78–80, 83–84, 86–87; other sources of, 56–58; patterns of, 22–24; quality-improving, 83; record of, 45–47; in service sector, 24–27; stagnant services and, 40–42; wages and, 21–22, 25, 41, 44

products: asymptotically stagnant, 112–113; disassembled, 36; disposable, 36–38; electronic, 49–50; innovative, 55–56

progressive sector, xx, 25; business services and, 124–126; cost disease analysis of, 119–120; job losses in, 24; labor productivity in, 80–81; share of output from, 80–82, 191n3

prosperity, 65–66, 73, 115

prostate cancer, 165–166, 171

prostate-specific antigen (PSA) testing, 166

psoriasis, 169

public, educating about cost disease, 63

public sector, increase in, 63–64

public services: decline in quality of, 33–34, 186n1; funding of, 44; privatization of, 64–65

purchasing power, 47, 48–53, 61, 65, 187n11

quality, service, 23, 92–93

quality-adjusted productivity, 83–84, 86–88, 91–92

quality improvement, 83, 86–93, 192n4

quality-improving productivity growth, 83

quality-unadjusted productivity, 83–84, 86–88, 91–92, 150, 192n5

radio frequency identification (RFID) technology, 147–148
ranolazine, 165
real costs: calculating changes in, 14–15; falling, 19–20, 21; versus nominal costs, 13–14; rising, 19, 21
real prices, 6, 116–117
Red Queen game, 55–56
Reinhardt, Uwe, 178
Renaissance, 45–46
repair services, 22, 37–38
research and development (R&D), 55–56, 111, 113–115
restaurant services, 22
resveratrol, 171
Revolutionary War, 125
Robbins, Lionel, 190n1
Robinson, Joan, xvii–xviii, xxi, 181
robotics, 40
robotic surgery, 88–89, 192n7, 192n8
Roman Empire, 46, 57
rosuvastatin, 167
Russia, 100

Sahl, Mort, 180
salt reduction, 171
sanitation, 22
Schumpeter, Joseph, 31, 55

sea level rise, 72
secretaries, 35–36
services: business, 120–137; productivity growth in, 24–27; progressive, 24–25; shifting output to, 72–73; stagnant, 22–29, 40–42, 60–61, 80–82
Six Sigma, 151–153, 199n12
Smith, Adam, 76
smoking, 171–172
software, 121–122, 195n3
Sony, 131
soy products, 171
specialists, 174–175, 178
spinal stenosis, 161
stagnant sector, xx, 22–24; asymptotically, 112–115; business services and, 122–123; fate of, 25–28; increasing costs of, 27–29, 60–61; labor productivity in, 80–81; share of output from, 80–82, 191n3; survival of, 40–42
standardization, 22–23
statins, 167–168, 202n35
Stimac, Vid, 97
strokes, 168–169
Sun World, 128–130

taxation, 191n7; increases, 44; restructuring of, 74–75, 191n8
technological change, 21, 118, 190n1

Technology Adoption Program (TAP), 135–136

telecommunications, 24–25, 117, 124–125, 190n6

television broadcasting, 112, 113, 185n15

terrorism, xx, 70–71

ThinkPlace, 133–134, 198n27

third-party payers, 98

"throw-away" society, 36–38

Toshiba, 131

Triplett, Jack, 86

Tufts Medical Center, 150–153, 199n12

type-2 diabetes, 161, 167, 170

typesetting, 39

uninsured, 59–60

United Kingdom: education expenditures, 9, 11; GDP per capita, 29–30, 45–46; health care system in, 62; health spending per capita, 10, 12; postsecondary education enrollment in, 41; real GDP growth, 47

United States: business services sector in, 124; GDP per capita, 188n13; health-care costs in, 5–11, 99, 155; health-care legislation in, 67; health spending in, 11, 12, 155, 184n3, 187n13; manufacturing job losses in, 81;

postsecondary education enrollment in, 41; poverty in, 59; purchasing power in, 47; uninsured in, 59–60

universal health coverage, 102–104, 107

universities, employee wages in, 11, 13

valsartan, 167

van der Gaag, Jacques, 97

Vassar Brothers Medical Center, 143–150

Veblen, Thorstein, 39

Verghese, Abraham, 154

vitamin D, 171

Voice-over-Internet Protocol, 143–144, 146, 199n6

wages: changes in, 21–22; of college and university employees, 11, 13; of health-care workers, 10–11, 13, 18; increases in, 34, 186n1; productivity growth and, 21–22, 25, 41, 44; in stagnant sector, 25–26

warfare, 70–71, 74

warfarin, 168–169

weapons, 69–71, 190n2

weapons of mass destruction, 66, 71

welfare programs, 22, 27

X-ray technology, 40